THE GREAT WAR COOK BOOK

May Byron,

introduction by Eleri Pipien

AMBERLEY

First published 2014

Amberley Publishing
The Hill, Stroud
Gloucestershire, GL5 4EP

www.amberley-books.com

Introduction copyright © Eleri Pipien 2014

The right of Eleri Pipien to be identified as the Author
of this work has been asserted in accordance with the
Copyrights, Designs and Patents Act 1988.

British Library Cataloguing in Publication Data.
A catalogue record for this book is available from the British Library.

ISBN 978 1 4456 3388 6
E-book ISBN 978 1 4456 3400 5

Typeset in 10pt on 12pt Sabon.
Typesetting and Origination by Amberley Publishing.
Printed in the UK.

Acknowledgements

Thanks go to Campbell McCutcheon (*CMcC*) and John Christopher (*JC*) of Amberley Publishing for the use of their collections of images and to the Discovery Museum of the Tyne and Wear Museums, Newcastle for their cooperation in providing an image from their circus animal photograph collection.

- E. P.

Every spare piece of land was taken over for growing vegetables. Here, mostly women can be seen planting a railway embankment. (*CMcC*)

Introduction

Baker: 'What's wrong with the little chap?'
Mother: 'I give it up. I've given him a bun – I don't know what more 'e wants. I can't get 'im to realise there's a war on.' (*CMcC*)

The First World War was a turning point both tactically and for civilian life in the countries involved. The availability of food was used as a tool by both sides to force each other to surrender and led to Britain's first taste of government-led, nationwide food restrictions. Food control was tentative at first, with more measures added as the war progressed, until the introduction of rationing shortly before its conclusion. As a consequence, by the time of the Second World War, there was already a template of food and information control to follow and the government knew how to act right from the start. The First World War, as a time of great change and uncertainty, forced people to learn how to live in a different way, including how to cook cheaply and most of all, creatively.

Although we are familiar with the literature inspired by the First World War – everything from the poetry of Wilfred Owen to comedy such as Blackadder Goes Forth – it is still the Second World War that holds our attention. We are acquainted, not only with its events, but also with the images produced at the time. The Ministry of Information, used throughout the Second World War, was responsible not only for ensuring through censorship that Britain's enemies did not gain any strategically sensitive information, but also that the British population was kept calm and educated about Home Front matters. This form of propaganda was designed to uplift the spirit of the British, make them feel empowered and create a feeling of cohesion and unity. Today, these images have made a return for much the same reasons in the face of the recession, and 'austerity nostalgia' has become a national obsession. Our resurrection of war-time principles has involved learning to cook wholesome budget meals, with various celebrity chefs and cooks teaching us how to do this. Yet as food shortage was a fundamental problem during the First World War, this style of cooking was not just an option, it was a necessity.

Preparing Birmingham's 900,000 meat cards in the Council House. (*CMcC*)

Diner (choking): 'Quick! Water! Crumb in me throat.'
War Waiter: 'Ah, Sir, if only the well-to-do would leave bread for the less fortunate.' (*JC*)

THE "IDLE" OF HIS COUNTRY.

War Lord: 'Why don't you do something? Don't you know the people are short of bread?'
Von Tirpitz: 'Nonsense! Why, nobody could have a bigger 'loaf' than I'm having!'

Alfred Von Tirpitz was Grand Admiral of the German Fleet from 1911 – 1916. He felt the German Navy was unable to take on the Royal Navy head-on and advocated unrestricted submarine warfare to break the British blockade of German ports, which had been causing severe food and communication problems. The construction of German submarines could not keep up with demand, however, and in 1916, he resigned. (*JC*)

German U-boats, including the one that sank the *Lusitania* (*second left*). (*CMcC*)

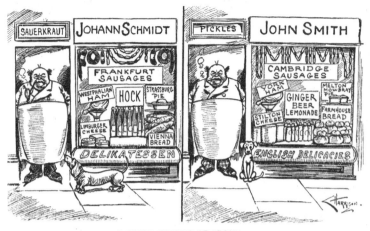

A QUICK CHANGE OF FRONT.

Punch magazine makes fun of Germans in Britain becoming more British than the British during the war. (*CMcC*)

The reality for a lot of Germans living in Britain was that they faced distrust and hostility even if they tried to blend in. Many German shops were attacked and ransacked following air-raids. (*CMcC*)

The Defence of the Realm Act (DORA) came into effect in August 1914 'for securing public safety'. This vaguely termed Act gave the government the power to prevent anything which was deemed to 'jeopardise the success of the operations of His Majesty's forces or to assist the enemy'. One of its clearer aims was to ensure that food shortages never happened. These were more guidelines than enforceable rules, however, and those with enough money could easily obtain and hoard more food. Poorer people and labourers were soon starving and malnourished, a problem that was not repeated in the Second World War. At the same time, the Royal Navy was aggressively patrolling the North Sea and also had in place a blockade of enemy ports in order to starve them into submission. They partly succeeded, with large parts of Germany suffering from malnutrition and the Austrian population facing starvation. However, in 1916, Germany retaliated by unleashing unrestricted submarine warfare. Prior to this point, Britain was able to import food from Australia, New Zealand, America and Canada (who put in place their own food restrictions in order to maintain the supply), but with this U-boat campaign, Merchant Navy ships were no longer safe. On average, U-boats were destroying 300,000 tons of shipping a month and in February 1917 alone, 230 ships were lost. Britain was facing severe shortages.

Created in 1916, the Ministry of Food was tasked with making Britain more self-sufficient. It worked hard to ensure that agricultural resources were better distributed and formed the Women's Land Army (WLA) to

Members of the WLA ploughing a field. (*CMcC*)

Potato queue. People were relying heavily on the potato, using it in place of flour and to bulk out meals. (*CMcC*)

work on the extra three million acres of land taken over for farming. By 1916, the demand for men on the Front was so high that conscription was introduced. Women – particularly young, single women who had no ties or responsibilities – were encouraged by David Lloyd George, then Secretary of State for War, and Emmeline Pankhurst, the leader of the Suffragette movement, to help the war effort by taking on the jobs that were usually done by men. Women became public transport drivers and conductors, they worked in munitions factories, took on clerical roles and farmed the land. Women had been able to work on the land previously through volunteer organisations such as the Women's Legion and the Women's Defence Relief Corps, but in 1917, the Board of Agriculture set up the WLA, a civilian organisation which paid its members. They recruited women from all walks of life to work in the fields and forests of Britain and by 1918 there were 250,000 women working the land, 23,000 of whom were members of the WLA. It was not enough and finally, in early 1918, rationing was imposed. May Byron published her 'Rations Book' the same year, joining the thousands of women who wished to help the war effort, although as a married woman, her role was limited. A seasoned author already, she turned her writing skills to compiling recipes that could be achieved with the limited resources available to the housewife.

Food demonstration showing the use of potatoes instead of flour. (*CMcC*)

Dairy products, meat and sugar were rationed and other popular ingredients were in short supply. It became a summary offence to waste wheat, rye or rice and the government considered making any food waste a punishable offence. The Ministry of Food was keen to cut back on consumption of bread in particular, as the majority of Britain's grain had been imported and was now in short supply due to the submarine blockade. They therefore issued a number of posters urging the British on the Home Front to not waste bread by cutting back by two slices a day. Housewives were also encouraged to make War Bread with GR flour, which was a less refined wheat flour, with other grains added, such as rye or barley. It was supposed to stay fresh much longer than the bread bought from the baker, enabling families to eat less bread without worrying that their loaf would go stale before they had finished it. May provides a recipe for this War Bread and bulks out her loaf with potatoes. She also comments on its longevity, stating that while bought bread goes stale after only twelve hours, her homemade War Bread stays fresh for a whole week. Food posters issued by the government made no mention of shortages or the threat of defeat, but instead stated that if you could save on bread, for example, you could 'defeat the U-boat'. These posters were designed to make the British at home feel that they could actively help win the war.

For those on the Front Line, the food situation contributed to the dire living conditions in the trenches. At the outbreak of war, each British soldier was given ten ounces of meat and eight ounces of vegetables a

German Pirate: 'Gott Straße England!'
British Potato: 'Tuber über alles!' (*JC*)

day, which dropped to six ounces of meat a day by 1916. By the end of the war, meat was only permitted once every nine days. Some soldiers, fed up with their meagre rations, would hunt, fish and forage whenever they could, and some even planted vegetable patches in disused trenches. Inefficient food transportation meant that supplies often reached the trenches stale or spoiled. Although the kitchen staff did the best they could with the poor quality and insufficient quantity of food, the meals produced were extremely unappetising, consisting mainly of weak soups and stews – the most frequently made of which, was pea soup with chunks of horse meat. Additionally, the kitchen staff had to make all the meals for their battalion in the same two large vats, and carried it to the Front Line in pans, petrol tins and jars through the communication trenches, so by the time it reached the men, it was cold and it all tasted the same. Despite Britain providing 3,240,948 tons of food to their soldiers, and the army attempting to provide the 3,574 calories to each soldier per day on the recommendation of dieticians, the soldiers were frequently hungry and dissatisfied with their food. The poor food also cause outbreaks of illness – in 1916, for example, there was a shortage of flour, so bread at the Front was made from ground parsnips that caused diarrhoea. The Home Front shared rationing with the soldiers, yet experienced little of the intense misery of the trenches.

Although the First World War drastically changed British cooking, it was not the first food-upheaval we had faced. Until the eighteenth century, the majority of the population had lived in the countryside, with great reliance on the land for food and work. The Industrial Revolution made a majority of rural living redundant and caused a mass migration to towns and cities, where people worked in factories instead of farming. The food of the working-classes became mass-produced instead of fresh and many regional dishes were lost. With industry came the rise of the middle classes, who were eager to climb the social ladder and, with the aid of publications such as *Woman's World* magazine, they were able to emulate the upper classes without the expense and the aid of servants. The upper classes were the main employer of good quality cooks and when the First World War reduced the lifestyle they were used to, these cooks either made the move to work in large hotels, or found themselves unemployed. Added to food shortages and rationing, this meant that Britain's quality culinary traditions had to be put to the side and were forgotten.

The state of British food was not helped by the rigorous rationing imposed during the Second World War, which continued for nine years after the war was over. Rationing actually meant that the British population on average was healthier than before, due to a carefully balanced diet with less fat and sugar. However, the post-war years saw a population deprived of sugar and indulgent foods compensating for the long years of rationing. Tooth decay, obesity and heart disease soared. The reputation of British food was so bad following the Second World War that George Orwell felt compelled to write an essay in defence of it, entirely unsuccessfully as we are still suffering from much the same reputation today.

The British attitude to food in the twentieth and twenty-first centuries has largely been shaped by the world wars. Rationing forced us to eat healthily and sparingly and when it came to an end, we over-compensated, causing severe health concerns. Combined with our current austerity measures, this has given rise to the subject of cheap-but-healthy cookery. Our on-going nostalgia for wartime culture has led us full-circle as we look to ration-cookery for inspiration.

Banana rationing, Second World War. (*CMcC*)

Similarly, those writing cookery books during the Second World War could draw inspiration from their First World War counterparts, reusing or adapting their recipes. But where did May get her inspiration from? Did she draw on traditional British recipes, or did she create her own? The main challenge she faced was limited means for experimentation – how could she devise recipes, try new things out and perfect ideas while experiencing rationing? It is likely that old recipes were simply adapted to suit the types and quantities of ingredients available, with an interesting twist given to make up for the shortages (making marmalade with carrots or parsnips for example, pp. 220–221). She also appears to have collected recipes from other people and publications, as she mentions that she has never made sugar-beet syrup before, but provides several recipes in the book. Her first austerity cook-book, May Byron's *How to Save Cookery Book*, published in 1915, contains some of the same recipes, indicating that she recycled her ideas, altering them to suit the ingredients available with rationing. Both her wartime cookery books were in a similar vein and, much like the recipes of the celebrity chefs today, show readers how to be economical in the kitchen while still creating tasty meals.

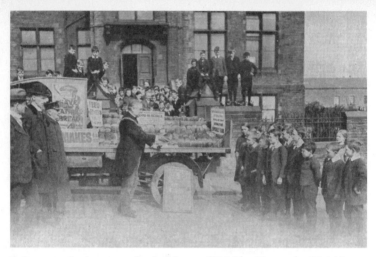

'A lesson on food economy by the Mayor of Keighley. The town of Keighley set a fine example of loyalty to the Food Controller's edicts.' (*CMcC*)

It is evident that May was taking full advantage of the war-time climate to sell her books as they were published following the implementation of DORA and rationing. Before the war, an austerity cook-book would have been impossible to sell as the content would have been suited to the working-classes, yet they would have been least likely to waste their money on buying a cookery book. The food restrictions were, to an extent, a social leveller and meant that the middle and upper classes would need to change the way they thought of and prepared food (as most had lost servants to the front line) and, of course, they had the disposable income to spend on buying a book teaching them how to accomplish this. This genre of cookery-book, encouraged by the wartime environment, has been seen in abundance since, with television personalities, cooks and chefs all taking it on. Fanny Cradock in the decades following the Second World War; Mary Berry, who has been writing about food since the 1970s; and the Hairy Bikers and Jamie Oliver, whose presence is highly publicised and on-going, have all given tips on how to create good meals for less.

Unlike the cookery books of today, which have big glossy pictures and clearly laid out recipes, with the steps listed one by one, May Byron's is unillustrated, short and delivered with a matter-of-fact attitude. It is her 'Preliminary Remarks' and short introductions to each section which hold the most character and are both informative and amusing to read. May does not shrink from giving her opinion and almost scolds her readers into the right mind-set: that of hard work, skill and imagination. Also unlike our celebrity chefs and cooks, May does not try to make cooking fun, quick or easy, stating instead in her opening sentence that cooking with rations will be difficult, yet she encourages her readers to take on the challenge with 'a sense of cheerful enterprise' as she very much does in this book. She is eminently practical, but she also has a sense of humour, sharing with us her thoughts and the occasional anecdote. She recalls, for example, hearing a man complain that he was eating so much fish to replace meat in his diet that he had 'become an aquarium'.

Wife of Profiteer: 'Er – can you tell me if – er – really *nice* people eat herrings?' (*CMcC*)

The recipes themselves take into account the shortage of butter and other fats for cooking, eggs, sugar, meat, bread, cheese and milk, using as little of these as possible. Although she makes clear her distaste of vegetarian food, most of her recipes are padded out with vegetables, pulses, rice or cereals. She also takes care to try to keep her recipes nicely balanced and often comments on their nutritional value. However, despite her horror of waste and disapproval of indulgence, she describes puddings as 'indispensable' and does not consider the option of doing without. In

**What does "S.O.S." mean?
Shortage of Sugar!**

Bamforth postcard depicting the consequences of sugar shortages. (*CMcC*)

fact, she states that 'one is tempted to tear one's hair above a reeling brain' while trying to think of something to make into a pudding. We would now not go such lengths to produce puddings in such circumstances, but May makes it clear that just because there is a war on, there is no excuse for letting standards slip. This attitude permeates her book and it is with such determinedly optimistic practicality that she writes.

Although May was published more than 100 times in her lifetime, very little information remains about her. We know that she was born Mary Clarissa Gillington in Wenbury, Cheshire, in 1861, the oldest of four siblings. In 1892 she published a collection of poems with her sister Alice and the same year married George Byron. During her career as a writer, she published biographies and works of poetry, children's fiction and cookery under her maiden name, her married name and the pseudonym of Maurice Clare. She was best known for her revised editions of J. M. Barrie's Peter Pan books for a child audience of varying reading abilities, but her other works were also generally highly thought

The government urged the public not to be wasteful throughout the war – May was also particularly scornful of wastage and constantly gives tips on how to use up leftovers, for example, using the water that vegetables, cereals, or pulses have been cooked in as the basis for soups. (*CMcC*)

of. Her series of biographies describe 'A day in the life of' various great authors, poets, composers and other famous personalities and although they were well received, they confused some critics, who could not tell if they were works of fiction or based on research. Her poetry appeared in both dedicated books and in newspapers and a poem entitled 'At Bay' in her collection Wind on the Heath was described as 'a cry, not from the heart of a woman, but from the heart of Woman'. This describes a passion not seen in her cookery books, but it is evident from the volume and variety of work produced that she was a very creative and dedicated individual.

Her cookery books covered everything from puddings to cooking for the ill, and in addition to her How-to-Save and Rations books she also wrote a wartime supplement for her Vegetable book. She describes her cookery books as a series and she certainly covers most forms of British cookery at the time. As her wartime cookbooks coincided with food-shortage measures, it seems that she was also a canny business woman. However, other than what can be gleaned from her publications, little remains about her life and personality. Her Rations Book though, was written in such a conversational manner, directly to her readers – in a way that few authors use now – that throughout the course of the book, we really get a sense of who she was. She was an opinionated woman, determined to 'make the best of a bad job,' and full of advice for the struggling housewife.

Out of her collection of recipes, some are familiar and have stood the test of time, but many will be completely alien. There are not only recipes for such modern favourites as Cornish Pasties, Shepherd's Pie and Chocolate Pudding, but also for dishes that we will have never heard of, such as Stewed Calf's Feet, Mock Crab and Mattress Pudding. May might be a little too fond of currying ingredients and the recipes involving offal might turn the modern stomach, but her book neverthe-less provides a valuable insight into the diet and mind-set of the British public on the Home Front.

– Eleri Pipien.

In rare cases, circus animals were also used to plough the land – elephants and camels were used in the place of horses to pull heavy loads. (*Discovery Museum*)

Different classes of women were employed in more hard physical labour than ever before. They had taken over many traditionally male roles – in both rural and urban settings. These women are carriage cleaners. (*CMcC*)

Basil: 'Mummy, aren't we exceeding the speed ration?' (*JC*)

CONTENTS

CHAPTER I

PRELIMINARY REMARKS

CHAPTER II

MEAT

WAR-TIME PIES, VARIOUS

CHAPTER III

FISH

CONTENTS

PAGE

MIXED FISH DISHES

VARIOUS FISH DISHES

CONTENTS

CHAPTER IV

SOUPS

CHAPTER V

EGGS AND CHEESE

CONTENTS

PAGE

315. Triped Eggs 105
316. Turkish Eggs 105
317. Home-made Cheese, No. 1 106
318. Home-made Cheese, No. 2 106
319. Home-made Cheese, No. 3 106
320. Bread and Cheese Custard 107
321. Celery Cheese 107
322. Cheese and Onions 107
323. Cheese and Onion Pudding 108
324. Cheese and Rice Pudding 108
325. Cheese and Potatoes 108
326. Mock Crab 108

CHAPTER VI

POTATOES AND OTHER VEGETABLES

327. Potato Balls 112
328. Potato Cakes, No. 1 112
329. Potato Cakes, No. 2 113
330. Potatoes, Curried 113
331. Potato Custard 113
332. Potatoes Delmonico 113
333. Potatoes Duchesse, No. 1 113
334. Potatoes Duchesse, No. 2 114
335. Potato Dumpling 114
336. Potato Dumplings, No. 1 114
337. Potato Dumplings, No. 2 115
338. Potato Fritters 115
339. Potatoes, Hashed 115
340. Potatoes with Herrings 115
341. Potato Mirotin 116
342. Potato Pancakes 116
343. Potato Savouries 116
344. Potatoes Stewed in Milk 117
345. Potatoes with White Sauce 117

OTHER VEGETABLES

346. Artichokes, Chinese (or Japanese) 117
347. Artichokes (Jerusalem) and Onions 117
348. Beans and Carrots 118
349 Beans and Rice 118
350. Bean, Roast 118

SALADS

CHAPTER VII

CEREALS

PORRIDGES

B

CHAPTER VIII

PUDDINGS, PASTRY, AND SWEET DISHES

CHAPTER IX

BREAD, CAKES, AND BISCUITS

CHAPTER X

VARIOUS :   NUTS, JAMS, BEVERAGES, HAYBOX COOKERY, WEIGHTS AND MEASURES, ETC.

CHAPTER I

PRELIMINARY REMARKS

I AM not going to minimise the difficulties which lie in wait for the rationed housewife. The making of bricks without straw is notoriously a hard job ; and the concocting of palatable dishes with a deficiency of those ingredients which we were wont to use so freely, is not at all an easy task. No amount of imagination will make baked haricots the least bit like roast mutton. No extent of make-believe will turn vegetable stock into good beef gravy. The question of nutriment is one thing, that of texture and taste quite another. Of course, professional optimists will say it is very good for you *not* to have this, that, or the other ; they will chill your blood by talk of proteins and calories and carbohydrates, and will declare that all you really need for health is to be found in split peas and sago. I have even seen tapioca recommended as a *substitute* for fat ! But nobody ever yet tried to fry potatoes in tapioca.

In this book, however, " there is no deception, ladies and gentlemen," as the conjuror says. I am not intent on assuring you that " everything is for the best in the best of all possible worlds " ; I am out to help you, frankly, to make the best of a bad job. Nearly all the most valuable component parts of our usual daily food are either very scarce or very dear. We must see what we can do with the quality and quantity vouchsafed to us. There is no reason why we should not rise to the occasion, and make a success of things. If necessity is the mother of invention, let us justify our existence by our skill. If makeshifts are the order of the day—at least let us have satisfactory makeshifts.

To this end we shall be obliged to take more trouble and more thought, much more, than of old ; and a sort of Robinson Crusoeish interest will invest our experiments in these days of dearth. Never a thrifty nation, we have dwelt for half a century in a fools' paradise, believing that " to-morrow shall be as this day and much more abundant." Now, when faced with the crude incontrovertible fact that we live in an island, and that nearly all our food has been coming from *outside* that island, there is no doubt that the present rude awakening should—in the long run—be very much to our advantage. " It's an ill wind that blows nobody good." To begin with, a fools' paradise is a weakening and demoralising habitation ; to go on with, we are now compelled, willy-nilly, to learn the use and value of expedients, of substitutes, of skilful cookery—in a word, of brains. I conjecture that, sooner or later, we shall emerge from this dire emergency a great deal cleverer than we were before ; having acquired all sorts of knowledge, and exploited all manner of possibilities, which we should have regarded with a stare of blank bewilderment in 1913.

So, not with a long face, but with a sense of cheerful enterprise, let me proffer you the following suggestions. It hasn't been at all easy to discover them ; but a feeling of adventure in unknown lands has carried me through. And I don't put them forward as a confirmed vegetarian, or an anti-carnivore, or a pulse-eater, like Daniel at the court of Nebuchadnezzar. For—to indulge in a momentary confidence—farinaceous foods are odious to me, and pulse foods pretty nearly poisonous, and most vegetables unattractive, to put it mildly. So my hearty sympathy is extended to others in like case, and I have borne them largely in mind, when collecting the recipes in this volume. There are plenty of books for the vegetarians. This one is intended as a sort of stand-by in what the Apostle calls the " present distress."

Of course, the fundamental idea of rationing was standardisation, equalisation : *i.e.*, that nobody shall have more than

anybody else. Equally of course, like all theories of stand-
ardising and equalising, it won't work out in practice—even
for a single day. Because, not only does the "heavy manual
worker" obtain a larger ration ; not only does the producer,
or capturer, of certain foods secure more in that way ; but
the small household has to tackle a much harder problem
than the large one. As usual, "to him that hath shall be
given," and the large family is, in many cases, conscious of
no difficulty at all : rolling in coupons, and getting on
supremely all right, beloved of its butcher and butterman ;
whilst the households numbering from one to three persons
have a desperate struggle to make ends meet on meat-ends
and scraps. It is, therefore, of these last that I have chiefly
thought in compiling this book : the people with very few
coupons. Their perplexities are multiplied in inverse ratio
to their tickets. No amount of arithmetic (which is notoriously unreliable), as regards fewer people wanting less food,
will alter or ameliorate the question of how small households
are to manage. This is a question only to be solved by good
management.

With reference to meat, bacon, fowl, etc., I do not state
the prices or exact amounts rationed and obtainable, because
these vary as time goes on. I can only generalise.

FATS are a very serious crux. I most emphatically advise
that butter and margarine rations (at present four ounces a
week per head) should be only used at table, especially at
breakfast, and never encroached upon for cookery, unless you
happen to have an extra good supply. For tea, the less one
eats the better, and one can make shift with jam (when procurable), or with treacle, or with one of the "fake" honeys
—real honey being exceedingly expensive.

Butter and Margarine, therefore, we will rule out. If you
find them mentioned in any recipe, it is purely by inadvertence,
and you must substitute something else.

The question is, what ?

Fat is particularly necessary, because it is what supplies *energy* to the human body—four times as much energy as bread does. Goodness knows, most of us could do with a bit more energy, but I daresay you have noticed how marvellously energetic some very fat people are—the last thing one could expect of them.

Well, certain foods, of course, furnish more fats than others, as follows (per cent) :

Lard	.. 95	Pork	.. 40	Eggs	.. 9
Butter	.. 85	Cheese	.. 30	Salmon	.. 9
Margarine	.. 84	Mutton	.. 25	Herrings	.. 4
Suet	.. 82	Nuts	.. 22	Milk	.. 4
Bacon ..	.. 60	Beef	.. 20		

Cocoa butter would probably top the list.

I have already suggested that some coupons should be used for the purchase of suet and of fat for rendering down into dripping. In roasting or baking meat, you must be careful not to use up the dripping by putting potatoes, onions, or Yorkshire pudding into the pan. Save every scrap you can : remove and render every bit of fat from the meat when cold. It is possible for a very small household, by care and thrift, to keep a little dripping of sorts in hand. Dripping can still —very seldom—be bought, but you don't know what it is made of.

Lard and " lard substitute " (which seems to me to be cotton-seed oil, hitherto largely employed in fried fish shops) are also precious when obtainable. Preserved Suets, such as " Atora," seem to have disappeared from the market : so it is of no use considering these. We must, therefore, fall back upon that new and much-discussed substitute—Cocoa Butter.

Cocoa butter is the fat which results from cocoa nibs during the process of converting them into cocoa. It is not so digestible as butter or margarine, but considerably richer. It has always existed as a vehicle for certain medical preparations. As a medium of cookery it has been hitherto unknown. Of course, the crude stuff, as we buy it by the pound, is nothing like the highly-refined article used by the chemist.

The problem is, how to get rid of the cocoa flavour. It is all right when you are using the cocoa butter for cakes or puddings, though, even then, one grows rather tired of its persistent chocolateness. But how to make it useful for salt dishes and for pastry ?

A great deal has been written on this subject, and most people end by confessing that you never do *quite* obliterate the cocoa. Even if the taste be practically gone after repeated clarifying, the smell is slightly there. The bother is, that clarifying makes it set so hard. It is then suggested that you should add to it, in the liquefied state, any lard, oil or dripping you can spare, to soften it. But who *has* any lard, oil or dripping to spare ?

Until cocoa butter can be softened into a malleable condition, it is too hard for pastry : it makes the pastry hard when cooked.

If you use it (after clarification) for frying, shred it or flake it into the pan, and add a little salt.

For puddings and cakes it is all right, until you get tired of it, and remember that it is much richer than margarine, or even than suet, so can be employed sparingly.

The various vegetable fats, such as "nutter," seem to have disappeared off the market. Remains only that treasure of the careful cook—

Salad or Olive Oil.—This, if good, is very dear ; and, if bad, is hateful. It is the best frying medium (especially for salt dishes) which can be found ; and can be used again and again if it is not allowed to become smoked or burned. (It is less liable to burn than lard or dripping.) It can be clarified by letting it heat through slowly at the side of the stove, and then putting in some thin slices of potato, which will remove all impurities. Of course, any crumbs or particles should be removed : there are not likely to be any if you use a frying basket.

It is most important for such articles as require deep boiling fat, that you should be able to use your oil, or whatever it is, again and again. Olive oil is exceedingly expensive, but not when you use it repeatedly. I recommend that you reserve it for *salt* frying, and use cocoa butter, clarified or not, for *sweet* frying.

If you can add a little olive oil to the cocoa butter, in frying, you will do well, because the oil will soften and modify the cocoa butter.

A good many people have written to the newspapers, explaining how you can double your butter or margarine by beating it up with milk : half-a-pound to half-a-pint. I have tried this plan, and I cannot conscientiously recommend it. It takes a mighty long time : it *apparently* doubles the bulk of the butter by incorporating that much milk—but the result is like a cream. It sinks into bread and does not, consequently, go so far as a more solid article. Its increase is a deceptive matter, to my thinking. Still, some folks believe in it, so I can only state my own experience. Other plans are suggested, which will be found below.

The fat which is skimmed off stock when cold, answers admirably for frying anything of a salt or savoury nature. It can also be run down along with mutton dripping, and helps to soften and improve the mutton dripping, which is otherwise rather tallowy.

All odds and ends of cooked fat should be clarified and kept for use ; never let any go to waste.

To *clarify fat*, cut it into pieces and put them in a saucepan with half a pint of cold water ; let them boil gently for one hour, stirring from time to time. Then remove the lid and let the water boil till it has all evaporated, this will be shown by no steam rising when you stir. Let it stand a few minutes to cool and then strain it into a basin.

To *clarify dripping*, pour it while hot into a basin containing some cold water. When it has hardened, remove the top, scrape it underneath and it is ready for use. Dripping should be examined every second day or so.

NOTE.—Whenever the word " fat " is mentioned throughout this book, it means *whatever kind of fat you can lay your hand to*—rendered-meat-fat or dripping, lard, lard substitute, olive oil, preserved suet, fresh suet, bacon fat, or cocoa butter.

TO CLARIFY COCOA BUTTER

Cocoa butter should be clarified before using it for salt dishes or frying. Many recipes have been put forth, but the following are the simplest :

1. No. I

Break up small, or grate, or flake, the cocoa butter into a basin; pour on sufficient boiling water to cover it; set in a cool place. Next morning, drain off the water, again break up the cocoa butter, which will have set hard, and repeat the process. After this second time of clarifying, the taste and smell of cocoa should be almost imperceptible.

2. No. II

Place one pound of cocoa butter in a pan with one flat dessertspoonful of salt, and one breakfastcupful of water (or lime water). Let it come to the boil ; then place at the side of stove and let simmer for two hours. Remove, and when cold, drain off the water.

3. No. III

Boil the cocoa butter as in No. II., and when it is cold break up and pour boiling water on it as in No. I. I have found this a successful plan. But I doubt that one ever *wholly* gets rid of the chocolate taste. Some of the finer makes of cocoa butter are more susceptible to treatment than others ; but one must be thankful for so excellent a fat, flavour or no flavour.

4. No. IV

Another method is to use as much water as possible. Break up two and a half pounds of cocoa butter, put it into one and a half quarts of water, let come to the boil; add one ounce of carbonate of ammonia. Mix four ounces of cornflour smooth in a little cold water, stir this into the cocoa butter; remove pan from fire and stand it in a larger pan with cold water. Whisk it as it cools. This will incorporate some of the water and render it easier to spread.

5. No. V

And yet another way is to boil the cocoa butter, broken up, in a double-saucepan (or in a large jam-pot placed in a saucepan of boiling water), and then strain it through butter-muslin.

TO INCREASE OR AUGMENT BUTTER

6. No. I

Wash four ounces of butter or margarine in cold water; drain, and work into the butter half a teaspoonful of salt. Then add four ounces of cooked sieved potatoes, still warm but not hot, and go on beating till they are thoroughly incorporated with the butter. Leave it in a cool place, and when cold, shape into pats.

7. No II

Cream the butter in a basin, add an equal quantity of cooked sieved potatoes and a little salt. Beat well until thoroughly blended, then put aside to cool.

8. No. III

Take eight ounces of margarine, and cream or gently melt it; dissolve one dessertspoonful of gelatine in a little milk (warm); add one breakfastcupful of milk, and mix all with the margarine. Continue to beat until the mixture sets firm, and form into pats.

9. No. IV

Mix one ounce of cornflour smooth with a very little milk, deducted from half a pint, the rest of which must be brought to the boil; then add the cornflour, and boil, stirring well, for ten minutes. Remove and let cool; do not let it film over on the top. Meanwhile cream six ounces of butter with a wooden spoon, and mix it very gradually into the milk, etc., when the latter is nearly cold, with salt to taste. Beat well till thoroughly blended, and keep in a cool place.

Sugar is another case in which actual standardisation is impossible; because some people desire to make their tea into a regular syrup with it, and others hate tea that even dimly tastes of sugar. So that the regulation rationed half-pound each is far too little for some households, and abundance for others. While on this point, let me assure my readers, from personal experience and that of many friends, that if they once had the self-denial to do without sugar in tea for one week, they would find the habit broken for ever. They would do very well without sugar till Doomsday. For it is, after all, only a habit; and the idea of sugar in tea is, in the East—whence tea comes to us—considered a sheer barbarism; as much so as sugar in stout would be considered here.

However, be this as it may, it is best to save your sugar for puddings and for the sweetening of fruit dishes especially, which are most unpleasant to a cultivated palate if saccharine or glucose is employed. For the sweetening of puddings and such-like, there are various proprietary preparations with quaint names—there are saccharin, saxin, etc.—there are the " fake " honeys, made from wax and glucose—there is glucose itself, which is a product of maize ; and, very sparingly, one can invoke occasional jam or treacle.

Again, there is a thin syrup made from sugar-beet—I give some recipes, pp. 10, 11—and it appears to involve a lot of labour, but may be quite worth while in the long run. I

C

have not tried it myself.   Some people make a similar syrup from parsnips.

Glucose (or corn syrup) is about two-thirds as sweet as cane sugar.   It is made, I believe, out of starch derived from maize.

Saccharin is derived from coal-tar ; so are many other proprietary articles.

Date stones, simmered in a little water, will produce a thin sweetish syrup.

SUGAR-BEET SYRUP

10.   No. I

Sugar-beet syrup is rather a bother to make, and will not keep longer than a month, and then only in an air-tight vessel.   You can't possibly " hoard " it !   Still, any port in a storm.

Peel and scrape the sugar-beets ; when you have got them absolutely clean, cut them up into thin strips, place in a pan with enough water to cover them, and boil for two hours ; then simmer for eight hours.   Then strain off the juice, and bottle, and cork it closely.

Chop up the drained strips very small, and dry them in a moderate oven.   They are said to be usable in puddings instead of raisins, but will need soaking.

11.   No. II

Having washed and thinly peeled the beets, slice them up, and place in a large earthenware jar with a lid.   When the jar is half full, pour in cold water almost to the top, put it in a moderate oven, and leave it there for twenty-four hours.   Then strain off the liquid, and add, for every pint, a large tablespoonful of glucose.   Place all together in a saucepan over a good heat, stir till the glucose is melted, then let boil fast for thirty minutes, or until the mixture thickens,

12. No. III

Wash the beetroot, peel it thinly, wash it a second time; dry it well in a clean cloth, chop it up fairly small, and weigh it. Cook it slowly for three hours, skimming frequently; then add half a pint of cold water for every pound originally weighed, and simmer two hours longer; strain through a sieve.

A second boiling can then be made; put to the beet two pints of cold water for each pound, and boil for five hours. This will be nothing like so good as the first liquid, but still usable.

13. No. IV

Wash and peel the beets as if they were potatoes, slice them into a casserole (with lid), with enough water just to cover them, and simmer them in the oven until a thick brown syrup results; probably in about five hours.

Sugar-beet itself can be used, boiled and mashed, or sieved, for puddings, and for preserves. See also p. 219.

CHAPTER II

MEAT

MEAT—including butcher's meat, game and poultry, bacon and ham, tinned and cooked meat, brawn, sausages, etc., and also, what are quite as important, suet, bones and " offal "—tripe, liver, heart, etc.

Well, you must buy the cheapest pieces (so long as they are nutritive) if yours is a small household ; if you have a large family, you will probably find joints (carefully doled out and dished up) will serve you best, for you will then, in addition to the meat, obtain bones and dripping.

If you cannot manage joints, I advise you occasionally to sacrifice some coupons to buy bones, which must be thoroughly well broken up and used for stock.

Suet should also be bought ; it is just as valuable as meat. Fat for rendering down into dripping is equally precious, although in pre-war time it was an extravagance to buy fat for dripping at the price of meat.

Tinned and cooked meats do not afford anything beyond what you see of them ; I mean you will get no bones, dripping, or stock. And they are expensive in coupons. Sausages are welcome—if one can be certain of their age and quality.

Bacon—back, streaky, hock, or gammon—is a priceless possession *if you boil it* and use it cold. By this means you secure stock, bones eventually, the fat skimmings off the stock (practically lard) and an excellent and wholesome piece of meat. Rashers, in these days, are sheer recklessness ; so is fried ham. Save for certain exceptional cases. You will find a few rasher recipes later on.

Fowl is not an economical purchase, however cheaply

you may happen to obtain it, because it is very much less nourishing than either butcher's meat or bacon. The same remarks apply to game. Rabbits are better value, if procurable fairly easily, but of no great worth from a food standpoint. Goose and duck are superior to fowl, from their fattier nature. One has to take all these points into consideration, when fats are so scarce.

METHODS FOR MAKING THE MOST OF MEAT

However much we may deplore the fact, there is a limit to the methods one can employ—especially under present conditions. Roughly speaking, they are as follows :

For larger Joints, or whole Fowls, Rabbits, Game, etc.—

Roasting or Baking.
Boiling or Steaming.
Braising or Stewing.

For smaller quantities, and for cold meat cookery—

Grilling or Boiling.
Frying.
Stewing.
Mincing (for rissoles, etc. Minced meat is better used as an ingredient of a larger dish).
Chopping (for curries, or for pies, with ordinary crust or potato crust).
Thinly slicing (for various dishes).

By whatever fancy name one may call a dish, it is bound to come under one of the above heads. So you will see that for small quantities of meat, whether fresh or cooked, your resource must be to make them into grills, stews, pies, rissoles or croquettes, curries, etc., etc. And the more vegetables you can employ without swamping the · meat, the more economical your dish will be. The favourite form of treatment recommended by all experts, is stews.

Stews may be made very nice or very nasty, according to the amount of care you give them.

The first point is to fry your meat *quickly* and *slightly* before putting it into the stew-pot or casserole. This hardens the outside just sufficiently to keep in the flavour of the meat; it also improves the flavour. You can use the fat in which it is fried, for the subsequent thickening with "roux" for the liquid in which it is stewed; nothing need be wasted.

Second—having put the meat into the stew-jar to keep warm, put your vegetables, cut up small and neatly, into the frying-pan, and toss them until they begin to brown. Then dredge in your flour, allowing three-quarters of an ounce of flour for every three-quarters of an ounce of fat, and let it slowly cook till it is a good brown; then very gradually stir in your stock (or water), one pint for every three-quarters of an ounce of flour; let it boil; skim, and put into the stew-jar. Stew very slowly, maintaining an even, regular heat all the while.

The result will be wholesome, appetising, and well-flavoured.

A casserole or covered earthenware jar is better than any tin or iron pot, because it retains heat and flavour to a wonderful degree.

A hay-box is also useful, because of its even maintenance of heat and saving of fuel. But you *must* have a coal fire or gas fire to begin with, because no boiling or frying can be done by means of a hay-box.

The most economical and (to some extent) the most tasty way of cooking meat is, undoubtedly, to stew it in a casserole. This retains all the essential juices of the meat (as of any vegetables which may be cooked with it), ensures its being tender, and is in all respects praiseworthy.

And yet one can get most dreadfully fed-up with stews!

So that, where and when you can afford to cook an old-fashioned joint in the pre-war way, do it occasionally, if only for a change. Variety is *everything* in cookery; and a constant unremitting course of casserole and hay-box cookery is therefore not to be recommended. "The life is more than meat"; and while not sharing the British workman's repugnance to stews, one can sympathise with his deep desire to " get his teeth into something," however leathery it might be.

Rissoles are generally termed so when they are salt; croquettes are the same thing, sweet; *i.e.*, small balls of various ingredients, fried in deep fat. The inside should be moist, and the outside crisp. Dry stuff and wet stuff are equally to be avoided. You can use up almost anything in a rissole, provided it is minced finely, well mixed, and well seasoned. Whatever solid ingredients you use, should be *hot* when mixed ; if need be, heat and thicken a little stock, and warm up your ingredients in that. Vegetables should be riced or sieved, meat passed through the mincer. Scraps and leftovers of boiled rice, of maize " mush," of polenta, of oatmeal porridge—last drops of sauce, will all come in handy. Don't forget seasoning of salt, pepper, minced parsley, minced onion, minced herbs, etc. Having thoroughly blended everything hot, leave it to go cold. Then it will be stiff or stiffish. Shape it into balls, dip them into beaten (dried) egg, and roll them in fine oatmeal, in maize flour, or in grated crusts. Fry them (in a wire basket, if possible) in sufficient boiling fat to cover them ; and don't put too many in at once, or they chill the fat.

If cooked in a wire basket, they need not be drained on paper ; you can drain them into the frying-pan, and thus save some fat. Serve at once on a hot dish.

The average amateur method is to mix the ingredients *cold and dry*, and then bind them with a beaten egg. The result is not half so good.

For very small households of say, three people, there is nothing more appetising and nourishing than shin of beef. It is much tenderer and usually cheaper than stewing steak. Two pounds of shin at 1s. 4d. and two ounces of suet (same price) will cost you five coupons. With that, a small family should manage four dinners. One pound of the meat to be made into a steamed pudding, eked out with sliced potato, onion and carrot ; a crust made of dripping or other fat, potato, and flour.

This, with plenty of vegetables, should serve for twice. Use the other pound to make a potato pie (or a paste pie, if you have a little dripping, lard, or other fat) or a casserole stew. A little well-boiled macaroni is a good ingredient, or any cold cooked haricot beans. There will be some of this left over ; and it can all be cut up and curried, or made into rissoles, or treated in any of the simple ways which you will find in this book.

The above is a mere suggestion as to how things may be done ; but it shows that you will have seven coupons (hypothetically) left over for bacon or anything else.

Again, a leg of mutton may be produced in three or four forms, as follows :

14. LEG OF MUTTON—THREE DINNERS FROM

A leg of mutton, if properly apportioned, will furnish three hot dinners for a small family (without counting the various ordinary ways of re-heating cold meat, such as hashes, curries, rissoles, etc.) This can be done either as follows : (1) Cut off the fillet end and bone it, replace the bone with veal stuffing, and roast it. (2) Cut a thick slice from the remaining portion, fry it to a good brown, and stew it in a casserole with turnips, onions, carrots, and herbs. (3) Roll up the knuckle end in a thick paste (should be a suet paste, but use what fat you can), tie it up in a floured cloth, and boil for three hours. Serve with baked or boiled onions.

Or thus : (1) Cut the leg right in two, with the knuckle end the largest. Bake the fillet end along with potatoes and Spanish onions (which should be parboiled first). (2) Cut a thick slice from the knuckle end, divide it into small equal strips, flour them and dip in beaten (dried) egg, and fry. Tomatoes or tomato sauce will be nice with these. (3) Boil rest of shank end with carrots, turnips, onions, and a bit of celery, and serve masked in parsley sauce. There will probably be enough scraps left from these three dishes to make a fourth. The liquid from the boiled shank should have all the bones (broken) added to it, and be boiled up again. It will make excellent stock, and with pearl barley, rice, or spaghetti, will supply a fine family soup.

Curries are a very admirable method for disposing of odds and ends. The hateful word hash, suggestive too often of dull insipidity and lack of invention, is not included in this book, save here in this paragraph.

Curries, bolstered up with vegetables, rice, and potatoes, have a savour and flavour which endears them to most people. And they need not be super-currified to ensure this result.

Minced meat is now too precious to be treated otherwise than as an ingredient in other dishes. Accustomed as you are to regard cold cooked meat as something to be camouflaged and got rid of, you will be amazed to find what an interest a very little of it lends to an otherwise " bald and unconvincing " dish.

As regards " offal," tripe, heart, liver, etc., that should be treated with equal reverence to other meat. No longer served in a plain, unvarnished condition, but tinkered up and made attractive in a variety of pleasing ways, and induced to go as far as it possibly can. I recommend sheep's hearts, calves' feet, calves' heads, ox tail, tripe, and liver, as eminently satisfactory to deal with, but *they must be above suspicion* as to condition. Anything horrider than " high " liver you will never wish to see.

15. LOIN OF MUTTON—SEVERAL DISHES FROM

Procure a piece of loin of mutton between two and three pounds (I am presuming that you are three in household), remove any fat that can be spared. Divide it into three pieces.

(1) Bone the first piece, which is for braising, flour it, and brown it in a stewpan in two ounces or so of the fat. Put it into a casserole, with seasoning of salt, pepper, and nutmeg or mace ; add half a breakfastcupful of heated stock, and any vegetables you may fancy, cut up fairly small ; such as onion, turnip, and carrot. Tie up in muslin two cloves, six peppercorns, a spray of parsley, some celery odds and ends, or celery seed, and a teaspoonful of minced fresh herbs or mixed dry ones. Place this with the rest in the casserole, cover, and cook very slowly. When the meat is tender, remove the muslin bag, sieve the vegetables and liquor, and serve them over the meat ; or, at pleasure, serve them as they are. Anything left over, including the seasoning (and of course the bones) will come in for soup.

(2) Bake the second piece of loin, with Yorkshire pudding made with dried eggs. The most economical way to bake it is in a double tin ; if you have not got one, cover whatever baking tin you use with another, the same size or a little larger, so as to retain all the heat and steam while the meat is cooking. It is the same idea as paper-bag cooking, only much better because you get more heat. The oven should be very hot for the first ten minutes ; then you require to lower the heat and let the meat do very slowly. Just at the last, remove the cover and brown the joint.

(3) The third piece can be either boned, and stuffed with a simple forcemeat ; or it can be steamed, and served with plenty of parsley sauce and vegetables. Or it can be boned, and the meat (browned in a little of the fat) can be made into a small mutton pie with potato short-crust ; or into a mutton pudding, using the fat to make a suet crust.

(4) There will be enough odds and ends over to make a fourth dinner at least ; consisting of rissoles, or potato pasties, or curry, or shepherd's pie. (5) And there should be enough stock, with the remains of these four days' meals, to result in an admirable soup.

16. BRISKET, BRAISED—SEVERAL DISHES FROM

(1) Take two to three pounds of brisket, and place in a casserole, on top of chopped fried onions, tomatoes, and carrots, with salt, and a teaspoonful of vinegar ; add enough stock of any sort to cover the vegetables but not the meat. Cover and cook very slowly indeed for two hours. Pulse, well soaked overnight, or cereals, can then be added ; such as two ounces of rice, or four ounces of haricots ; and another hour should see the whole dish ready to serve.

(2) Second day ; make some of what is left into curry, with boiled rice. (3) Third day ; mince, and serve with macaroni and tomato sauce. Or mince, enclose in mashed potato balls, and bake, smeared with a little fat.

17. BABOTIE

One onion, one cupful of milk or white stock, one thick slice of bread, six sweet almonds blanched and pounded, two eggs, any sort of meat minced, one small spoonful of curry-powder, a little bit of fat, pepper, and salt. Set a slice of bread to soak in the milk, pound the almonds, fry the onion after cutting it up very small, beat two eggs, and add to them the milk which remains from the cupful, part of which was used for soaking the bread ; mix these ingredients well together, and add the minced meat, curry-powder, fat, salt, and pepper. Rub a pie-dish with a lemon or some vinegar, put in the mixture, and bake for one hour in a hot oven.

18. BACON PIE

Mash some potatoes, and place them in a pie-dish in layers ; between each layer place thin slices of bacon, a little chopped onion, and either parsley or sage cut very fine, and some pepper ; moisten with stock, or water, or milk, as you proceed. Let the last layer be of potatoes, over which place little bits of bacon fat. Bake in a hot oven for about one hour.

19. BACON BATTER

Have twelve sound mushrooms cleaned and trimmed, place in a deep pie-dish and strew with minced sage and onion, salt and pepper. Lay two rashers of bacon on these; then add a second layer of mushrooms, seasoned as before, and two more rashers. Have ready a batter made with one (dried) egg, four ounces maize flour, one tablespoonful suet or other chopped fat (but this may be omitted), salt to taste, one breakfastcup milk. Pour this in, and bake one hour. To be served in the same dish.

20. BEEF, BOILED, WARMED UP IN FLEMISH FASHION

Fry three onions cut in slices; let them cook slowly without getting brown. Cut the cold beef in pieces about an inch square, put in the pan, adding some stock, flour, pepper, and salt, a spoonful of vinegar, and a small quantity of sugar; just before serving add a little fat.

21. BEEF, LEG OF, STEWED

Take about two pounds of fresh leg of beef and cut it small, removing any skin or gristle. Put it in a pie-dish, with a little flour dredged upon the pieces of meat, and a good pinch of salt. Cover it with cold water to top of dish, cover all closely with a dish, and let it cook gently in the oven for three hours. Add more water if it sinks. This can be eaten along with plain suet pudding, and is particularly satisfying and nourishing.

22. BEEF AND LENTILS

Fry some beef steak cut small, or some slices of underdone cold meat, with some onions, pepper, and salt. Have ready one pound of lentils boiled and mashed; make a wall of them on a dish, and place the fried meat, etc., inside. If preferred, tomato sauce can be served with the beef.

23. BEEF MINCED WITH TOMATOES

The remains of any cold beef minced fine; fry two or three onions cut in rings, and two tomatoes in slices; add the minced beef (about half a pound) and one pint of stock, pepper and salt to taste; stir well; make a wall of mashed potatoes on a dish, and pour the contents of the saucepan in the middle.

24. BEEF MIROTIN

Cut a small onion into very thin slices and fry in fat. When it begins to colour, stir in a tablespoonful of flour. Then add a breakfastcup of brown stock, pepper, salt, a pinch of sweet herbs, and two tablespoonfuls of tarragon vinegar. Stir till the sauce has boiled two or three minutes, and is of the right consistency, then strain it into another saucepan. When cold, put in some thin slices of cooked beef. Set the saucepan by the side of the fire, let the contents get warm, without boiling. When nearly simmering, add some sliced gherkins. The longer the mirotin takes to warm, the better it will be.

25. BEEF RAGOÛT

Fry an onion in some dripping; add to it one pint of stock thickened with one tablespoonful of flour, salt, pepper, and a pinch of clove powder. Have ready about half a pound of minced cold beef, and stir; just ten minutes before serving add to the ragoût one pint of hot boiled and peeled chestnuts, and mix well. Serve very hot.

26. BEEF, STEWED SHIN, WITH MACARONI

Take two pounds of shin of beef, cut it up in even pieces, and place in a stewpan with three pints of cold water. Let cook very slowly until nearly boiling, and then simmer gently for four or five hours, covered closely. Break up into two-inch lengths four ounces of macaroni, and parboil it, then add it to the stew quite half an hour before serving. Add pepper, salt, and a teaspoonful of minced parsley. An economical and nourishing dish.

27. BEEF, STEWED SHIN, No. I

Cut up half a pound of shin (or leg) of beef, one sheep's kidney, and one onion; dredge the meat with flour, and place in a casserole which has a close-fitting lid. Add two sticks of macaroni broken small, and half a pound tomatoes cut up (fresh or tinned), or tomato sauce to taste. Season with pepper and salt, put in just enough water to cover ; place casserole in moderate oven for two hours.

28. BEEF, STEWED SHIN, No. II

The whole shin is required for this ; if you can obtain it, it will be good value, being exceedingly nutritious. The shin-bone should be sawn across (but not the meat) in three separate places. Put it in a stewpan with water *nearly* to cover it, and let it heat through till just on boiling, then add a head of celery cut up, four onions, a bouquet of herbs, and seasoning of salt and pepper (or two teaspoonfuls pepper-corns in a muslin bag). Cover up closely, and let cook slowly for three hours, when cut-up carrots may be added at pleasure, and cut-up turnip. Stew one hour longer and serve. Some of the liquor may be thickened to make a sauce, and seasoned with made mustard and ketchup of any kind.

29. BEEF, BRAZILIAN STEW

Take one pound of shin of beef, cut it into dice, dip the pieces into about two tablespoonfuls of vinegar. Stick one clove in an onion, take one carrot, one strip of celery, and add half a pint of water. Put the whole in a jar and cook slowly in a cool oven, or stand the jar in a saucepan of water.

30. BUBBLE AND SQUEAK

Slices of either cold boiled beef or of roast beef can be used. Fry the slices of meat gently in a little fat, and arrange them nicely round a centre of fried greens ; these should be boiled till tender, well drained, minced, and then placed in a frying-pan with a little fat, a finely sliced onion, and seasoned with pepper and salt. When the onion is done, the greens are ready to serve.

31. BULLOCK'S HEART

Soak the heart, which must be thoroughly cleaned and emptied, in warm water for an hour and a half. Have ready a saucepan of boiling water, in which plunge the heart; let it boil up, and then only simmer slowly for two hours. Drain it, and either leave it till next day or until quite cold. Dry the heart inside and out with a hot cloth; fill the inside with sage-and-onion stuffing; sew it up, so that the stuffing keeps in; put some dripping on the top, and bake it in a very hot oven for two hours. If it acquires too much colour, place a piece of paper on the top. It must be basted very often, and sent to table very hot, and with a sauce tureen of gravy.

32. CALF'S FEET, BOILED

Take two calf's feet, the rind of a lemon, mace, cloves, mignonette and pepper to taste.

Boil till bones drop out. Then place pieces of meat on the dish it is to be served in. Boil liquor till it clarifies, and reduce to just sufficient to serve each piece. Last of all sprinkle with chopped parsley. Sufficient for four persons.

33. CALF'S FEET, STEWED

Divide two calf's feet into even pieces, place them in a stewpan with one sliced onion, a little thyme and parsley and bayleaf, a saltspoonful of mace, salt and pepper; pour in a pint of water, and simmer very slowly for two to three hours. When nearly ready to dish up, stir in one tablespoonful minced parsley, and two tablespoonfuls crumbs (soaked and drained pieces). Shake up the pan well.

34. CALF'S HEAD, STUFFED

Take half a calf's head, bone it, and fill with following stuffing; three ounces crumbs (soaked and drained crusts), one tablespoonful minced parsley, half a teaspoonful of mixed herbs, grated rind of half a lemon, nutmeg, pepper, and salt to taste. Bind with one (dried) egg. Roll up the head in a cloth, tie it, and place in boiling water containing two carrots, two turnips, two onions, and a bouquet of herbs. Let simmer for two hours, or until all is cooked. Serve masked in parsley sauce.

35. CHICKEN RISSOLETTES

Cook two ounces of rice in half a pint of weak stock, until the rice has absorbed the liquid. Then fry a slice of onion in two ounces of fat, without allowing it to brown; add one ounce of flour and a saltspoonful salt. Cook until well blended, and pour in half a pint of milk, or good stock, or tomato purée; stir till it boils; then remove the onion, and add half a cupful of the sauce to some finely minced scraps of chicken. Into the rest of the sauce put sufficient rice to make it stiff enough to form into balls; add one beaten yolk. Turn both the rice mixture and chicken out on plates and set aside. When sufficiently cool, form the rice into balls, with a hollow in the top of each, which must be filled with the chicken, and covered with rice. Roll twice in flour and beaten (dried) egg, let stand for a time. Fry in deep fat.

36. CORNISH PASTIES

Have a nice piece of potato short crust ready, roll it out not too thin. Cut up small any remains of cold meat, potatoes, onions, carrots, turnips—place a little of each on half the rounds of pastry, sprinkle salt and pepper over, fold the other half of pastry over, and pinch edges together. Make a couple of slits in top with knife, pour just a little cold gravy in, and place on greased kitchen paper in hot oven till pastry is cooked.

37. CORNISH PIE

Cut up one pound of pork or any other fresh meat; also cut up one pound of apples and one pound of onions; lay these all in a pie-dish with some pepper and salt, and a very little water or stock. Cover with pastry, and bake for an hour and a half,

38. COW-HEEL, No. I

Scald one cow-heel, but do not let it boil. Take it from the saucepan, split it, and simmer gently for four hours in two quarts of water. Dish up the cow-heel, pour over it some parsley sauce, and serve very hot.

Note.—The liquor must be saved either for soup or jelly.

39. COW-HEEL, No. II

Scald one cow-heel; boil it for an hour in very little water; take it out and dry it well; cut it into pieces about two inches long; dip them in chopped parsley, and then in batter, and fry them a nice brown.

40. CURRY, BAKED

Fry a sliced onion in a little dripping or other sound fat. Have a small slice of bread (or baked crust) soaked in a little water. Beat two dried eggs into one teacupful of milk or milk and water: add six sweet almonds grated, and the bread. Stir to this as much minced meat as you can spare (eight ounces is the proper quantity), with a little lump of margarine, chestnut-size, and one tablespoonful curry. Grease a pie-dish, sprinkle the juice of a lemon in, put the curry in, and let bake it for thirty minutes in moderate oven. Boiled rice should be served separately, as a vegetable.

41. CURRY CROQUETTES, BAKED

Have eight ounces of rice boiled in a pint of water, along with one finely-chopped onion, one teaspoonful of curry powder, half a teaspoonful of salt. Meanwhile mince any cooked mutton odds and ends, up to eight ounces, add a little minced thyme and parsley; and mix this into the hot rice as soon as it is done. Shape the mixture into balls: roll them in maize-flour; brush with a well-beaten dried egg, set in a baking-tin, and bake brown. A nice brown gravy, or a sharp sauce, will go well with this dish.

D

42. DOLMAS (SPANISH)

Chop some mutton or beef very fine ; add one large onion, also chopped (after being boiled), pepper, salt, and some boiled rice (about as much rice as meat). Take some cabbage leaves and put them in boiling water for two minutes, dry them and put the meat into them, and roll up the leaves like small sausages ; then stew them in thin stock. Take the rolls up carefully, place them on a dish, keep them hot, thicken the gravy with a little cornflour, and pour round the dolmas.

43. FAGGOTS

Put one pound of pig's fry into a saucepan with half a pound of onions and enough cold water to cover. Bring to the boil, let boil fifteen minutes, then remove the fry. Continue to boil the onions till they are tender, then put them, with the fry, through the mincer. Mix in six ounces soaked stale bread, one tablespoonful of sage (finely minced fresh, or powdered dry), one teaspoonful of pepper, one and a half teaspoonfuls of salt. Place the mixture in a baking-tin, strew with some little bits of fat and a little of the water in which the fry was boiled ; put into a moderate oven, and bake forty minutes. The mixture can be cut into oblongs or squares, either before or after baking.

44. FOWL, BRAISED

This is a good method when a fowl is not in its first youth. Truss it for boiling, and put it in a casserole or stew-pan, on top of a sliced onion and carrot, and a slice or two of salt pork, and a rasher or two of bacon. On top of the fowl place another slice of fat meat, seasoning, of peppercorns (eight or so), cloves (six), mace (a saltspoonful), salt half a teaspoonful), thyme and parsley to taste, two or three bay-leaves, and a pint of water. Put greased paper, cover closely with lid, and simmer steadily for two hours. Strain off the gravy and thicken it before serving.

45. FOWL AND RICE

Any pieces of cooked fowl can be used thus : Boil one pound of rice in stock, add salt, pepper, and mace to taste ; when it has absorbed almost all the liquor, line a greased baking-dish with it, place the pieces of fowl in, cover with the rest of the rice. Pour a very little stock over, smooth the top, and cook in a slow oven until quite set.

46. FOWL, STEWED

Procure an untrussed fowl, and cut it up into as many small joints as possible. The legs, thighs, wings, and breasts are divisible into two pieces each, and the back into three. Have a medium Spanish onion finely minced and stewed with two ounces of fat, and salt and pepper, for an hour or so. Place the pieces of fowl in this, let cook gently for thirty minutes, then transfer to a (heated) casserole, and let them finish cooking, if need be, in the oven. Add the juice of half a lemon, and serve in the casserole.

47. FRENCH TOAST

One pound of shin of beef, half a pint of soaked and drained bread, half a pound of tomatoes. Mince the beef, mix with the breadcrumbs and tomatoes chopped up (previously scalded to remove skins), bind with one beaten (dried) egg. Press into pillow form, place in a baking-tin, cover, and bake for one hour. Remove cover, put a little fat on the top, and let it bake until brown. Make a nice gravy.

48. GOOSE, MOCK

Take half a pound of pig's liver, one pound of potatoes, one good-sized onion, a little flour, four or five leaves of chopped sage. When you have washed and wiped the liver, slice it and add a little salt and pepper ; dredge a very little flour over the pieces, and put them in a pie-dish, with a little onion between the layers—the onion should have been half cooked and well chopped. Half fill the dish with water, and mash the potates (with a little dripping or margarine *ad lib.*) to make a crust. Bake the " mock goose " for about forty-five minutes in a good hot oven.

49. GOOSE, POOR MAN'S

Take half a pound of liver ; wash, wipe, and slice it evenly ; dredge it with a very little maize or barley flour; season with pepper and salt ; place the slices in layers in a greased pie-dish, and between each layer put minced parboiled onion mixed with minced sage. Have the dish half-way full of water ; and cover the top with sliced parboiled potatoes (one pound will be required) ; a little fat should be sprinkled on top if possible. This is said to taste just like goose.

50. HARE, BAKED

Have the hare skinned, cleaned, and washed. Make a forcemeat of soaked, drained (stale) bread, suet or fat, parsley, onion, etc., and stuff the hare. Sew up and truss ; if you can spare any slices of fat bacon, put them over it ; if not, wrap it in a greased paper, and bake for an hour or so.

51. HARE, HARICOT

Fry the inferior joints of a hare in one tablespoonful of fat. Add to them one turnip, one carrot, and one shallot or small onion, sliced ; a little thyme and parsley, and seasoning of salt and pepper, also a pint of stock or water. Place in a stew-pan or casserole, and simmer for two hours.

52. HARE, JUGGED

Have the best joints of hare cut up into small even pieces or joints about three inches long (the inferior joints can be used otherwise). Wash and dry them, fry them in one table-spoonful of fat. When nicely browned, place them in a casserole, with pepper and salt to taste, five or six cloves, a bayleaf, a pinch of cinnamon, the juice of one lemon, and two pints of good stock. Put a greased paper over, and cover with lid ; cook for two hours.

53. HEAD, POTTED

Take half a sheep's head, removing the brains ; wash the head thoroughly, and soak it for an hour or two in warm water ; then break it up and lay it in a pan with just sufficient water to cover it well ; bring to the boil, skim well, and simmer steadily, closely covered, till the bones will slip from the flesh. Now lift the meat out, remove the bones, cut into dice, seasoning it as you do so, with the following mixture ; two teaspoonfuls of salt, one of freshly ground black pepper, one of powdered allspice, and, if liked, a salt-spoonful of cayenne. Return the meat to the pan, allow it to simmer uncovered for a few minutes, then pour it, with its liquor strained, into a wetted basin or mould, putting in with it the tongue, which should have been cooked separately, and leave till set. If liked, the liquor may be sharply boiled up to reduce it, while the meat is being cut up.

54. IRISH STEW

This popular dish is made with onions, potatoes, and with sliced breast, jointed scrag, or neck of mutton. Very few people succeed with it. The point is, to parboil the onions and potatoes (separately) for fifteen minutes each, and drain off the water, before slicing them thickly and placing in the casserole. The bottom layer should be onions, next potatoes, the next meat ; season each layer of meat with salt and pepper, and pour in a little cold water three-quarters of a pint to three pounds of potatoes. Cover closely and bake in quiet oven, or place on stove to simmer very slowly, for three hours.

55. JAMAICA FRITTERS

Take a small slice of cold meat, about one ounce, one dried egg, the equivalent of half a slice of bread in soaked, drained stale bread. Mince the meat finely. Beat the egg, add to the bread some minced parsley and onion, or any other flavouring. Have ready boiling fat in frying pan.

Drop the mixture in by tablespoonfuls, turn when sufficiently set, so as to brown both sides—or it may be made in one large fritter, filling the bottom of the pan. Any sort of meat or fish may be used. The above is enough for two persons.

56. KIDNEY PUDDING

Take half a pound of fresh ox-kidney, cut it up in small equal cubes, dust with salt and pepper. Have six ounces of flour mixed with three ounces of chopped suet or other fat ; add one beaten egg (dried) and enough water to make the whole into a thickish batter. Mix in the pieces of kidney ; place all in a greased (or rinsed) basin, cover and tie down, place in boiling water ; let boil quickly for three hours.

Double the above quantities can be used at pleasure, and a little finely minced onion and parsley can be added.

57. KIDNEY AND ONION SAVOURY

Take a Spanish onion, cut out the centre, and insert a kidney which has been carefully washed and skinned. Bake in rather a hot oven, basting frequently with fat ; serve with thick brown gravy.

58. LEEK AND PORK PIE

Cut up small one bundle of leeks, wash, and place them in salted boiling water. Let boil twenty minutes, and drain thoroughly. Cut up one pound of salt lean pork in small equal pieces, boil for twenty minutes in enough water to cover ; then empty meat and liquor into a deep greased pie-dish ; add the leeks, half a breakfastcupful of soaked drained crumbs, one beaten (dried) egg, and mix thoroughly. Cover with a potato crust (see No. 486) and bake for one hour in moderate oven.

59. LIVER AND BACON

Cut up one pound of bullock's liver into thin slices, and half a pound of bacon into small strips. Lay a piece of bacon on top of each strip, roll up tight, and skewer it. Have

some hot fat ready in the frying-pan and cook the rolled
pieces until they are a nice brown. A thick gravy and a
wall of mashed or riced potatoes are correct with this dish.

60. LIVER AND ONIONS

Cut up one rasher of bacon into small squares and fry it ;
put in one large onion thinly sliced, and when this has browned
add eight ounces of calf's liver, cut up into strips or slices
a quarter of an inch thick. Let these cook slowly until well
browned both sides and thoroughly cooked ; transfer them,
with the onion, to a hot dish. Thicken the liquor in the
frying-pan, add gradually a little stock of any kind ; continue to stir until it boils and browns ; add pepper and salt,
pour it over the liver, and serve at once.

61. LIVER AND POTATO TURNOVERS

Boil some potatoes, dry and floury ; mash them smoothly,
make into a paste with a dried egg, adding a little salt and
pepper. Roll out and cut into rounds about five inches
across ; prepare a stuffing as follows : Finely chop or mince
some boiled liver, add a few breadcrumbs, season with a
little chopped onion and powdered eggs, lay a little mixture
on each round, fold over and wet the edges of one half to
make it adhere to the other, and bake in a quick oven.

62. LIVER, STUFFED

Take a calf's liver, and stuffing (sage and onions). Make an
incision through the centre of the liver to the depth of half
its thickness ; now put the knife into the opening, and, by
holding it flat, cut round on each side. This will make a
pocket to hold the stuffing. Bake in a hot oven, well basting
with good dripping.

63. MEAT CAKE

Mince half a pound of cold underdone meat ; add two
ounces of breadcrumbs, the same of cooked rice—or macaroni
cut small ; beat a dried egg into a cupful of gravy mixed with

half an ounce of flour. Add salt, pepper, fried onions, a
teaspoonful of celery sauce, a few tinned mushrooms, or
anchovy sauce, or mixed pickles. Grease a cake-tin, coat it
well with grated crust crumbs, pack in close, cover with
breadcrumbs and bake about an hour.

64. MULLIGATAWNY STEW

Fry four onions sliced small and a head of garlic of a
light brown, then put them into a stewpan with the meat,
which should be fowl or any white meat. Three spoonfuls of
curry powder and two of flour mixed together, likewise a
spoonful of lemon juice and cayenne pepper to your taste.
Pour over it a pint of boiling water and let it simmer slowly
for a short time, then add a sufficient quantity of broth made
without vegetables to make a tureen of mulligatawny. The
ingredients must then stew together an hour. To be served
with a dish of rice as for curry. Cold fowl can be dressed
this way extremely well.

65. MUTTON, BREAST OF, STUFFED AND BAKED, No. I

Have a piece of breast of mutton, put into warm water,
and simmered slowly until the bones can be removed (but
not enough to cook the meat entirely). Carrots, turnips,
salt and pepper should be placed with it. Meanwhile prepare
a stuffing, according to amount required, with (soaked and
pressed) crumbs, finely-minced onion, parsley, and thyme,
and a little chopped fat, such as scraps of bacon. Put the
meat on a flat board, remove the bones, dredge with salt
and pepper, and spread evenly with the stuffing. Then roll
and tie it, and bake until tender and a good brown.

66. MUTTON, BREAST OF, STUFFED AND BAKED, No. II

Have a breast of mutton boned, and substitute for the
bones (which must be broken up and used for stock) a turkey
stuffing of crumbs, grated lemon-peel, thyme, parsley, chopped
fat of some sort, and seasoning of salt and pepper. Spread
this an inch thick, roll up the meat the short way, tie or

skewer it, and bake, allowing thirty minutes for a pound
Baste now and then.

67. MUTTON CASSEROLE

Mince any scraps of cold roast mutton, up to eight ounces ;
add one teaspoonful each of chopped parsley and of capers,
one medium onion (boiled) and chopped, salt and pepper,
half a pint of good stock or brown gravy. Place in a casserole and cover with one pound of potatoes mashed with a
little fat. Place in a hot oven, until the potatoes are golden
brown.

68. MUTTON CHARLOTTE

Slices of cold cooked mutton, however few, will make this
appetising dish.

Have a greased pie-dish, put some grated crusts or dried
soaked crumbs at the bottom, then a little mutton, then
some slices of tomato ; sprinkle with minced onion, salt and
pepper. Repeat, from the breadcrumbs, as before. The
last layer must be tomatoes, thinly strewn with crumbs.
Bake for forty-five minutes.

69. MUTTON KEDGEREE

Chop (not mince) any kind of cold mutton scraps, up to
six ounces in weight. Have one ounce of rice boiled and
drained. Put one ounce of fat in a stewpan, melt it, fry a
small minced onion till it is golden brown ; stir in the meat,
and let fry for three or four minutes ; add the rice, with
seasoning of salt, pepper, and nutmeg. Have ready two hard-
boiled eggs ; chop up the whites, and stir them to the rice,
etc. Pour on to a hot dish. Pass the yolks through a wire
sieve, and strew them into the kedgeree, with some finely-
minced parsley. Put the dish in the oven for five minutes or
so, and serve. Any other odds and ends of meat, game, or
poultry can be treated as above.

70. MUTTON AND MACARONI

Boil two ounces of Naples macaroni in fast-boiling salted
water, drain thoroughly ; butter six small moulds thickly

and line them with the macaroni, coiling it round the bottom and sides. Take any remains of cooked mutton, remove skin, fat or gristle, mince finely, and mix with a third its quantity of bread crumbs. Also pepper, salt, a dessert-spoonful of chopped parsley, a seasoning of chopped herbs. Beat up a dried egg in a little thick gravy, add to the meat. Turn the mixture into the moulds, cover with greased paper, and steam for twenty minutes. Turn out the moulds on a very hot dish, pour good thick tomato sauce round, and serve.

71. MUTTON, MINCED

Take half a dozen ripe tomatoes, the size of an egg, break them up into a lined saucepan, with an ounce of fat, a chopped shallot, two cloves, a few herbs, a pinch of salt and of sugar, and a gill of gravy. Let simmer until cooked, then rub through a sieve, make a roux of an ounce of butter and a large tea-spoonful of flour, add the purée, and boil up well; put in any scraps of cold mutton, cut in dice, keep the mixture well under boiling point for an hour. Then bring it barely to the boil, and dish up in a pile garnished with boiled macaroni.

72. MUTTON OLIVES

Take slices of cold roast mutton, trim neatly, dust on one side of each pepper, salt, and a little allspice. Put a small piece of stuffing on each and roll up, tying firmly with cotton. Place the rolls in a baking-tin, pour some good gravy over, cover with greased paper, bake for half an hour. Make a mound of mashed potatoes on a dish, arrange the olives round, thicken the gravy and pour round.

73. OX-BRAIN FRITTERS

Boil an ox-brain in fast-boiling water for half an hour. When quite cold, cut it in pieces, and fry in batter until it is a golden brown.

74. OX-CHEEK

Wash a cheek well, but do not soak it; put it on the fire with plenty of cold water, and with two pints of split peas that have soaked all night ; onions, carrots, turnips, celery, salt and pepper, are also added, but not at first, as the cheek and peas will require four hours' boiling, and the vegetables not more than two. Dish up the cheek, lay the vegetables round it (all except the peas), and serve very hot, with a sauce tureen of liquor from the saucepan. The liquor with the peas makes a very good soup for the following day.

75. OX-CHEEK MOULD

The remains of an ox-cheek cut into slices, and laid in a mould with pepper, salt, powdered herbs, and hard-boiled eggs cut in slices. Proceed with these ingredients, and a few slices of boiled ham or bacon, until the mould is full ; have half an ounce of gelatine dissolved in one pint of the liquor in which the cheek was boiled ; add it to the meat, etc., in the mould, until it is quite full ; bake one hour in a hot oven. When cold, turn it out of the mould, and serve.

76. OXTAIL, STEWED

Have the oxtail cut into small equal pieces, place in a saucepan with two quarts of water, seasoned to taste with salt and pepper. Let boil, and then simmer three or four hours. Then put in any vegetables you like, such as carrots, onions, green peas, parsley, etc., and let boil for another hour.

WAR-TIME PIES, VARIOUS

77. CURRY PIE

Minced meat mixed well with the same quantity of stale bread soaked in warm water, a small onion minced, a little curry powder. Put all, well mixed, into a pie-dish, over the top put a beaten dried egg, bake, turn out, and serve with rice, tomatoes, macaroni, or fried onions.

78. HARICOT PIE

Pour boiling water on one pint of haricots ; leave to soak overnight ; boil for about one hour next day. Have one

large onion and four ounces of bacon (say, two rashers) finely
chopped, place in a pie-dish, with a teacupful of water ; cover
with the beans, adding chopped parsley, pepper, and salt.
Make a potato shortcrust, cover the pie, and bake a nice brown.

79. SQUAB PIE, DEVONSHIRE

Take a pie-dish, put at the bottom a layer of sliced apples,
strew over them a little sugar, then a layer of fresh mutton
(well seasoned with salt and pepper). Then another layer
of apples. Peel some onions and slice them, lay them on
the apples, then a layer of mutton, then apples and onions,
Pour in a pint of water, cover all over with a potato crust,
and bake.

80. SQUAB PIE, KENT

Take one pound of the best end of the neck of mutton,
cut it into small pieces, flavour with salt and pepper, and put
a layer of it at the bottom of a pie-dish ; next add a layer
of sliced apples and onions, with about a dessertspoonful of
brown sugar, then another layer of mutton. Cover with a
good pie-crust, and bake.

81. POOR MAN'S PIE

Have half a pound of beef " pieces," nice and fresh ; stew
them very gently until quite tender. Cut it up small. Make
a plain short-crust with two ounces of dripping or other fat,
enough to line and cover a shallow (greased) pie-dish. Have
four potatoes and one onion (if parboiled, so much the better)
cut up and mixed with meat. Place meat and vegetables in
dish ; season with salt and pepper, add some of the stock
that the meat was stewed in. Cover with paste, and put
into a gentle oven for an hour.

82. SAUSAGE POTATO PIES

Take half a pound of sausages, place in a quarter pint
(half-breakfastcupful) of boiling water, let simmer for twenty
minutes, take out, skin, and cut each in two. Have two pounds
of potatoes boiled, mash them, and beat them with about half

a breakfastcupful of milk until they are very light. Then lay each piece of sausage upon a tablespoonful of potato, and cover it up roughly with more potato. Place in a greased tin, and bake to a nice golden brown, which should take about twenty minutes.

83. SEA PIE, No. I

Have one pound of shin of beef cut into equal pieces, and dredge with a little flour of any kind, seasoned with salt and pepper. Cut up one carrot, one turnip, and one onion into small cubes. Place all in a wide earthen jar, and pour in enough cold water to cover meat and vegetables. Let it come slowly to the boil, and then stew very gently for an hour. Then have ready a paste, made with six ounces of flour, pinch of salt, half a teaspoonful of baking-powder, and three ounces of chopped suet or other fat. Moisten it with cold water. Cover top of stew with this crust, put lid on, and replace in oven for one-and-a-half hours. Serve in the casserole.

84. SEA PIE, No. II

Take eight ounces of shin or neck of beef, cut into equal pieces; dip (but do not soak) each piece in vinegar. Have one large onion and one carrot sliced, at the bottom of an earthenware pot; next put in the meat, then half a pound cold boiled sliced potatoes, and any cold cooked haricots or green peas. Add salt and pepper to taste, pour in a pint of stock or cold water to taste. Let it come to the boil, then simmer gently for one hour. Put a suet crust on, and let it cook two hours more.

85. SHEPHERD'S PIE

Any sliced cold meat will do for this. Have ready a seasoning of salt, pepper, and finely-minced parsley and thyme. Place the meat in a pie-dish, alternately with layers of sliced parboiled onion and sliced cold potatoes. Pour in one gill of stock of any sort, or water. Cover with mashed potatoes that have been beaten with pepper and salt, a little

hot milk, and a little fat, dripping for preference. Smooth
the potato with a wide knife, and place in a moderate oven
until it turns a golden brown.

86. TRIPE PIE

Take cold stewed tripe, and place it in a pie-dish, with
the jellied liquor ; add salt and pepper, and a little bit of
uncooked ham if possible ; also a few little bits of fat, and a
few spoonfuls of brown stock, or gravy. Cover with a potato
crust (see No. 486) and bake in a good oven till the pastry
is done.

87. PIGEON PIE

For this, the pigeons (four at least will be required) should
be stuffed with a forcemeat of soaked drained stale bread,
fat of some sort, finely minced parsley, pepper and salt.
Steak is usually added, at top and bottom, to supply gravy,
but is too extravagant now. Still, if you can manage a little
leg or shin of beef in the bottom of the pie-dish, it will make
a more nourishing dish. Hard-boiled yolks are also usual,
but can be dispensed with. Put the pigeons breast down-
wards in the dish, and pour in half a pint of stock. Cover
with a potato crust if you cannot manage a short crust.
Puff paste was the pre-war usage.

88. PIGEON PUDDING

For this, two pigeons will suffice ; and steak is commonly
included, (see above recipe), and a chopped kidney is an
improvement. The pigeons should be each divided into
four pieces, and the meat (if any) cut up small, and all should
be dredged thickly with flour of any sort, salt, and pepper.
Place the pieces in a basin lined with suet crust, or potato
crust ; pour in a teacupful of good stock or gravy. Cover
with paste, tie over with scalded floured cloth ; boil gently
for two hours.

89. PIGEON, STEWED, No. I

Take 2 pigeons, and cut them in half, down the middle or
back. Cut up half a pound of shin of beef (if you can spare

it) into little equal pieces ; place in a casserole, with pepper, salt, and a sliced onion, and just enough water to cover. Simmer until tender—probably two hours—thicken the liquor and serve in same dish.

90. PIGEON, STEWED, No. II

Take a piece of dripping or other fat, about as large as an egg. Dredge it with flour, salt and pepper, and put it inside the pigeon. Have sliced vegetables in a casserole—onion, turnip, potato, and any others to taste. Put the pigeon upon these, add a little stock, and simmer for an hour. Remove pigeon, dredge it with flour, and put it in the oven until brown. Strain off the liquor from the casserole (the vegetables can be sieved for purée), season with salt, pepper, and mushroom ketchup ; pour it over the pigeon upon a hot dish.

91. PIG'S FRY, BAKED

Cut up a pound of pig's fry, lay it in a pie-dish, chop finely two onions and a few sage leaves, season to taste, mix these ingredients and sprinkle over the meat. Cut up a pound and an half of part-boiled potatoes, and cover over the meat with them ; fill the dish with water or stock, bake for two hours and a half in a moderate oven.

92. PIG'S TROTTERS

Place two pig's feet in cold water (salted), and when it just boils, remove, scrape them, and place in a saucepan with just sufficient hot water to cover them. Put in one onion, one carrot, one small turnip, all sliced ; salt and pepper to taste, a saltspoonful of ground mace, a small tea-spoonful of powdered or chopped fresh thyme. Let all simmer slowly until the trotters are quite tender. Take out and serve (hot or cold) ; if hot, with peas pudding. Reserve the liquor for stock.

93. PILAU

Put one breakfastcupful of rice to soak in cold water for an hour ; then drain off the water, and put the rice into a double boiler, with two breakfastcupfuls of stock and half a smallish onion. Let simmer until the rice has absorbed all the stock. Meanwhile, stew half the contents of a tin of tomatoes, add salt and pepper, and a little fat. Mix this with the rice. Have pieces of cold cooked fowl or turkey lightly fried, put them into the centre of the rice, let stew for twenty minutes, and serve, retaining the rice around the meat.

94. PORK AND BAKED BEANS

Soak one pint of butter beans or haricot beans in cold water overnight. Next day wash and rinse them, then boil until they are just soft enough to prick with a fork. A teaspoonful of bicarbonate of soda should be added. Then rinse them in boiling water, and put half of them into a large stew-jar. Have ready half a pound of salt pork, score the rind half an inch apart, put it into the beans, and put the rest of the beans on top. Mix one teaspoonful of salt, one teaspoonful of mustard, and one teaspoonful of sugar (or treacle) with hot water, and put it over the beans; then pour in enough boiling water to cover them. They must be kept covered with water, and you must replenish it if it sinks; but towards the last hour of cooking you may bring the pork to the top, so that it gets browned; but do not leave the cover off. Bake in a moderate oven for not less than eight hours.

95. PORK CHOPS, BAKED

Put the chops in a baking-tin, and cover them with slices of apple, tomato, and onion—about one pound of the first two, and half a pound of onion will suffice for four chops; add pepper and salt, and about a tumblerful of cold water. Cover up with another tin or flat dish, and bake in hot oven for about one hour and a half.

96. PORK AND HARICOT BEANS

Take one quart of haricot beans and soak them all night in water; next morning put them into boiling water in a saucepan, and boil them slowly for half an hour, or longer; take them out and drain them; have ready an earthenware jar with a lid; put three-quarters of a pound of pickled pork into the jar, and one onion cut in quarters; add the beans and enough cold water just to cover the whole; bake the pork and beans in the oven for four hours with the lid on, or until they both are perfectly tender. Dish up the pork in the middle of a dish, and cover with the beans.

97. POTATO PUFFS

Mince some cooked meat, and flavour it, according to taste, either with pickles or mushrooms cut small; moisten with stock or gravy, mash some potatoes, roll them out with a very little flour, cut them into the shape and size of a saucer, place the meat in the centre of a potato saucer, cover over with a similar piece, pinch the corners together, and fry them a light brown in some boiling fat.

98. POTATO AND MEAT ROLLS

Have enough cold potatoes as will fill a breakfast cup when mashed, mix in a little dripping, work into a smooth paste with a little milk, roll out half an inch thick, and cut into squares. Have ready any scraps of meat or bacon, or odds and ends of vegetables, finely minced, seasoned with salt and pepper and a few drops of sauce; put a little upon each square, and bake a golden brown in a good oven.

99. RABBIT, BOILED WITH RICE

Have a young rabbit boiled gently for thirty minutes, then remove the meat from the bones. To a breakfastcupful of (hot) boiled rice, add a lettuce shredded small, one little leek chopped finely (white part only), half a teaspoon each of finely minced parsley, onion, and lemon peel; salt and pepper to taste. Mix well, then stir in the pieces of rabbit meat. Place the mixture in a scalded cloth, and let boil slowly in the rabbit stock, which must well cover it, for about two hours, not longer. For a small rabbit, one and a half hours will suffice.

E

100. RABBIT, CURRIED, No. I

Cut up the rabbit into joints, dry, and flour them. Have one onion and one apple peeled and chopped. Heat one ounce of fat, add the onion, rabbit, one dessertspoonful of flour, and two teaspoonfuls of curry powder; fry a light brown. Add the apple and one breakfastcupful stock. Let simmer one and a half hours, or until the meat is tender. Add salt to taste, and a few drops of lemon juice or vinegar. Serve at once.

101. RABBIT, CURRIED, No. II

Take a rabbit, cut up, fry the pieces a light brown, with sliced onion and strips of bacon. When they begin to colour, dredge in flour, with curry-powder *ad lib.*; add stock and salt. Let all simmer gently till done. (The flour and curry-powder may also be mixed smoothly into the stock.) Serve with a wall of plain boiled rice around. Some people add slices of apple.

102. RABBIT, JUGGED

Cut up a rabbit into joints, place in a deep stew-jar, with two large sliced onions, parsley, pepper, salt, and a very little mace. Add any bacon bones and bits of bacon that you can spare. Fill up with enough water or stock to cover all. Place lid on, and let cook about three hours in a slow oven. The liquor can be drained off, thickened, and put back to the meat, before serving.

103. RABBIT AND ONION SAUCE

Blanch the pieces of rabbit for ten minutes in boiling water. Put them into a saucepan with an onion stuck full of cloves, thyme, parsley, pepper, and salt. Cover with boiling water. Let them simmer about three-quarters of an hour. Serve on a dish piled, with plenty of onion sauce poured over them.

104. RABBIT, STEWED

Cut up a rabbit into small pieces; fry it in some dripping with a sliced onion and tomato. When the rabbit is done through, take it out of the frying-pan, and place it in a clean saucepan ; add some stock, lemon peel, spice, herbs, pepper, and salt to the ingredients in the frying-pan ; boil these for an hour, and then strain them over the rabbit in the saucepan ; thicken it with flour, simmer for half an hour, and serve very hot with sippets of fried bread.

105. RICE MOULD WITH MEAT

About three-quarters of a pound of any cold meat (if chicken or veal, a little cold ham or bacon as well), finely minced ; add to it three ounces of boiled rice, one onion scalded and chopped, one teaspoonful of chopped parsley. Salt and pepper ; mix well ; add two dried eggs well beaten, and two tablespoonfuls of gravy. Pour into a greased basin, and steam for one hour. Thicken some stock with fat and flour, add one teaspoonful of sauce, turn out the shape, and pour gravy over.

106. RICE MOULD SAVOURY

This is a very tempting and nutritious dish. To half a teacupful of rice boiled in milk, add two ounces of minced cold mutton, one ounce of ham, one hard-boiled egg minced, one tablespoonful of chopped parsley, one beaten dried egg, pepper and salt to taste. If not moist enough, add a little milk. This may be baked in a pie-dish or steamed in a mould.

107. RICE SAVOURY

Boil a breakfastcupful of rice for twenty minutes; drain it ; grease a pudding basin, and place in it a layer of rice, and as much as will stick to the sides of it as well. Have ready any cold meat, minced and seasoned with spice, pepper and salt ; place this on the rice in the basin, and cover it over with the remainder of the boiled rice. Steam it for an hour. When cold, turn out and serve, garnishing the dish with parsley.

108. RICE PIE

Boil a breakfastcupful of rice in stock or water for twenty minutes (rice must always be put into boiling liquid); **drain** it; grease a pie-dish, and put in a layer of rice; on this lay some cold meat chopped very fine, one onion and some parsley (also chopped), pepper and salt; fill up the pie-dish with the rest of the rice, carefully pour in a cupful of stock or gravy, place some little pieces of fat on the rice, cover the rice with a dish to prevent its getting hard, and bake for one hour or rather less. It ought not to be brown on the top.

109. RISSOLES AUX HERBES

Minced cold meat of any kind. Place in a greased pie-dish, with a thick sprinkling of common and lemon thyme, pepper and salt, and a very little gravy; strew breadcrumbs thickly over, place dabs of fat on the top, and bake for half an hour in a quick oven.

110. SAUSAGES, CURRIED

Have one pound of sausages fried; add one teaspoonful each of curry powder and flour; mix smooth with a little water in the saucepan, simmer for ten minutes, and pour off all upon a hot dish.

111. SAUSAGE DUMPLINGS

Mash some potatoes with milk, make them into a thick crust with some flour, roll up one sausage into each piece of potato crust (after taking off their skins), and bake in a tin dish until the potatoes begin to colour, which will be in about one hour.

112. SAUSAGES AND LENTILS

Soak one pint of lentils in cold water for twelve hours. Drain them, and put them in a saucepan with one cut-up carrot, one stick of celery, one piece of parsley, one teaspoonful of salt, and three pints of cold water. Let all simmer for two hours closely covered; then take out all the vegetables.

Melt half an ounce of dripping in a saucepan, stir in two table-spoonfuls of flour, add a small onion minced fine, and let this colour to a pale brown. Drain off to this all the liquor from the lentils ; stir and boil a few minutes. Now add the lentils, and let them boil ten minutes more. Meanwhile fry one pound of sausages, and, having arranged the lentils on a large heated dish, place the sausages on top. This is a tasty and nourishing dish.

113. SAUSAGE RAGOÛT

Fry two onions and two tomatoes in a saucepan ; add to them one pound of pork or beef sausages and one pint of stock, thickened and flavoured. Let all simmer for an hour and a half. Have ready a wall of mashed potatoes or boiled rice on a dish, and place the contents of the saucepan in the centre.

114. SAUSAGE SURPRISES

Take half a pound of sausages, prick them, and cook them for twenty minutes in a quarter of a pint of boiling water. Skin them and cut them in two. Have ready two pounds of hot mashed potatoes, mixed with a quarter of a pint of milk and a little dripping (a little finely chopped parsley is an improvement), with salt and pepper to taste. Lay each piece of sausage in a tablespoonful of potato, and cover it with potato ; let these be laid in a greased baking-dish and baked a good brown.

115. SAVOURY PUDDING

Half a pound of stale, soaked, drained bread, three dried eggs, three ounces of flour, three ounces of suet or fat, one ounce of fine oatmeal, one pint of cereal stock, a small shallot, chopped very fine, a little salt, a pinch of sweet marjoram, and enough lemon to give a flavour. Mix all thoroughly well together, not too moist ; turn into a basin or (better) a floured cloth, and boil or steam for three hours.

116. SCALLOPED MEAT

Mince some cold meat very fine. Have ready some mashed potatoes ; place a layer of them at the bottom of a scallop shell, with the meat in the middle, seasoned according to taste, and moistened with either gravy or milk ; cover up with more mashed potatoes and little pieces of fat, and bake.

117. SCRAP ROLLS

Take any pieces of cooked meat (two or three different sorts if you happen to have them) ; mince through the machine ; season with pepper, salt, and herbs or parsley, according to taste. Make a crust with cold boiled potatoes, flour, and milk ; place little pieces of the seasoned meat inside the crust, which must be cut according to the size you wish ; roll up tightly, and bake in the oven for one hour.

118. SHEEP'S HEARTS, BAKED

Clean some sheep's hearts, place in boiling water, and let simmer twenty minutes. Remove, and fill with veal stuffing. Let them grow cold, then roll up each in a piece of paste (made with lard if you can get it) and bake about twenty minutes.

119. SHEEP'S TROTTERS, BAKED

Boil six sheep's trotters until the bones can be easily removed ; replace the bones with veal stuffing, of which four ounces will be required. Fry half a sliced onion in two ounces of fat ; add a teaspoonful of minced parsley, plenty of pepper and salt, and one breakfastcupful of stock. Put the trotters, floured thickly, into an open casserole ; add one teaspoonful of vinegar to the contents of the pan, and pour it over the trotters. Sprinkle with a few crumbs, and if possible, a little grated cheese. Place in a good oven, and serve in casserole when nicely browned.

120. TOAD-IN-THE-HOLE

Mince any kind of meat ; season well with pepper, salt, one onion minced, and parsley chopped, also two large tomatoes sliced. Place this in a buttered pie-dish; make some batter several hours before it is wanted, and just before you require the "toad" cooked, add the batter, and bake in a quick oven for an hour and a half.

121. TRIPE BOILED IN MILK

Boil one pound of tripe in water, *i.e.*, place it in cold water until the water boils; take it from the saucepan, and cut it in small pieces. Cut four large onions in slices, and put them in a saucepan with the tripe and one pint of milk; let it simmer for two hours (it must boil), then dish up the tripe, and keep it hot. Cut the onions very small, thicken the milk with a dessertspoonful of flour made smooth first in cold milk; put back the onions into the milk, let them boil up, and then pour over the tripe and serve very hot.

122. TRIPE, CURRIED, No. I

Prepare the tripe as above. While it is simmering, fry one large onion and one apple in some dripping, adding one ounce of flour, one dessertspoonful of curry-powder, pepper and salt; then add half a pint of the liquor in which the tripe simmered, and stir until it becomes nice and thick; into this put the slices of tripe, a pinch of brown sugar, and a strip of lemon-peel, and let all simmer together for two hours. Serve very hot, with a border of boiled rice.

123. TRIPE, CURRIED, No. II

Curried tripe is both economical and nutritious. Take two or three large onions, and fry them in dripping till tender. Chop them very fine, or, if preferred, pass through a sieve, and dredge with a dessertspoonful each of curry powder and peaflour mixed. When quite smooth, add gradually one pint of stock and stir till it boils. Now take one-and-half pounds of boiled tripe, cut it into pieces about one inch square, and put it into the sauce. Let all stew together for one and a half hours. Have ready some well-boiled rice, make a pile of it on the dish, pour the tripe into the centre and serve. Squeeze a little lemon juice over the whole.

124. TRIPE FRICASSEE, No. I

Take the whitest tripe you can get, and cut it in long pieces; put them into a stewpan with a little good gravy, a few breadcrumbs, a lump of butter, a little vinegar to taste, and a little mustard if you like it. Shake it up altogether with a little minced parsley, let it stew slowly till done.

125. TRIPE FRICASSEE, No. II

Take the whitest *and* thickest tripe, cut the white part in thin slices, put it into a stewpan with a little white gravy, lemon-juice, shred lemon-peel, and a tablespoonful of white wine. Take two dried eggs and beat them very well; put to them a little minced parsley, and two or three (minced) chives if you have any. Shake it altogether over the fire till it is as thick as cream, but don't let it boil for fear it curdle. Garnish with sliced lemon, or mushrooms. This will eat like chicken.

126. TRIPE, STUFFED

Have a piece of tripe large enough to double; wash and trim. Prepare a stuffing of sage and onions, crumbs (soaked and strained pieces), pepper and salt, according to require-ments. Lay this on half the tripe, double over the other half, and sew the two together round the edges. Place in a greased tin, put three rashers of bacon on top, and bake for an hour or so. Remove the tripe to hot dish, thicken the liquor in the tin, browning it, pour it over the tripe, and serve.

127. (VEGETABLE) MARROW PUDDING

Péel a young vegetable marrow, cut in half, remove seeds from either half, and replace them with any odds and ends of ham, bacon, or meat, finely-minced along with onion and parsley, with pepper and salt to taste. Place the pieces together again, roll them up in a thin suet crust, and boil for three to four hours.

CHAPTER III

FISH

Fish has now too often to be our *pièce de resistance* ; it seems poor fare after the Roast Beef of Old England—even after the lamb of Canterbury, N.Z. It is very dear, but still it can be had. The red oily fishes are the most nourishing, and as a rule the cheapest ; but unfortunately they are often unsuitable for delicate digestions. They include herrings (fresh, pickled, bloaters, kippers, red), sprats, mackerel, and salmon.

To these may be added so-called sardines, which (whatever they may have been named in their native jungle) are tinned in oil, extremely nutritious and tasty. They are dear ; but it is cheaper to buy a large tin, which will serve a small family for two meals. Pilchards, or herrings (with tomato), tinned prawns—and of course tinned salmon—can also be made to provide two or three dishes each tin. So can tinned cod's-roe (larger sizes), which makes particularly dainty fish croquettes along with potato sieved or riced.

Eels are oily and nourishing, but not to everybody's taste.

Freshwater fish for the most part is dull stuff unless provided with a veal stuffing. The earthy taste peculiar to freshwater fish can be obviated by several methods, of which, for the average housewife, the easiest are : (1) careful cleaning as soon as caught, or (2) by washing and cooking in an acid—such as vinegar or lemon juice.

There are many sea-fish which in palmier days we disdained, but which are really quite decent if one takes a little trouble over them. Amongst these are sea-bream, fresh haddock, skate, ling, and the now very expensive hake. I believe lemon-sole contains less nourishment than any other fish.

Clarified cocoa butter is satisfactory for frying herrings, whose powerful taste and odour overcomes that of the cocoa. I have also found it all right for fried fish-cakes ; and I should suppose that cocoa butter, used as suet, would do very well for fish stuffings.

Remember that a little nice sauce goes a long way towards redeeming the character of the least interesting fish. I heard of a man the other day who said he had *become an aquarium,* and was sick of the very name of fish. But indeed this might have been rectified. A little pickle, or beetroot in vinegar, the plainest of parsley sauce, a few drops of anchovy essence —are invaluable when one can't afford the better sauces.

While on the subject of fish, let me recommend you to make liberal use of bloater paste. It is cheap, and intensely appetising ; it lends a flavour and a savour towards stolidly farinaceous dishes. Salmon-and-shrimp paste is useful, but does not go half so far. Anchovy paste is best of all, but also dearest of all.

It is inadvisable to have fish trimmed or filleted at the shop. By doing it at home, you obtain the bones and trimmings for fish stock.

Fish Stock is made of bones, trimmings, heads and tails, lobster-shells, shrimp-shells, prawn-heads, and any other scraps, provided they are perfectly fresh, and do not belong to " red " fish, such as herrings, sprats, salmon, etc. It must be cooked a shorter time than meat stock, and used more quickly, as it has a tendency to go bitter. A few vegetables can be included, cut up small ; also a little parsley, bayleaf, lemon-rind, salt and a few peppercorns, may be used to flavour.

The pieces should be well washed and cut up quite small, then place in *cold* salted water, and brought slowly to boiling point before skinning and adding the vegetables, etc. Let simmer about one and a half hours ; then squeeze in the juice of half a lemon, and strain.

The liquor is very useful, not only for soup and for stewed

or casseroled fish, but for fish sauce, using it when possible instead of milk.

RULES IN SELECTING FISH

1. Fish which is fresh, is firm, and the eyes are bright.
2. When stale, the eyes are sunken and dimmed by a film, and the flesh is flabby.
3. The smell of fish when fresh is scarcely apparent.
4. Mackerel, herrings, sprats, whitebait, and smelts should be bright and silvery.
5. If the colour has departed, the fish is stale.

The most economical method of cooking fresh fish, is boiling or stewing, whole or in slices.

The most extravagant, probably, is filleting. The most appetising, is baked and stuffed. The most popular, perhaps, is frying.

There is no need to employ egg and breadcrumbs for the last purpose. Milk and flour—or vegetable stock, or cereal stock, and flour—any kind, but oatmeal is excellent—will do perfectly well; and grated baked crusts will also supply the place of crumbs.

As regards the various ways of " making up " cold left-over fish, they are much the same as those employed for meat; and are always appreciated if nicely done.

A point often ignored, however, in the making of fish cakes, is that you can add almost any vegetable (riced or sieved), and improve the thing. Parsnips are especially suitable.

When fish is to be boiled, remember the water must be boiling, and slightly salted, and flavoured with vinegar, before the fish is put into it. The water must be kept boiling for five minutes, then drawn aside and simmered until the fish is done.

128. BRILL, BROILED

Wash, trim, and well dry the brill. Prepare in a deep dish a marinade as follows : three tablespoonfuls of salad oil, the juice of half a lemon (or its equivalent in good vinegar), pepper and salt; all well mixed. Dip the fish in until well coated with the mixture, brush some of the marinade over a grill or gridiron, and broil the brill over a clear fire for ten minutes; then turn it over, and let cook another twelve to fifteen minutes.

129. BREAM (SEA), BAKED

The fish must be well washed inside and out, and gently dried with a cloth. Make a forcemeat of dried grated crusts (or plain biscuits powdered), one teaspoonful of chopped mixed herbs, a little onion, pepper and salt; moisten with good stock, mix thoroughly, and stuff the fish, binding carefully with narrow tape. Roll the fish in maize, oat, or barley flour, put it in a baking-tin with two tablespoonfuls of stock, and three little bits of margarine or dripping on top.

Bake for thirty minutes, with frequent basting, in a moderate oven. An ordinary veal stuffing may be used if circumstances permit, made with suet; this will make the dish more nutritious.

130. BREAM (FRESHWATER), BOILED

Clean and trim, but do not remove scales. Wash and dry well, dredge with maize or oatflour; place on an oiled gridiron and grill slowly for thirty minutes.

Anchovy sauce should be served with it.

131. COD CASSEROLE

Cut a small onion into small slices and put it in a saucepan, containing a pint of white stock; then add a stick of celery, a blade of mace, a few thin strips of lemon peel, one or two pieces of parsley, and a little salt and pepper; when the milk has boiled draw the pan to the side of the stove and let it simmer very gently for twenty minutes. Melt two ounces of fat in a saucepan, then scatter in gradually an equal quantity of any flour, and mix to a smooth paste; strain the stock and pour it by degrees to the paste, and stir until the sauce has boiled and thickened ; add a teaspoonful of tomato ketchup. Remove the skin from a piece of cod (preferably the middle cut) weighing about two and a half pounds, put it into an earthenware casserole and pour the sauce over it ; cover it with a piece of thick greased paper, cover and put the casserole into a moderately hot oven for half an hour. When the fish is done, remove the paper, scatter some finely chopped parsley over the surface and serve the fish at once. The sauce for fish served in a casserole can be varied considerably, the tomato ketchup can be replaced by a large teaspoonful of anchovy essence, and garnish of shrimps can be used instead of the parsley. Just before serving, a squeeze of lemon juice should be stirred into the sauce. A thick brown sauce can be substituted for the white.

132. COD CUTLETS

Take thin steaks or slices from the tail end ; have them well washed and dried an hour before they are cooked. Mix one teaspoonful each of minced parsley, and of onion scalded and minced, with a little salt, pepper, grated nutmeg, and fine oatmeal, or maize flour ; moisten with a little milk, and lastly add a few drops of anchovy essence. Dust the cutlets with any flour, and coat them on both sides with the mixture ; then dip in crumbs (grated dried crusts) and fry in boiling fat.

Serve with sauce.

133. COD'S HEAD, BAKED

Wash and clean a large cod's head and shoulders. Place it in a baking-tin, and sprinkle well with bits of dripping. Bake for about an hour ; frequent basting will be needed. Remove fish to hot dish, strain liquor into a small pan, add one tablespoonful of chopped parsley, two tablespoonsfuls of vinegar, pepper and salt to taste. Let heat thoroughly, and serve as sauce with the fish.

134. COD ROCK

Slice an onion, and put it into a saucepan with a little fat until it is soft, but not browned. Have ready some cold boiled cod, freed from skin and bone, and flaked as small as possible. Add it to the minced onion, with pepper and salt and three cold potatoes mashed very fine. Stir well, and add a little fat. Serve it raised roughly on a dish, and garnish with narrow strips of pickled beetroot.

135. COD'S ROE, No. I

Take a good fresh roe, wrap it in butter-cloth, and put it into salted boiling water in a fish kettle. Let it boil gently for thirty minutes ; then take it out, but leave the cloth on until it is almost cold. When it is completely cold, skin, and slice it in pieces about half an inch thick. Dredge the slices with flour of any kind, and fry crisp in boiling fat.

136. COD'S ROE, No. II

Boil the roe for fifteen minutes in salt and water and a little vinegar. When cold, cut it in slices. Moisten and flour each slice, and fry for about ten minutes. (See also tinned cod's roe, p. 49.)

137. COD SOUNDS

Soak six cod sounds in cold milk and water all night. Next day boil them slowly in fresh milk and water or stock for two hours. Make some egg sauce, put the sounds into it, and serve with a wall of mashed potatoes round, or with boiled parsnips cut small.

138. COD STEAK, BAKED

Take a cod steak weighing one pound to two pounds. Wash, dry, and trim, tie it up into shape, dredge it with maize or barley flour, and place in a greased pie-dish or baking-tin. Have ready two tablespoonfuls of crumbs (soaked and pressed), mixed with two teaspoonfuls of minced parsley, one teaspoonful minced mixed herbs, salt and pepper to taste, and two ounces chopped suet or other fat. Shred this thickly on top of the fish, cover with a piece of greased paper, and bake for about twenty minutes.

139. COD (SALT), CURRIED

Wash and dry two pounds of salt cod, cut up into small equal pieces. Have two ounces of finely-minced onion fried in two ounces of margarine or other fat until light brown. Add half a large apple thinly sliced and two teaspoonfuls of carry powder. Stir for four or five minutes, then put in the fish. Season with salt and pepper, gradually add one gill of broth or meat stock. Place all in a stewpan and let cook gently for an hour, stirring occasionally.

140. COD (SALT), STEWED

Wash and dry three pounds salt cod. Cut it up in smallish equal pieces, dip them in oat or maize flour. Have ready two ounces of minced onion fried in two tablespoonfuls salad oil and two ounces of dripping (or other good fat). When the onion is pale brown, put the fish into the frying-pan, and let it cook for six to eight minutes, with gentle stirring. Then gradually add one teacupful of warm broth (or Oxo) and one wineglassful of sherry or Marsala. Add a very little cinnamon, and season with pepper. Place all in a stew pan, and let stew slowly for twenty-five minutes, with the lid not quite closely on.

141. CRAB, BROWNED

Clean and grease a crab shell. Mince all the crab meat with some parsley, one small onion, and two or three mushrooms ; brown these in a saucepan with some fat, and add pepper and salt. Keep stirring until it is quite hot. Put the mixture into the shell, cover with breadcrumbs and little dabs of fat, and bake about twenty minutes (until the breadcrumbs are brown) in a very hot oven. Serve in the shell.

142. EELS, FRIED

Skin the eels, remove backbones, wash and dry well, cut in 3-inch pieces ; dust with salt, pepper and grated nutmeg. Roll in maize or barley flour, fry for five minutes in boiling oil or lard.

143. EELS, JELLIED

Have two pounds of skinned and cleaned eels, cut up into two-inch lengths, and boil for twenty minutes in water, slightly salted, containing one bayleaf, one sliced onion, and about one teaspoonful of vinegar. Then drain them, remove the bones without breaking the flesh, and place the pieces in a mould, with a hard-boiled egg or two, thinly sliced. Strain the water in which the eels were boiled, measure it ; boil up again, skimming carefully, and stir in a quarter of an ounce of isinglass for each half-pint of the broth. As soon as the isinglass is dissolved by stirring, let boil fast for five minutes ; remove and let it cool off, and before it sets, fill up the mould with it. Serve when quite set and cold.

144. EEL, STEWED, No. I

Have the eel cut up in small pieces. Place in a saucepan enough milk-and-water to cover it, flavoured with one sliced onion, a little thyme and parsley, one bayleaf, pepper and salt, and any odds and ends such as bacon rinds, meat trimmings, etc. Let this liquor boil, then put the eel in. When it has simmered half an hour, remove eel to hot dish, strain off liquor, return it to the pan and boil up again ; thicken with a little flour mixed smooth, stir well, let boil, pour over eel and serve.

145. EEL, STEWED, No. II

Cut up an eel in three-inch pieces, dip them in maize or other flour, and put in a stew-pan with a little (meat) stock, salt to taste, an onion stuck with cloves, the thin peel of a lemon, and a glass of red wine. Let stew gently for half an hour ; then remove the eel to a hot dish, squeeze a few drops of lemon juice into the liquor, and strain it over the eel before serving.

146. EEL, STEWED, No. III

Cut up a skinned eel into pieces two inches long ; stew it gently in good stock, flavoured with pepper and salt, herbs, and a spoonful of mushroom ketchup, also a strip of lemon peel, for one hour and a half. When the eel is done, dish it up, and strain the gravy over it. Serve very hot.

147. HADDOCKS, BAKED, No. I

Have two middle-sized haddocks filleted. Put half of the fillets into a greased baking-tin, strew thickly with flour (any kind), minced parsley, salt, and pepper ; put the rest of fish on top, and season as above. Sprinkle with little bits of good fat, and bake for thirty minutes in a moderate oven.

148. HADDOCKS, BAKED, No. II

Cut off the heads and fins of two or three haddocks, and put into a stew-pan, with an onion, salt, pepper, and two anchovies cut up fine, a little flour, two tablespoonfuls of French white wine, and a little ketchup. Boil this all well up together, and when the fish has been skinned and cut into pieces, lay them in a deep pie-dish ; pour the above sauce over them, and bake in an oven. Strew the bottom of the dish with breadcrumbs and some more on top, having seasoned well with pepper and salt and a little grated nutmeg.

149. HADDOCKS (FRESH), FILLETED

Have two middle-sized haddocks filleted. Place two of the fillets in a greased baking-tin, and sprinkle them with fine oatmeal or grated baked crusts, with chopped parsley, pepper, and salt to taste. Then put in the other two fillets, and treat them the same, but more thickly. Put little bits of margarine or dripping on top of the fish, and round the sides of the tin. Bake thirty minutes in a moderate oven.

150. HADDOCK WITH SAUCE

Fillet two fresh haddocks ; boil the skins, heads, bones, etc., with seasoning and some parsley ; strain off the liquor

F

and season it with milk and flour. Have one egg whisked up in a tureen or deep dish, and some finely chopped parsley. Take the fish fillets, and when the liquor is boiling, place them in it and boil for ten minutes; gently stir some of the sauce into the tureen among the egg and parsley, taking care not to let it curdle. Add the fish, with the sauce that remains, and serve very hot.

151. FINNAN HADDOCK SAVOURY

Soak a finnan haddock for four hours. Skin it and remove all bones, and break the fish into flakes, slice a small onion and two tomatoes, chop up a little parsley, season with pepper, stew in a little fat till quite soft, then add the fish and cook for ten minutes.

152. FINNAN HADDOCKS, STEAMED

Instead of boiling a finnan haddock the usual way, lay it in a deep basin or dish, and *pour boiling water upon it* to cover it completely. Cover it up with a dish, lid, or thick cloth, and leave it for ten minutes. At the end of that time it will be better done, tenderer, and infinitely more digestible than if cooked the old way. Smear it with fat, and a dash of pepper, and serve on a very hot dish.

153. HAKE, STEAMED

Put about three-quarters of a pound of hake into a small casserole, with two tablespoonfuls of milk, and stand the dish on a saucepan of boiling water. Let it steam in the milk until tender. Drain off the milk into a little saucepan, mix smooth one teaspoonful of cornflour in a little cold milk (or water), add one teaspoonful of tomato sauce, salt and pepper; stir into saucepan, let boil, and serve as sauce.

154. HERRINGS, BAKED

Take six fresh herrings, which must be scraped, washed, and cleaned, the heads and tails removed, the fish split, and the bones and roes taken out. Lay the fish at the

bottom of an earthenware jar, with the roes in the middle.
Strew over them one thinly-sliced small onion, six peppercorns, six whole allspice, a saltspoonful of salt; pour in
sufficient vinegar to cover the fish (half a pint should be
plenty), tie down with doubled brown paper, or cover with
a close-fitting lid, and bake for thirty minutes. To be served
cold.

155. HERRINGS, BOILED

Clean the herrings, and having removed the eyes, put the
tails through the eyeholes, and let boil slowly in water containing half a teaspoonful of vinegar and a teaspoonful of
salt.

156. HERRINGS, BROILED

Split and bone the fish, dust them with pepper and salt,
lay them flat open on a gridiron, and broil quickly, cooking
both sides. Place in heated dish. Have ready the following
sauce: One tablespoonful of chopped parsley, one teacupful
of vinegar, one ounce of fat (melted), salt and pepper to taste
—and pour it over the fish.

157. HERRINGS, MARINATED

Clean the fish well without washing. Open them so as to
remove the backbone, and season them well with salt, pepper,
and onion chopped very fine. Roll them up tight, and place
them in a jar, and pour over them some vinegar and water
in equal quantities; tie over the jar with paper, and bake
in rather a slow oven for an hour. When they are cold, pour
over them a little cold vinegar. They may be pickled in the
same way as mackerel (*see* Mackerel).

158. HERRINGS, POTTED

Take six fresh herrings, wash, dry, and split them open,
removing heads and backbones. Dust them with flour,
pepper, and salt, chopped parsley or powdered mace. Roll
them up tightly with a small piece of fat in the centre of
each. Place them in a pie-dish, pour over half vinegar and

water, but not to cover them. Cover the pie-dish, and bake
in a slow oven; then remove cover and let them brown a
little. Two bay leaves may be put in the pie-dish instead
of mace.

159, HERRINGS (RED), BAKED

Soak the red herrings in water for twelve hours. Scale,
wash, and dry well; lay the herrings in a dish, and rub them
well with a mixture of pepper, salt, and a teaspoonful of
mixed spices. Place in a deep baking dish, pour over vinegar
and water (equal proportions), enough to cover, put in three
or four bay leaves, lay a paper on top, and bake for half an
hour in a moderate oven.

160. HERRINGS (RED), BROILED

Soak the fish as above, dry, bone, and split them. Prepare a marinade of three tablespoonfuls of salad oil, two
teaspoonfuls of finely-minced herbs, pepper, and salt: all
thoroughly mixed. Dip the fish into this and broil them
over a clear fire, brushing them once or twice with the marinade, and turning them twice at least.

161. HERRINGS (PICKLED), BOILED

Clean the fish, remove head and tail, and soak for forty-
eight hours in cold water, which must be frequently changed.
Hang the fish up to drain. Wash thoroughly, and put them
in a saucepan of cold water. Bring it to the boil, then throw
away the water, replace it with cold, then bring it to the
boil again, and let simmer gently for a quarter of an hour.

162. HERRINGS AND POTATOES

Wash and boil some potatoes in their skins, carefully, so
that they do not break or get too soft. Drain them, peel,
and slice them rather thickly. Keep them hot. Fry lightly
a chopped onion in one ounce of fat. Dust in some flour,
add three tablespoonfuls of vinegar, salt and pepper, and a
bay leaf, and not quite a pint of water. Put the pan to

simmer at the side of the stove. Take two red herrings, wash them well, cut them lengthways, and remove the bones. Cut up the flesh small, and let it simmer in the sauce for a few minutes. Put in the potatoes next, stirring carefully so as not to break them. Then add two ounces of fat and one gill of milk, and stir all well over the fire till it reaches boiling-point.

163. HERRING, SAVOURY ROE

Take some soft bloater roes, place them in a slightly-greased dish, and bake for about ten minutes in a moderate oven. Then mash them well with some fat and season to taste. A little cayenne pepper is an improvement. Spread the mixture over some rounds of toast, lay a fried egg in the middle, sprinkle a little minced parsley over, and serve hot.

164. JOHN DORY, BAKED

Remove the head, clean and trim the fish, lay it in a fire-proof dish, with a sprinkling of pepper and salt and two ounces of margarine or dripping cut small. Let it bake for twenty minutes in a moderate oven. Fry four chopped mush-rooms, lay them evenly on the fish, bake ten minutes more, and serve in the same dish.

165. LOBSTER, BASHAWED

Take any remains of lobster and cut them up. Chop up a piece of onion about the size of a nut, and a little parsley. Mix all together with a little anchovy sauce and cayenne pepper. Cut up in small pieces a bit of fat and mix, and then put all into the shell of the lobster. Cover over the top with bits of fat, and shake a few raspings on the top. Bake for about ten minutes, or a little more, and serve hot.

166. LOBSTER FRITTERS

Chop up the meat, with the red part and the spawn, of two large lobsters, very fine, with finely-grated crumbs and a little fat, and season with pepper and salt, and a very small quantity of chopped sweet herbs; make this into a paste with a beaten egg, and having formed it into pieces about two inches in length and an inch thick, dip them into a good thick batter, and fry.

167 LOBSTER RISSOLES

Take one tin of lobster; mix the fish with equal weight of mashed potatoes, pepper, salt, and a little liquor of the lobster if not sufficiently moist; form into flat cakes, and fry in boiling fat until nicely browned.

168. LOBSTER, SCALLOPED

Line your dish well with lobster (tinned or fresh), put some breadcrumbs next, then lobster, and so on, alternately with little bits of fat, salt and red pepper. Cover well with bread-crumbs, and then put little bits of fat all over, and pour vinegar over all. Bake for about half an hour or more, or brown nicely before the fire. You can heat it up a second time, pouring in milk or gravy or anything to moisten. One tin of lobster makes two small dishes. Serve very hot.

169. LING, STEWED, No. I

Make brown, in a casserole, one ounce of minced onion, two ounces of dripping, and one tablespoonful of flour. When coloured, put in fillets, steaks, or slices of ling—fillets for preference—along with three bay leaves, a pinch of minced or powdered thyme, half an apple, finely chopped, and six or eight peppercorns. Let cook slowly for eighteen to twenty minutes, and add gradually one wineglass of white wine and one teacupful warm (not hot) stock. This results in a delicate and tasty dish.

170. LING, STEWED, No. II

Cut up three pounds of ling into eight steaks or fillets, coat them with maize or oat flour. Have ready in a frying-pan one ounce of chopped onion and a small quantity of parsley fried in two ounces of fat. When the onion browns, add the

fish, and fry until each side is a golden brown. Then put
in a little thyme, three bay leaves, half an apple finely
minced, one wineglassful of sherry, and about the same of
stock (these should be added gradually). Salt and pepper.
Let simmer quietly for twenty minutes. Serve at once.

171. MACKEREL, PICKLED, No. I

Six rather small mackerel, four bay leaves, four cloves,
one level teaspoonful of peppercorns, one pint of vinegar,
thyme, parsley, fennet (if possible), salt and pepper.

Fillet the mackerel, wash and dry, strew over them the
herbs finely minced, and a little pepper and salt. Put in a
dish with a little fat, and bake till cooked. Try with a
skewer and see if they are done. Boil the vinegar, bay leaves,
cloves, and peppercorns together for ten minutes. Stir in
a teaspoonful of extract of meat, and when cold, strain over
the fish. Let it stand for several hours before serving, then
drain, put on a clean dish, and garnish with parsley.

172. MACKEREL, PICKLED, No. II

Having cut and split the mackerel, cover them with a little
thyme, parsley, and shallots, chopped fine ; then fry the fish
carefully. When done, pour over them some vinegar boiled
with black pepper, a few cloves, and three or four bay leaves ;
this liquor is not to be poured upon them until it is cold.

Another mode is to cut the fish into pieces, and to cover
them with a mixture of black pepper, nutmeg, mace, and
salt, reduced to a fine powder ; then fry them brown in oil,
and when cold put them into a jar, and fill it with strong
vinegar previously boiled. This is a rich preparation. The
quantities of spices required for six middle-sized mackerel
is : three nutmegs, six blades of mace, and an ounce of black
pepper. A good handful of salt should be used.

173. MACKEREL, STEWED

Cook three smallish onions in half a pint of water in a
stew-pan. When they are done, put in two pounds of

mackerel, with pepper and salt to taste, and let cook till partly done. Then add one teacupful of brown vinegar and the same of treacle, which have been previously well mixed (a little gingerbread crumbled into this is an improvement), and let the whole mixture simmer until the fish is done. The pan will require occasional shaking to prevent sticking. This dish is to be served cold.

174. MULLET, BAKED, No. I

The red mullet is the only one worth using, the grey mullet being somewhat poor and coarse. Grease sheets of white paper, sprinkle them with a little salt. Clean the mullet, wipe them dry, and roll each in a separate sheet. Broil them, and send them to table in the papers, and serve with them a tureen of good sauce.

175. MULLET, BAKED, No. II

Wash and clean, but do not scrape hard. Dip each fish into a preparation of salad oil and minced parsley, salted and peppered. Wrap each separately in greased paper, lay in a baking-tin, place in a good oven for twenty minutes. Serve at once in the paper cases.

176. MUSSELS, BOILED

Remove the heads and boil the mussels in their own juice, with a seasoning of chopped parsley, garlic (or onion), and fat. Strain the liquor over the mussels before serving. No water is needed.

177. PERCH, BOILED

Wash the fish in tepid water, clean and trim it thoroughly; scrape off scales. Put it into a pan of boiling water deep enough to cover it, with five or six chives or spring onions and a handful of parsley. It must boil (according to size) from ten minutes to half an hour. Serve with parsley sauce.

178. PERCH, FRIED

Clean, wash, scale and dry two middle-sized perch. Lay them in a marinade of oil, pepper and salt, (*see* Brill, Broiled) for thirty minutes. Drain, and roll in oatflour containing a little powdered thyme, grated nutmeg, pepper and salt to taste. Fry in boiling fat ; and when they are golden brown, drain and serve with piquante sauce.

179. PLAICE, BAKED, No. I

Remove the black skin from a good plaice, butter a fire-proof dish well, sprinkle lightly in some very fine bread-crumbs, a little finely chopped parsley, onion, pepper, salt, and if at hand two or three chopped mushrooms. Lay the plaice on this, sprinkle the same mixture over it and bake for twenty minutes. Serve very hot on the dish on which it was cooked.

180. PLAICE, BAKED, No. II

Roll small fillets of plaice, lay them in a casserole, and cover them with parsley sauce. Put cover on casserole, and bake in moderate oven for forty minutes or so.

181. PLAICE, BAKED, No. III

Take a large plaice, grease it all over thickly, sprinkle with breadcrumbs, chopped onions, parsley, pepper and salt, and bake for an hour. Serve with the gravy that comes from it.

182. PLAICE, WITH TOMATOES AND ONIONS

Butter a pie-dish, put in a thick layer of sliced tomatoes and onions, then a layer of plaice filleted and skinned, then another layer of tomatoes and onions ; sprinkle bread-crumbs, cheese, and a little fat over them. Bake for three-quarters of an hour.

183. SALMON, BAKED

Take the required number of slices from the middle of a salmon and wipe with a clean cloth, sprinkle them with salt, pepper and finely chopped parsley, then place side by side in a greased baking tin, lay small pieces of fat on the top, and put in a well heated but not fierce oven. Bake for three-quarters of an hour, basting frequently. Serve on a hot dish and pour the following sauce over:

A teaspoonful each of chopped mushrooms and salad oil, a small bunch of parsley, thyme, a little salt and a few pepper-corns. Stir over the fire a few minutes, then add four large tomatoes cut in slices and a teacupful of stock. Stir till the tomatoes are dissolved, and pour over the fish very hot.

184. SALMON CECILS

The contents of one tin of salmon freed from bone, a few potatoes mashed very smooth, a hard-boiled egg cut into small pieces, some chopped parsley, pepper and salt to taste, a little anchovy sauce, and sufficient of the liquor in the tin to moisten the whole; knead into little flat cakes, and fry until both sides are nicely browned.

Note.—This recipe can be applied to any cold fish.

185. SALMON CROQUETTES, No. I

Take half a pound of tinned salmon, pound it, rub it through a fine sieve. Have ready in a stewpan one ounce of margarine or dripping stirred until smooth with one tablespoonful flour; add one teacupful milk. Stir all the time until it boils; let simmer ten minutes; add the fish, with pepper and salt, and one well-beaten egg. Stir fast until all is well mixed, then pour on to a dish until cold; shape and fry.

186. SALMON CROQUETTES, No. II

Turn salmon out of tin and prepare as in No. I. Mix into it six ounces of well-boiled rice, a small onion minced, a dessertspoonful (or more to taste) of chopped parsley, pepper, salt and a beaten egg. Beat thoroughly till the mixture is well blended, shape into small rissoles or croquettes, and fry in boiling oil until they are a good pale brown.

187. SALMON, CURRIED

Have a pound tin of salmon drained of the liquor and
broken small. Slice a small onion and fry it in two ounces
of dripping or margarine. Add two teaspoonfuls of curry
powder, and stir in gradually a teacupful of warm stock.
Let it simmer for ten minutes, then add the salmon
and when it has stewed gently for a quarter of an hour, serve
inside a border of rice.

188. SALMON CUTLETS

Half a pound tin of salmon mashed with a fork, one cup of
hot mashed potatoes, with salt and pepper to taste ; form
into cutlets, dip in egg and breadcrumbs, and fry in deep lard
or in oil.

189. SALMON MAYONNAISE

Open a tin of salmon and remove the bones. Make the
following sauce : Boil one egg hard ; pass the yolk through
a sieve ; add to it a teaspoonful of unmade mustard, a small
spoonful of sugar and salt, cayenne pepper to taste ; add a
quarter of a pint of oil, stirring all the while ; then some
anchovy and Worcester sauce, a tablespoonful of vinegar,
and lastly a wineglassful of milk. Pour this sauce over the
salmon, cover it with young lettuces cut very fine, and place
over them the white of the egg cut in rings, and two tomatoes,
or a small beetroot, also cut in slices.

190. SALMON PUDDING

Pour off the liquor from a pound tin of salmon. Remove
the bones and skin, and shred finely, using a silver fork.
Add salt and pepper, four tablespoonfuls of melted-butter
sauce, one breakfastcupful of soaked and drained bread,
one beaten (dried) egg. Mix well. Place in a greased pie-
dish, press down tightly with a fork ; stand the dish in a
pan of hot water, and place in a good oven for about twenty
minutes. For sauce, boil one breakfastcupful milk in double
boiler ; thicken with one tablespoonful of cornflour mixed

smooth in two tablespoonfuls of cold water. Add one table-spoonful clarified cocoa butter, the juice of half a lemon, one dried beaten egg; and stir it until it thickens. Then, having warmed up the salmon liquor, add it to the sauce last of all.

191. SALMON STEWED, No. I

Remains of cold salmon, or a pound tin of salmon, two eggs hard-boiled, cut into slices. Put the salmon and the eggs into half a pint of stock, thicken with flour, and add one ounce of fat, salt and pepper; stir until it boils. Make a wall of mashed potatoes on a dish, and pour the contents of the saucepan into the middle of the mashed potatoes.

Lobster is excellent done in the same way.

192. SALMON STEWED, No. II

Slice the fish thickly and place in a large casserole, along with a small sliced onion, sliced carrot, sliced half-lemon, three bay leaves, and two or three sprigs of parsley; salt and pepper to taste. Cover the fish with vinegar and water (in equal proportions) and leave it for four or five hours. Place the casserole on range or gas, and let it come to the boil very gradually. When it boils, remove from fire and let all cool off slowly. When cold, serve on another dish, with salad of any sort.

193. SARDINES, CURRIED, No. I

One box of sardines; strain off the oil into a small frying-pan; add to this a dessertspoonful of curry-powder previously mixed with cold water. Thicken the oil with a little arrow-root, previously mixed with water. As soon as the curry and oil make a sauce about as thick as good melted butter, the sauce is ready. Pour this over the sardines, and place them in the oven long enough to get heated through. When quite hot, serve with pieces of toast.

194. SARDINES, CURRIED, No. II

Prepare the sardines as above ; put them on toast in the oven while you prepare the following sauce : Rub a saucepan with a clove of garlic ; place in it the oil in which the sardines were tinned. When it boils, put into it one teaspoonful of curry-powder and one teaspoonful of flour, made smooth with a little stock which has been seasoned with onions, and boil, stirring all the time until sufficiently thick ; add the juice of half a lemon, and pour the sauce over the sardines in the oven. Serve very hot.

195. SARDINES, DEVILLED

Split the sardines, take out the backbones, and spread each fish with mustard, salt, pepper, and lemon juice. Leave them for half an hour, and then fry them in the oil in which they were tinned, in which also fry some slices of bread, and in dishing up place the sardines on the toast, and serve very hot.

196. SARDINES, GRILLED

Remove the skins and bones from twelve sardines, and place them in a pie-dish in the oven, covered over, just to heat through. Pour the oil from the sardines into a saucepan ; thicken with flour ; add half a pint of stock, one teaspoonful of Worcester sauce, salt, and cayenne. Beat one egg with one teaspoonful of mustard and one of vinegar, pour the sauce boiling hot on the egg, etc., stir a moment, and then pour it over the sardines. Serve very hot.

197. SARDINE SALAD

Bone some sardines, breaking them as little as possible ; lay them in a bowl, and place over them some lettuces cut small and some cress. Boil two eggs hard ; mash the yolks with salt, pepper, mustard, and cayenne ; add gradually the oil from the sardine tin and the juice of a lemon, pour it over the salad, and ornament the top with the white of the eggs cut in rings and two tomatoes in slices. A few chopped capers laid on the sardines under the lettuce are an improvement.

198. SARDINE TOAST

Put some sardines in a covered pie-dish in the oven. Fry some toast in the oil from the tin, lay the sardines on the toast, shake a little cayenne and salt over them, and send to table very hot, and a cut lemon with them.

199. SKATE, CRIMPED

Clean, skin, and slice the skate in long pieces. Roll them up and tie with string, place in well-salted boiling water, which must boil fast for twenty minutes or so : the fish should then be done. Drain, remove string, serve at once with shrimp sauce.

200. SKATE, FRIED

Take some very fresh skate, divide it up into long strips, and separate these into pieces of equal size, two inches long. Roll in oatmeal flour and fry for six or seven minutes in boiling fat. Dust with salt and serve with sliced lemon.

201. SPRATS, BAKED

Clean some sprats, place them in a pie-dish with some whole pepper, salt, and a few bay leaves spread over them; cover them up and bake them for about half an hour; let them stand in the liquor which comes from them until quite cold, and then pour vinegar over them.

202. SPRAT CROQUETTES

Cold sprats, freed from skin and bone. Add the same weight in cold potatoes, mash and mix until quite smooth, make into round balls, cover with flour, and fry in boiling fat until well browned.

203. SPRATS, FRIED

Flour each fish, and lay them on a frying pan which has been standing on the range until it is quite hot, and before laying in the fish sprinkle it well with salt; lay the sprats in rows, turn once, and serve with cut lemon. Fresh herrings can also be done in this way, and will be found much nicer than when fried in fat.

204. SPRATS FRIED IN BATTER

Make some batter ; wipe some sprats and dip them in the batter, fry a nice brown, and serve very hot.

205. SPRAT PIE

Sprats (divested of their skin and backbones) which have been cooked. Mince them and mix with chopped parsley, pepper, salt, a little fat, and stock enough to moisten them ; lay in a pie-dish, and fill it up with mashed potatoes. Bake in the oven for one hour.

MIXED FISH DISHES

. BOUILLABAISSE

This celebrated dish *can* be made with cod only, and with mackerel only ; but, correctly speaking, it consists of a variety of fish. I give first the correct Marseillaise form, and then one of a somewhat simpler nature.

206. 1.—BOUILLABAISSE MARSEILLAISE

Take the meat from a one-pound lobster, cut it into six even pieces. Skin and trim two very fresh eels, cut them into two-inch pieces. Take a very small sea bass (or other firm-fleshed fish), clean, wash, trim, remove head, and cut flesh crossways in six equal steaks. Place all above on a plate in a cold place. Have three tablespoonfuls of oil heated in a saucepan ; add two chopped onions and three chopped leeks. Let these brown gently for ten minutes, stirring occasionally. Put in three tablespoonfuls of flour, mix well for two minutes while cooking ; then add one pint of tomatoes (tinned or fresh, crushed), one pint of water, the heads of the various fish, and the eel skins ; one tablespoonful of salt, half a teaspoonful of white pepper, half a teaspoonful of saffron, two crushed beans of garlic, and three sprays of parsley. Mix all with a spoon for three minutes; then let boil briskly for forty minutes, mixing now and then. Remove, strain the liquor into another pan, boil it up again, replace the fish in it. Mix lightly, cover pan, let boil gently for thirty minutes. Remove fish, and arrange it in a large deep dish, pour liquor over; arrange six little slices of toast around, sprinkle with half a teaspoonful of minced parsley; serve at once.

207. II.—BOUILLABAISSE ANGLAISE

Take a variety of fish up to two pounds weight in all; they must be quite fresh. A mixture of large and small fish is quite in order; some shellfish should be included. Dory, haddock, gurnet, brill, whiting, hake, lobster, mussels, may be suggested. The larger fish should be in slices or steaks, the smaller ones whole, the lobster cut lengthwise. Fry an onion or a leek in good oil in a saucepan; then put in the fish with a teaspoonful of flour, a little salt and pepper, and enough water just to cover it. Add two skinned and chopped tomatoes, one crushed garlic bean, a pinch of saffron, a spray each of thyme and fennel, and two bay leaves. Let boil fast for fifteen minutes. Add a teaspoonful of finely-minced parsley; remove from fire. Have some slices of bread laid in a deep dish, place the fish on these, and strain the liquor over all.

VARIOUS FISH DISHES

208. FISH BATTER

Any cold fish that has been slightly boiled and is quite firm; take out the bones, season with pepper and salt, and dip in batter made as follows: A quarter of a pound of flour, made very smooth with one tablespoonful of salad oil and a quarter of a pint of tepid water; add to this the whites of two eggs beaten to a stiff froth; make this some time before it is wanted, and beat it quickly from time to time;

dip the fish into it, and fry in boiling fat until it is nicely brown.

Note.—This batter is very superior to ordinary batter, and is equally good for meat or fruit.

209. FISH CAKE, No. I

The remains of cold fish, a few mashed potatoes, a little chopped parsley, a few breadcrumbs, pepper, salt, and anchovy sauce. Work these together until no lumps remain ; make into a flat cake and fry until nicely browned. Make a sauce with a little fat, salt, a squeeze of lemon, and a wine-glassful of stock thickened with flour ; pour this over the fish cake, and serve very hot ; or the sauce can be served in a sauce-boat separately.

210. FISH CAKE (STEAMED), No. II

Take one and a half pounds of any white fish, boil it, remove any bones and skin, and shred up the flesh very small. Mix it with half a teacupful of crumbs (soaked and drained pieces), anchovy essence, salt and pepper to taste, one ounce of fat of some sort, two well-beaten (dried) eggs, and nearly a teacupful of milk. Blend thoroughly, pour into a plain greased basin, put a greased paper on top, and steam for forty-five minutes.

211. FISH CAKES, No. I

Break up very fine any remains of cold fish, having carefully boned and skinned it. Pass through a sieve any cold potatoes, and mix an equal quantity of them with the fish. Moisten with any melted butter left over, or with a well-beaten egg ; add a few breadcrumbs to make the mixture firm. Season with pepper and salt. Make the mixture into balls or small round cakes. Roll in milk and flour, as for frying fish, and fry a light brown.

212. FISH CAKES, No. II

Pull to pieces with two forks the remains of any cold fish, carefully removing all bones and skin. Mix some well-mashed potatoes and a small piece of butter with the fish, season with pepper and salt to faste, adding a little cayenne. Form into small cakes and fry in hot fat to a golden brown colour, and garnish with fried parsley.

213. FISH CHOWDER

Take one ounce of bacon, cut it into dice, and fry for five minutes with a small thinly-sliced onion. Place both in a saucepan, along with six (raw) potatoes peeled and chopped small, one carrot, washed and chopped. Pour in enough boiling water (or stock) just to cover them, and let cook until the contents are tender. Then mix smooth two table-spoonfuls of flour (any sort) with a teaspoonful of cold milk, and thicken the liquor with it. Add one breakfastcupful of milk and one pound of fish of any kind, boned, and cut up small. Let cook for ten minutes or so, or until the fish is done. Serve at once.

214. FISH CURRY

Take two pounds of cod, hake, or other fish, and fry in two ounces of dripping. Take it out, and fry one sliced onion until brown. Add half a tablespoonful of curry powder, one tablespoonful of grated cocoanut, one ounce of flour, a pinch of salt, the same of sugar, and a breakfast cupful of stock. Let boil for a quarter of an hour, then separate the fish into large flakes, and add it to the mixture; let simmer for five minutes, add one teaspoonful of lemon juice, and serve at once.

215. FISH CUSTARD

Take any cold fish, remove all bones and skin, lay it in small pieces in the bottom of a pie-dish, with a little salt and pepper. Mix a dessertspoonful of flour smooth in a teacupful of milk; add one beaten egg and a piece of fat about as big as a walnut, creamed but not oiled. Pour it over the fish, and bake half an hour or so in a moderate oven,

216. FLEMISH FRICANDEAU OF FISH

One pound of chopped fish (cod, haddock, and a few shrimps); add quarter of a pound of bread crumbs soaked in stock, quarter of a pound of fat, two dried eggs, pepper, and salt. Make into the shape of a loaf and bake half an hour; serve with caper sauce.

217. KEDGEREE, No. I

Boil two tablespoonfuls of rice, add any fish previously cooked (salmon or turbot best); it should be well picked from the bone in shreds; beat up an egg and stir it in just before serving, but don't let boil after the egg is added. Serve with egg sauce.

218. KEDGEREE, No. II

Take half a pound of cold fish, break it into flakes, and remove all the bones. Then take three ounces of cold boiled rice, two hard-boiled eggs, cut the whites into dice and put them with the fish and rice into a saucepan with one and a half ounces of fat, pepper, salt, and nutmeg. When well heated, put it into a dish, and squeeze the yolks of eggs through a sieve over the top. Then put it into the oven to brown.

219. KEDGEREE, No. III

Boil two ounces of rice till tender and let it remain till cold. Mix with it a teaspoonful of curry powder and some pepper and salt. Melt two ounces of fat in an enamelled saucepan, break two dried eggs into it and add the rice and stir until it is stiff, which will be in a few minutes. Have a large square of toast ready on a hot dish and pile the kedgeree on it. Sprinkle chopped parsley on the top, and serve very hot. The remains of a cold finnan haddock, removed from the bones and mixed with the kedgeree, make a very tasty supper-dish.

220. FISH MACARONI

Take any cold fish; free it from skin and bone; add seasoning of salt and pepper and a little chopped parsley;

have ready some boiled macaroni; mix the fish with it in a pie-dish, adding a little stock and fat; grate crusts thickly over the top with dabs of fat, and bake in a hot oven about three-quarters of an hour.

221. FISH MOULD, No. I

Cold fish freed from skin and bone; weigh it, and take half the weight of cold potatoes; mash them through the masher, and mix with the fish cut very small; add some fat, one teaspoonful of anchovy sauce, pepper, and salt. Grease a mould, press the fish, etc., into it, and bake for one hour in a hot oven with the mould covered over; turn on to a hot dish, and sprinkle thickly with chopped parsley.

222. FISH MOULD, No. II

Have one breakfastcupful of cooked fish (of any kind) shredded, and bones carefully removed. Whisk two eggs well, add half a teacupful of milk; stir in the fish, a breakfast-cupful of crumbs (soaked, drained crusts), a little minced parsley, seasoning of salt and pepper. Mix well, steam in a greased mould for one hour. Serve hot. Sauce should be poured over the mould—a piquant sauce for preference.

223. FISH MOULD, No. III

At the bottom of a wetted mould put a little aspic jelly (or flavoured gelatine). Next put a layer of cooked fish, either shredded or in small pieces, also some sliced hard-boiled eggs and minced parsley; when this has set, put in more jelly. Have ready the following: One beaten yolk of egg, one tablespoonful salad oil, salt and pepper, one teaspoonful of tarragon vinegar, one tablespoonful of white vinegar, well blended. Stir into the above, more eggs, fish, and jelly, until the mould is full up. Steam for half an hour, put aside to grow cold. Turn out and garnish with parsley.

224. FISH PASTY

Make a short crust ; line a baking-tin, put pieces of filleted or cold fish, a very thin layer of veal stuffing and a good thick gravy ; cover with crust.

225. FISH PIE, No. I

To half a pound of cooked fish (shredded) add half a pound of cooked macaroni (broken into two inch lengths). Add pepper and salt to taste, one ounce of fat of some sort a beaten (dried) egg, half a pint of hot milk, and a few drops of lemon juice. Sprinkle with grated crusts or oatflour, strew with minute pieces of fat, and bake until the mixture is well set and nicely coloured.

226. FISH PIE, No. II

Take half a pound of any cooked fish, or a half pound tin of salmon. Remove bones and shred the fish very small. Mix with the following : one teaspoonful each of chopped parsley and of grated lemon-rind, one hard-boiled egg minced finely, pepper and salt to taste, and two tablespoonfuls of any sauce left over from the fish when previously served—white sauce for preference. If you have no sauce, bind the mixture with a very little flour and milk. Have ready half a pound of paste of any kind, formed into a square. Put the fish mixture into the middle of this, and bring the corners to meet in the middle, or make a triangular " turn-over " of it. Bake in good oven.

227. FISH PIE, No. III

Fresh-water fish—either roach, jack, or eel, one pound of onions, half a pound of rice, three eggs, quarter of a pound of fat, paste.

Boil rice. Lightly fry onions, cut into small pieces. Boil eggs hard, then slice them, and bone fish. Fill pie-dish, first with layers of rice, then onions, fat, fish, and eggs. So on. Cover in with paste, and bake. Very good, hot or cold

228. FISH PIE, No. IV

One pound of cold boiled fish (no skin or bone). Stew in two ounces of fat very gently; steep one thick slice of stale bread in boiling stock, add to it the fish and fat, then beat these ingredients in a mortar; add pepper and salt, and two eggs well beaten; place the mixture in a greased tin; bake for an hour in a quick oven.

229. FISH PIE, No. V

Remove all skin and bone from any kind of fish (cooked), break into small pieces mixed with minced onion, previously fried in fat, add pepper, salt, and mustard, tomato sauce, and half a well-beaten (dried) egg, and pack into a pie-dish. Cover with mashed potatoes, brush over with egg. Bake for three quarters of an hour.

230. FISH PIE, No. VI

Put three quarters of a pint of milk into a saucepan with half a small onion, two cloves, a few thin strips of lemon-peel, and two or three pieces of parsley and some salt and pepper, and let simmer gently for twenty minutes. Make a paste in a saucepan with an ounce and a quarter of fat, and an ounce and a quarter of flour. Strain the milk and mix it gradually with the paste, thus making a thick sauce; ascertain whether more pepper and salt is required, and add a teaspoonful of anchovy essence. Grease a pie-dish and place a layer of cooked fish which has been divided into flakes into it, and cover it with some of the prepared sauce, a few shrimps and a little chopped parsley; then put more fish, and the remainder of the sauce, and some shrimps and parsley as before. Have in readiness some smoothly mashed potato which has been well seasoned with salt, pepper and nutmeg, and mix in some milk, fat, and an egg, then beat it until it is light and creamy, cover the fish with this, mark the top with a fork, and after pouring a small quantity of warm fat over the surface of the potato, bake the pie in a quick oven until it is evenly browned.

231. FISH À LA PORTUGUAISE

Take at least one pound of sliced or filleted fish, wash, dry, and place in a deep pie-dish. Strew it with pepper, salt, and chopped thyme to taste; dredge it with a little flour of any kind. Have ready two onions and three tomatoes, sliced and fried; put these on top of the fish, with one tablespoonful each of salad oil and of vinegar, and half a pint of stock. Sprinkle in a few little scraps of dripping or other fat, and cook in a very hot oven until the fish is brown, which will be at least an hour. Serve in the same dish.

232. FISH PUDDING, No. I

Any cold fish freed from skin and bone; add to it a quarter of a pound of chopped suet, a quarter of a pound of bread-crumbs, pepper, salt, and a little good gravy; mince one onion and some parsley very small; add it to the fish, etc. Beat up two dried eggs and work them into the other ingredients, press all into a mould, and steam it for two hours and a half.

233. FISH PUDDING, No. II

Take one pound and a half of cooked fish, half a teacupful of milk, one ounce of melted fat, a little anchovy essence, a teaspoonful of chopped parsley, pepper and salt. Break up the fish as finely as possible in a bowl, and add the rest—the eggs and milk last. When all is well mixed, put it in a greased mould, and let it steam for three-quarters of an hour. For a baked fish pudding, use an equal amount of well-mashed potatoes, and about twice as much milk and fat as is mentioned above.

234. FISH RICE, No. I

Save the liquor in which cod or any other fish has been boiled. On the following day fry some onions and tomatoes; add the fish stock and a bunch of herbs, and enough rice (about one breakfastcupful to one quart of liquor) to take up the stock. When the rice is nearly done, stir in any remains of cold fish, freed from bone, and serve very hot.

235. FISH RICE, No. II

Boil four ounces of rice until it can be mashed smooth ; and before it cools mix into it any remains of cold fish, finely shredded. Of course all bone and skin must be removed ; this is better done while the fish is still warm. Add salt, pepper, minced onion, and parsley, to taste. Blend thoroughly, put into a basin. When cold, turn out upon a dish ; a little sharp sauce can be poured over it.

236. FISH SCALLOPS

Take any cold fish remaining from the previous day, carefully remove all skin and bones, and break it as small as possible with two silver forks (steel ones will injure the flavour). Mix in any cold sauce left over, or use half a pint of milk and two ounces of fat ; add soaked, drained breadcrumbs to thicken it, and salt, pepper, and mace to taste. When all is well mixed, take some scallop-shells, or saucers, butter them well, and put in the mixture. Scoop a little hollow in the centre at the top, and put in a very small quantity of anchovy sauce. Dust over with very fine grated crumbs, and drop some tiny bits of fat over. Bake in a moderate oven, and serve very hot. These will be found most savoury and appetising. A little chopped parsley may be added at discretion.

237. FISH SOUFFLÉ, No. I

Mix the remains of some cold fish with a little mashed potato and two well-beaten dried eggs and sufficient milk to make a thin batter ; pour into a well-greased mould ; steam for half an hour.

238. FISH SOUFFLÉ, No. II

Take half a pound of white uncooked fish, remove the bones, and pass it through a wire sieve. Put one ounce of fat into a saucepan, and mix it well with two ounces of flour which has been dried and sifted, and pour in gradually rather less than half a pint of hot milk. Stir quickly until the sauce is smooth and thick. Let it simmer for five minutes, then add two beaten (dried) eggs, and strain it into a basin. Add the fish to the sauce, season with salt and pepper. Grease a small china soufflé dish, nearly fill it with the prepared fish ; cover with greased paper and steam very gently for fifty minutes. Serve the soufflé in the mould with a little chopped parsley over top.

239. FISH AND SPAGHETTI

Break up small four ounces of spaghetti, place in boiling water, boil for twelve minutes, and drain. Have any remains of cold cod or other fish well shredded and put into a pie-dish, mixed with the spaghetti. Beat two eggs very thin, blend with one breakfastcupful of milk, add a little pepper and salt, pour over the mixture, and bake for thirty minutes.

240. FISH, STEWED

Slice and fry one pound of tomatoes and one pound of Spanish onions (sliced cold potatoes may also be added). Put in any cold fried fish, broken small, and at least half a pint of stock, thickened and seasoned. Let simmer till thoroughly hot, and serve.

241. TWICE LAID

Take the remains of cold salt fish. Tear it into flakes ; mix it with double its quantity of mashed potatoes. Moisten with milk ; season with pepper and salt ; roll into balls ; dip them in egg ; roll them in flour, and fry them brown. Drain and serve on a folded napkin.

242. FISH TIMBALE

Flavour one and a half gills of white stock with half an onion, a small blade of mace, a few thin strips of lemon peel, and some celery, salt, and pepper. Then thicken it with one and a half ounces of any flour, which has been smoothly mixed with a small quantity of cold milk and water, and stir until it is very thick; then add one and a quarter ounces of fat, blend thoroughly, and rub the sauce through a gravy strainer into a basin, pressing the onion well to extract the flavour. While the milk is simmering, pass one pound of raw white fish through a fine mincer, season it lightly with sauce, pepper and nutmeg, and mix it with the prepared sauce; then add two unbeaten eggs, beating first one and then the other into the mixture. Butter a china soufflé mould and line it evenly with boiled rice, then fill it with fish and put a layer of rice over it; tie a thick piece of greased paper over the mould, place an inverted saucer or small plate on it, and steam gently for three-quarters of an hour. Turn it carefully from the mould, garnish with a little chopped parsley scattered over the middle, and surround it with some good white sauce flavoured with either lemon and parsley or essence of shrimps. Macaroni or spaghetti can be used in place of rice to line the mould.

CHAPTER IV

SOUPS

Soups are not a national institution with us, as they are with other nations. We don't care for them, and that's the plain truth. Yet they can be made extremely palatable; and they are a means of conveying nourishment, and vegetable salts, and animal juices, which otherwise would certainly be wholly wasted. They are also (when properly concocted) very satisfying. And as we have got to live on something, they supply an amount of bulk, or perhaps I should say they take up a certain amount of cubic space in the body, in a manner which nothing else can quite replace.

But soup need not be—it often is—mere tasteless wish-wash. It can be good, appetising, substantial fare. I maintain that soup to be the best which combines the greatest number of nutritive ingredients. For instance, a good bone stock, in which peas, haricots, rice, or other such materials have been cooked; which is subsequently enriched and flavoured by the addition of vegetables, herbs, bacon-rind, and any other suitable substance, and is then passed through a sieve. Of course, it then may be called a purée, not a soup : but what's in a name ? You will assuredly find your household clamouring for more.

If I dared refer to bygones, I would also mention that eggs, and milk, and wine, can all be pressed into the service and go to make the soup of double-extra food value. But we must confine ourselves to the solemn facts of the present.

The chief of these facts are that (1) you must never throw away anything which can possibly help to eke out your soup, and (2) you must not let your stock go sour by keeping

it too long. This especially refers to summer. It is far
better to make soup little and often, than to run any risks
with it. The more vegetable matter it contains, the more
likely it is to deteriorate, and even boiling-up will not prevent this. No pieces of vegetable should be left *in* stock
when it is put to cool. They must be strained off if they are
not sieved.

The words "soup" and "broth" are very loosely employed. The most up-to-date significance of "soup" is, as
already mentioned, what would formerly have been termed
"purée," *i.e.*, all the ingredients are sieved when tender
enough, and re-heated before serving. This makes the soup
very thick and nice. Broth, on the other hand, has the
vegetables, etc., floating loose in it. Some people prefer
it thus ; personally, I regard it as an untidy, slipshod method.
But it is a matter of taste. Clear soups are not to be encouraged in these days. We want something more "stodging."

There is practically nothing (except sweet things) that
cannot be used for soups. All the things that people throw
away, scraps and odds and ends of meat, bones, and bacon-
rinds, and cheese-rinds, outside leaves of vegetables, peelings
of vegetables and apples, bits of crust, etc., etc., etc., can all
be put into a pot with some water, boiled, simmered for three
hours or so, seasoned with salt and pepper, sieved and re-
heated ; behold, a particularly attractive soup !

Again, the water in which any cereal or any dried pulse
food has been cooking—rice, macaroni, haricots, split peas.
etc.—forms an admirable basis for soup. Most likely you
have always thrown it away before. Don't waste it any
more.

Rice, sago, tapioca, semolina, pearl barley, and macaroni
are excellent for thickening ; so are potatoes, and artichokes,
and parsnips (cold cooked, sieved or riced). Rice, pearl
barley, and sago should be well soaked before adding to
soups. Half a teacupful of either will suffice for three quarts

of soup. Herbs of some sort should never be omitted. If the vegetables are fried first and added to the soup with the fat they were fried in, so much the better.

Vegetable soup is not in itself a perfect substitute for soup from bones (whatever the scientific experts may say). But it can be made very tasty and satisfactory.

All bones should be broken up small with a hammer, and used *before they can get sour*. Don't save them up, but put them on at once in the water, keeping the pan covered, and boil fast until they become perforated with little holes (this may take hours). Then drain off the stock, and *keep the bones*—the Government wants them.

The water in which ham or bacon has been boiled is invaluable for stock.

Fish trimmings and bones can also be made into stock. But fish soups are not popular in Britain. Fish stock will supply the place of milk in making fish sauce.

Whenever *milk* is indicated in the following recipes, either fish stock or cereal stock can be substituted. Milk is dear and scarce. If, however, the soup is for children, you should try and give them real milk in it (or what passes for that seldom-seen liquid).

Grated cheese is a great improvement to soup. But, unhappily, there is none to be had, as ordinary cheese is too scarce, and Parmesan is at fancy prices—10s. a pound or so.

Keep soup or stock in earthenware, not in metal, vessels.

To conclude: in making tasty soups out of formerly unconsidered trifles, you have a chance to show how clever you are. It really is a most interesting job to prove this; you try, and you'll see !

243. ARTICHOKE SOUP

Take some liquor that ham or bacon has been boiled in (if not too salt); add to it an onion and some pepper, six pounds of artichokes, and let them boil until quite tender; take them out; pass them through a sieve into a basin, adding as much of the stock in which they were boiled as will make the purée of the right thickness. Return to pan and boil up.

244. BARLEY SOUP

Two quarts of stock, a quarter of a pound of pearl barley, parsley, four onions, salt and pepper. Simmer gently for four hours; sieve, reheat, and serve.

245. BELGIAN POTAGE

Cut two white onions in halves, finely slice and place in a saucepan with three finely sliced fresh leeks, an ounce of fat and brown for fifteen minutes, stirring quite frequently meanwhile. Add four finely-sliced peeled raw potatoes, moisten with two and a half quarts stock, season with a teaspoonful salt, a half teaspoonful pepper, and a saltspoonful grated nutmeg, mix well and let boil for forty-five minutes. Add a teaspoonful of freshly-chopped parsley, lightly mix, pour soup into tureen and serve.

246. BREAD SOUP

Cut up four onions and four tomatoes, and fry them in dripping. Add as much water or thin stock as required, also herbs, pepper, and salt. Let it boil about two hours. Cut up some pieces of stale bread, put them in a tureen, put some of the stock to the bread; stand it close to the fire with the lid on for ten minutes, then add the rest of the soup.

247. BOUILLABAISSE (AS SOUP)

Take some fresh-water fish—perch or roach. Boil twenty minutes; free them as much as possible from bones; strain the water in which they were boiled, and return the fish to it, with two or three onions, two tomatoes, a few cloves, allspice, whole pepper, cayenne, anchovy sauce, one ounce of parsley, and two bay leaves. Boil one hour, strain the liquor, add the fish, and simmer gently for a few minutes, care being taken not to break the fish. Place a thick slice of bread in a tureen; soak it with the liquor. Take out the fish, serve in a separate dish, and fill up the tureen with the rest of the stock.

248. CARROT SOUP

Take three pints of stock, and add the following : one onion finely minced and four carrots grated, fried in one ounce of fat ; one ounce of rice, one teaspoonful of maize flour ; herbs and parsley to taste ; bacon rinds and scraps. Boil up, and add salt and pepper to taste, let simmer one and a half hours ; put through a sieve, re-heat, and serve.

249. CAULIFLOWER SOUP

Break up a sound medium cauliflower, and put it into a quart of boiling stock (any sort). Boil again, and let simmer for an hour. Then rub the soup hard through a sieve, return to pan. Mix one tablespoonful of cornflour smooth in a little water, and add to soup. Stir continuously until it boils and thickens, then add pepper, salt, and nutmeg or mace to taste, one teacupful of hot milk, and one table-spoonful of grated cheese. Serve immediately.

250. CELERY SOUP

Take a head of celery, which need not be a very good one fit for the table ; cut it up roughly, and place in a pint of boiling water (salted). Boil for three-quarters of an hour. Meanwhile boil half a Spanish onion in one pint of milk ; thicken with one tablespoonful of flour mixed smooth in a little cold water, and subsequently let boil for ten minutes. Rub celery and onion through a sieve, replace, with their liquor, in one of the pans. Season with salt, pepper, and mace ; serve very hot.

251. CHESTNUT SOUP

Boil one pound of chestnuts till they burst open. Throw them into cold water, peel them, crush them into a paste (moistening with a little milk when desirable), put them through a fine sieve. Set them in an earthenware pan with an onion already cooked in a little fat. Add a teaspoonful of sugar, a saltspoonful of salt, a little pepper, a light hint of spice, and as much white stock or milk as will make up the requisite amount. Stir continually, and when it boils, add a spoonful of rice-flour made smooth in cold milk.

252. CUCUMBER SOUP

Take two cucumbers, peel, slice, and seed them. (Be careful not to let your fingers come in contact with the peeled flesh of the cucumber, or it will turn bitter). Place in three pints of boiling cereal stock, and simmer until thick enough to sieve. Return to pan and thicken with one and a half ounces of cornflour melted in one ounce of fat. The soup, boiling, must be gradually poured to this, stirring continually until it has boiled again. Then put in salt and pepper to taste, one ounce of fat, and one yolk beaten up with one teacupful of milk. The soup must not boil after this is added, or the egg will curdle. Serve at once.

253. CURRY SOUP

Fry two large onions. Add one pint of stock previously flavoured with vegetables ; thicken with one teaspoonful of curry powder and two dessertspoonfuls of flour mixed with cold water. Strain through a sieve. Boil a teacupful of rice, and add it to the soup about five minutes before dishing up.

254. FISH SOUP

Take the liquor in which codfish has been boiled, and add to each quart half a teacupful of tapioca, a carrot, half a head of celery, and a little parsley. Cut the vegetables up very small and boil until they are cooked. Then thicken with flour. Add pepper and salt to taste, and serve.

255. FLEMISH SOUP

Boil equal parts of potatoes and turnips in water, with one onion and a head of celery, pepper, and salt. When the vegetables are soft, pass them through a sieve. Return the soup to the fire, and as soon as it boils add some chopped parsley.

256. ITALIAN SOUP

Warm one quart of stock in which a cow-heel has been boiled. Cut up the meat into small dice, and add two tablespoonfuls of boiled sago. Put the cow-heel and sago into the stock, and let it boil. Place one tablespoonful of grated cheese into the tureen, pour the contents of the saucepan over it, and serve.

257. HARICOT SOUP

Soak one pint of haricots overnight. Next day, place in a saucepan with three pints of stock or water, and two rashers of bacon. Cut into thin strips (or some broken-up bacon bones). Add a boiled onion, sliced; two sticks of celery (or about a quarter of a head), pepper and salt. Let boil gently two to three hours, until all can be rubbed easily through a sieve. Return the purée to the pan, add a pint of milk and a squeeze of lemon-juice, and boil up for two or three minutes. Very nourishing.

258. HERB SOUP

Fry a large Spanish onion cut in rings, and two raw tomatoes; add as much hot water as required; herbs, pepper, and salt. Boil half an hour. Pass through sieve; boil up again and serve.

259. HODGE PODGE SOUP

Take a quantity of shelled green peas, with onions, carrots, and turnips, and a sprinkling of salt and pepper. Put these into a pot *with a lid*, with a quantity of stock corresponding to the quantity of soup wanted. Let it boil slowly or simmer for five or six hours. Rub through a sieve and re-heat.

260. HOTCH-POTCH

Have the liquor in which mutton has been boiled made thick with green peas, onions and leeks, grated carrots,

H

haricot beans, and two turnips; add one teacupful of soaked pearl barley when the vegetables are nearly done, and boil for one hour. Rub through sieve and re-heat.

261. LEEK SOUP

Put a pint of water and a pint of rice stock (or other cereal stock) to boil; when boiling fast, put in four or five leeks and an onion, well washed and chopped small. Simmer for an hour, rub hard through a sieve; re-heat, and season with salt, pepper, and mace. Mix three tablespoonfuls of ground rice quite smooth in one breakfastcupful of milk; when the soup boils, pour this in, stirring all the time. In about ten minutes the soup should be slightly thickened, and ready to serve. At the very last, stir in a quarter of an ounce of fat.

262. LENTIL SOUP

Soak half a pound of whole lentils in cold water all night. Boil them in as much stock as you require soup (and keep adding to it as it boils away); add onions, pepper and salt, and also seasoning, a few pieces of pumpkin or vegetable marrow cut small, or a few cold potatoes, to thicken. Let it simmer five hours. Strain through a sieve.

263. LENTIL FLOUR SOUP

Mince or grate one carrot, half a turnip and three outer stalks of celery. Fry in one ounce of fat in a stewpan for five minutes. Pour to them three pints of stock (any sort), add two cloves, three or four peppercorns, and salt. Simmer gently for one hour. Sieve, and return to pan. Mix two ounces of lentil flour smoothly in a little cold water, add it to the soup; boil up, stirring well; put in half a pound of cooked sieved potatoes. Work the whole mixture quite smooth, season, and serve.

264. MACARONI SOUP

Macaroni soup is one of those which taste best when made in the simplest manner. After the macaroni has boiled for ten minutes, it must be transferred to a pan containing two quarts of boiling stock. It should then be left to simmer for twenty minutes, after which it may be served.

265. MILK SOUP, No. I

Take four large potatoes, peel and cut into quarters, cut up one onion, and put them into two quarts of boiling water or white stock. Boil till done to a mash, strain through a colander, and rub the vegetables through with a wooden spoon, return the pulp and soup to the saucepan, and one pint of milk, and bring to the boil, when it boils sprinkle in three tablespoonfuls of crushed tapioca, stirring all the time. Boil fifteen minutes, and serve.

266. MILK SOUP, No. II

Peel two pounds of potatoes, boil them in two quarts of water, and add two leeks cut up small. When tender, rub them through a sieve. Place them in a saucepan with two ounces of fat, stir until the fat melts, and then add one pint of milk, pepper and salt. When it boils, stir in three dessert-spoonfuls of tapioca. Boil ten minutes, and serve.

267. MULLIGATAWNY SOUP, CHEAP VEGETABLE

Have two turnips and six middle-sized potatoes peeled and cut into half inch dice. Add a good-sized onion, thinly sliced, and two carrots, very finely shredded. Melt two or three ounces of fat in a saucepan, and put in the vegetables. Stir until they are nicely brown. Add one full tablespoonful of rice, salt and pepper, and a heaped teaspoonful of curry powder. Mix thoroughly. Pour in three pints of water; let it simmer two hours. Thicken with one dessertspoonful of cornflour. Add one tablespoonful of vinegar. Serve very hot.

268. NETTLE SOUP

Only the very young shoots can be used for this. Wash the nettles well; place in boiling salted water, just enough to cover them, with a little salt and a minute pinch of carbonate of soda. Boil for twenty minutes, rub through a sieve. Have a little flour and fat mixed smooth in a sauce-pan, put in the nettle purée, seasoned to taste; thin with a little stock of any kind; boil up and serve.

269. ONION SOUP, No. I

Boil four large Spanish onions in water. When tender, take them out and cut them small. Return them to the water with one pint of milk, and add more water if neces-sary; pepper and salt them, add one ounce of fat, stir until it is melted, and boil altogether two hours; serve with fried toast cut into dice.

270. ONION SOUP, No. II

Cut four Spanish onions in rings, and fry them; add a thickening of flour and one pint of stock, gently stirring the ingredients for a few minutes. Add pepper and salt and a few herbs; break up some pieces of stale bread in a tureen, and soak them with liquor; mash the bread, add the re-mainder of the soup, and serve.

271. PARMENTIER SOUP

Cut up four or five medium-sized very mealy potatoes, with two small carrots, one pound of ripe, well-coloured tomatoes, and a small head of celery. Put into a pan two ounces of fat, and as soon as this is melted put in the tomatoes and a medium-sized onion finely sliced, let cook in the covered pan for twelve to fifteen minutes, after which pour in three pints of stock (or water), together with the potatoes, celery, etc., and seasoning to taste, and let cook gently till the vegetables are in a pulp. Rub through a sieve, re-heat and serve.

272. PARSNIP SOUP

Peel and slice one pound of parsnips, cook them brown in one ounce of fat in a stewpan; add one ounce of rice and one quart of hot stock (any sort). Simmer gently for two hours, sieve, re-heat, season to taste with salt, pepper, and onion; stir in, last of all, one breakfastcupful of hot milk. Serve.

273. PEA SOUP, No. I

Take three pints of liquor in which beef or pork has been boiled; add two onions cut up in quarters, and some herbs. Let this boil until the onions are soft. Have a twopenny packet of pea powder and a teaspoonful of curry powder made into a paste with cold water. Stir this well into the soup for a few minutes; let all boil together for two hours longer, and serve.

274. PEA SOUP, No. II

Take four pints of water, one pint of dried peas, three onions, three carrots, two turnips, a bunch of herbs, six-pennyworth of beef bones (or stock from boiled salt beef). Soak the peas in two or three waters for twelve hours, wash the bones, put them in a clean saucepan with the water and peas, add salt and pepper, skim well while boiling. Scrape the carrots, peel the turnips, skin the onions, cut them all in dice, add to the bones and peas, simmer very gently for four hours. Remove the bones, season with dried mint if liked, rub through a hair sieve if a purée is required. The water in which a joint of salt beef has been boiled, or one pint of bone or of vegetable stock, can be used instead of the bones.

275. GREEN PEA SOUP, No. I

Take half a pint of shelled peas, one quart of the green shells, one and a half pints of water, two ounces of fat, one onion, two sprigs of mint, two lumps of sugar, half a pint of milk, one teaspoonful of cornflour. Shell the peas, rinse the empty shells, and with a sharp knife remove the strings. Melt the fat in a very clean saucepan, put in the peas, the prepared shells, the onion sliced, and toss (to absorb the flavour of the butter), over a slow fire for a few minutes, *but do not brown.* Then add the water, mint, sugar, and boil until tender. Rub all through a hair sieve. Blend the cornflour smoothly with the milk. Put the soup back into the saucepan, add the milk and cornflour, and stir until it boils. Season and serve.

276. GREEN PEA SOUP, No. II

Take two pounds of pea-pods (which should be young and green), wash well, and place in two quarts of boiling salted water, containing one dessertspoonful of sugar, one teaspoonful of salt, one spray of mint. Let boil for three hours; then rub the pods through a sieve, return this purée to the pan with the rest of the liquor, add a teaspoonful of fat and a teacupful of milk, and boil up again.

277. PEA-NUT SOUP

Roast one breakfastcupful of shelled pea-nuts, skin and mill them. Stir them into two breakfastcupfuls of the liquor in which rice, macaroni, haricots, or any cereal has been cooked, and two breakfastcupfuls of milk. Add enough flour to make as thick as cream; salt and pepper to taste, and (at discretion) a beaten egg. Bring just to the boil, and serve.

278. POMERANIAN SOUP

Soak and boil one quart of white beans until they are soft. Mash half of them in thin broth, and pass through a sieve. Add one head of celery cut small, some herbs and parsley, salt and pepper. Boil one hour longer, add the whole beans, and serve.

POT AU FEU (French)

279. No. I

(NOTE.—I give this recipe for completeness sake; but it is rather reckless unless you have a lot of meat coupons. The following will suffice for eight people.)

Put two pounds of brisket into a deep pan, cover the meat with cold water, and bring it slowly to the boil. Skim off all fat. Fry two sliced onions brown; cut up finely a small cabbage and two carrots; add these, with salt, minced

parsley, and herbs to taste, to the brisket, and simmer quietly
for three to four hours. Serve.

280. No. II

Proceed as above, but use three pounds of brisket and the
following vegetables, all neatly cut up; one large onion,
three leeks, one small cabbage, one stick of celery, one large
parsnip, one large carrot, two or three cloves, one dessertspoonful of salt; parsley, thyme, and bay leaf. In either
case the onion should be fried to dark brown.

Remove the meat and half the vegetables before serving,
to use as next day's dinner.

281. POT AU FEU (VEGETABLE)

Have a casserole which holds three pints of cold salted
water; into this put the following, sliced; one large onion,
one turnip, three carrots, half a small cabbage. Let boil,
then simmer slowly for three hours. Then put in a bit of
toast, very hard and brown and leave it for five minutes or so;
remove it before it breaks up. This is merely to improve
the colour of the liquid. Serve at once.

282. POTATO SOUP, No. I

Wash, peel, and slice one pound of potatoes, and one
medium-sized onion. Have one ounce of dripping melted
in a saucepan, add the vegetables, but stir them so that
they do not burn. Pour in one pint of water, and half a
teaspoonful of celery seeds tied up in muslin. Cover the
pan and let the potatoes cook gently until they are soft.
Stir often. Remove the celery seeds, rub the rest through
a sieve and return to pan. Add half a pint of milk, and
seasoning of salt and pepper. Boil up and serve.

283. POTATO SOUP, No. II

Boil one carrot, one onion, one head of celery, one large
spray of parsley, and three or four leeks, with a little fat, in
just enough water to cover. Have some floury potatoes

cooked, add these to the other ingredients, and rub all through a sieve. Return to pan, and thin the purée with stock; season, and boil up.

284. POTATO SOUP, No. III

Have two onions, three potatoes, and two ounces of bacon, very thinly sliced. Season with salt and pepper; boil in two quarts of water or stock for two hours; pass through sieve, boil up, and serve.

285. POTATO SOUP, No. IV

Fry two onions in a saucepan; add fourteen good-sized potatoes cut in quarters, and boil them in stock until soft enough to mash; return them to the saucepan, adding pepper, salt, and a large piece of dripping. Simmer for a few minutes, and serve.

286. PUMPKIN OR MARROW SOUP, No. I

Cut up and fry one large Spanish onion, in a saucepan with some dripping, and about six tomatoes; add a little water, and twelve pieces of pumpkin or marrow cut rather small, one sprig of thyme, and pepper and salt to taste. Boil until the vegetables are reduced to pulp. Pass through a sieve, and re-heat.

NOTE.—Wherever in these recipes tomatoes are used, tinned tomatoes or sauce can be substituted for fresh.

287. PUMPKIN SOUP, No. II

Boil a small pumpkin, after peeling it and cutting it up into small pieces, in salted water. When quite soft, rub the pumpkin through a strainer. Melt one ounce of fat in a saucepan, with a wineglassful of milk; add the pumpkin pulp and some pepper. Stir well, and serve very hot.

288. SEMOLINA SOUP

Peel and slice thinly two medium potatoes; chop up the outer stalks of a celery head, place in boiling stock of any sort, to simmer for one hour. Sieve, re-heat to boiling point, and gradually sprinkle in two ounces of semolina. Continue to stir until the soup boils up again, then let simmer slowly ; and at the end of thirty minutes, season to taste with salt, pepper, and mace. Add one teaspoonful of fat, and if possible a teacupful of hot milk. Stir well and serve.

289. STEW SOUP

Take the liquor in which tripe has been boiled ; add to it half a pint of split lentils (which must have been soaked the night previous), one or two turnips, a few potatoes, and a root of celery ; add pepper and salt. Let all simmer together gently for four hours, and then serve.

290. TOMATO SOUP, No. I

Take two pounds of fresh red tomatoes (or a quart of tinned ones), two ounces of crushed tapioca, two onions (medium size), a strip of celery, or trimmings, a bunch of herbs, one ounce of fat, one teaspoonful of salt, a quarter of a teaspoonful of pepper, a pint of milk, one quart of hot water.

Slice the tomatoes, peel and slice the onions, cut the celery in small pieces, tie together two sprigs of parsley, one each of thyme and marjoram, and a bay-leaf. Melt the fat in an enamelled saucepan, add the prepared vegetables, cover the pan, and cook all for five minutes over a gentle heat, but do not let them colour. Pour in the water, and cook slowly for three-quarters of an hour ; rub all through a wire sieve and return to saucepan. Wash the tapioca, and boil it in the soup until it is quite dissolved and clear, from eight to ten minutes. Lastly, add the milk and seasoning. If tinned tomatoes are used, twenty minutes instead of three-quarters of an hour will suffice for cooking them.

291. TOMATO SOUP, No. II

Fry four ounces of chopped onion in two ounces of fat, add one tin of tomatoes, let boil for half an hour, then add one

pint of stock and one teacupful of water. Salt and pepper
to taste after this has boiled. Rub the whole through a
sieve. Simmer about one hour. Thicken with rice if desired.

292. TOMATO SOUP, No. III

Cut up about fourteen large tomatoes and three large
onions; boil and mash them; add two quarts of stock,
a teaspoonful of sugar, one of salt, black and cayenne pepper,
thicken with flour, and serve.

293. TOMATO SOUP, No. IV

One tin of tomatoes, two ounces of lean ham, one small
onion, one ounce of butter, salt, and pepper, a few drops
of cochineal, and two ounces of tapioca. Slice tomatoes
and onions and ham into a saucepan, add the butter, simmer
one hour and rub through a strainer. Boil one quart of
stock, throw in the tapioca, and boil until it is clear; add
the tomato, etc., to it, season and colour it, boil ten minutes
and serve.

294. TURNIP SOUP

Boil some turnips till tender enough to mash. Fry an
onion till it is tender, but not brown. Place it in a saucepan with the mashed turnips, salt and pepper, and one
quart stock (or one pint of stock and one pint of milk). Boil
till thick, and serve.

295. VEGETABLE SOUP, No. I

Equal quantities of carrots, potatoes, and onions, a head
or two of celery, and some herbs. Slice and fry the vegetables
in a little dripping, add as much water or stock as is wanted;
put in salt, pepper, and the herbs. Let them all boil two
hours; then add a thickening of flour, mixed with a teaspoonful of mustard. Let the whole simmer for half an
hour longer, and then serve.

296. VEGETABLE SOUP, No. II

Fry a large slice of bread in some dripping; add two
quarts of stock, six potatoes, four turnips, three onions cut

in slices, one tin of mushrooms, two heads of celery, salt,
and pepper. Let the whole boil for two hours; mash the
vegetables, return them to the stock, just let them boil ten
minutes, stirring all the time, and then serve.

297. VEGETABLE SOUP, No. III

Cut up six carrots, six parsnips, six potatoes, and fry
them in dripping; add one quart of stock, boil for two hours,
and serve.

298. VEGETABLE SOUP, No. IV

Take a few sticks of celery, a large onion, a carrot, a turnip,
a pound of cabbage, cut into strips, a pint of split peas and
a rasher of streaky bacon. Boil these in a gallon of salted
water, and when the fat has been skimmed off, add a little
sugar and pepper. The bottom of the tureen should then be
covered with slices of bread, over which the soup is poured.

299. VEGETABLE SOUP, No. V

Boil some bones for six or eight hours, then strain off,
and, when cold, take all the fat off. Mince small a couple of
turnips, a tiny onion, a piece of shallot, and some outside
pieces of celery. Let the stock boil for twenty minutes, then
throw in the vegetables and a tiny bit of fat. Let boil rapidly
for half an hour, and if the stock is not sufficiently thick
with the vegetables, mix a teaspoonful of flour smoothly
with cold water and strain it into the soup. Let it simmer
at once, then strain it into the soup-tureen.

300. VEGETABLE MARROW SOUP

One slice of raw ham or bacon boiled in one quart of stock
or water; one vegetable marrow, peeled and cut into small
pieces and mashed; add a pint and a half of boiling milk
or stock to the bacon and marrow; mix well; flavour with
pepper and salt and a very little nutmeg. A bay leaf must
be boiled in the milk or stock. Remove the ham, and serve.

301. VERMICELLI SOUP

Boil for a quarter of an hour two ounces of vermicèlli in one pint of stock; add salt and pepper. Add a pint of stock. Boil five minutes and serve.

302. SCOTCH BARLEY BROTH

Take one pound of scrag of mutton, chop it into even pieces, place in a saucepan with one teacupful pearl barley, one large onion sliced, and one quart of water; pepper and salt to taste. Simmer gently for two hours.

303. SCOTCH BROTH

Take six quarts of cold water, any bones of meat or a ham bone, two carrots, two turnips, two onions, one small cabbage, half a teacupful of pearl barley, half a teacupful of parsley, half a teacupful of shelled peas, a bunch of sweet herbs. Any other vegetable in season. Put the water in a large pan with the bones and the barley. Let boil with the lid on until the barley is nearly tender. Wash the vegetables, cut the carrots, turnips and onion into neat dice and the cabbage into shreds, tie the herbs together. Put all the vegetables into the pan, put on the lid, and cook for about one and a half hours. About ten minutes before sending it to table, add the parsley coarsely chopped. Season carefully and serve.

304. VEGETABLE BROTH

Vegetable broth is composed of greens or cabbage, shorn or cut into small pieces, onions, carrots, and turnips, or one or more of them as can be got, also cut into small pieces, with pearl barley boiled slowly in a portion of water corresponding to the quantity of broth wanted, to which a sprinkling of salt and pepper is added, a small quantity of dripping is also added, when that can be procured; and vegetable broth, if properly made, is a nourishing and palatable food.

CHAPTER V

EGGS AND CHEESE

THIS subject is particularly awkward to handle, because eggs are so very dear, and cheese so very rare. We cheerfully pay 4d. to 6d. each for so-called new-laid eggs now—in 1916 3d. seemed an exorbitant and preposterous price. Real eggs, therefore, should be regarded as on a level with meat—and of almost equal value, which, indeed, they are ; one new-laid egg is said to be equivalent to a quarter of a pound of fresh meat. They must be used as solid articles of food—poached, boiled, shirred, fried, or curried ; and never lightly used for culinary purposes.

Boiled eggs are (or should be) eaten with bread and butter. But we want to save the butter.

Poached eggs are (or should be) served on buttered toast. Butter again.

Fried eggs can only be cooked in fat of some sort. Fat is precious.

Shirred or baked eggs must be put into greased cups, etc., in order to bake them. They are not so easily digested as the rest ; and they don't go so far, in actual bulk.

Omelets are nowadays too great a luxury. It follows that *hard-boiled* eggs, included with other ingredients in a dish, will go the farthest and be the best value. Next to these I should place fried eggs.

Most fortunately for us in our present dilemma—when we are even forbidden to " hoard " eggs beyond a certain number, by putting away the usual store in water-glass—dried eggs have been invented, and are (comparatively speaking) cheap and plentiful. They are available for most culinary purposes instead of "real" eggs; but I have not found them very successful for pancakes, fritters, or omelets, or such dishes as should have the yolks and white separately beaten. It is obvious that they could not be the ideal eggs for these.

For custards, cakes, and many puddings, custard and egg powders are quite good enough. They don't profess to be made from eggs; but they will serve their purpose right enough for the time being.

305. CAIRO EGGS

Take four hard-boiled eggs; have ready cold boiled lentils, seasoned with minced herbs, pepper and salt. Coat them half an inch thick with this mixture; then brush with milk, roll in fine oatmeal, and bake for about ten minutes on a greased tin in a quick oven. They can be served as they are, with a nice gravy separate; or halved and set upon flat cakes of hominy or polenta.

306. COCOTTE EGGS

Take four good eggs, and four little earthenware egg-pots. Line the dishes with a thin layer of anything you have handy —such as scraps of meat or bacon finely minced and mixed with chopped parsley and crumbs—or a plain forcemeat. Break each egg and drop it into its pot; the pots must then be placed in a shallow pan of boiling water in the oven, until the eggs are well poached and set. Serve in the same dishes, with a little tomato sauce or ketchup on top of each egg.

307. CURRIED EGGS, No. I

Take four hard-boiled eggs, one sour apple, one large onion, one ounce of fat, one ounce of flour, one dessertspoonful of curry-powder, one small teaspoonful of salt, half a pint of milk or milk and water, a quarter of a pound of Patna rice. Boil the eggs for ten minutes; shell and lay them in cold water, to keep white. Peel and chop finely the apple and onion; fry them in the fat for five minutes, using a saucepan; stir in curry powder, then the flour and salt; lastly, the milk, and simmer gently for a quarter of an hour. Add the eggs, which should be cut in quarters. When quite hot, serve in a border of boiled rice.

308. CURRIED EGGS, No. II

Slice finely a couple of onions, and fry them a delicate brown in two ounces of fat, rub together till smooth two ounces of curry-powder, two teaspoonfuls of good vinegar, and a teaspoonful of castor sugar. Stir into it, over the fire, about a breakfastcupful of good stock and bring it to the boil. When nicely blended, break into it five eggs, and let them cook gently in this about one or two minutes. Serve at once with boiled rice.

309. CURRIED EGGS, No. III

Take six eggs, boil them for twenty-five minutes; then place in cold water for fifteen minutes. Next, remove the shells carefully, and put the eggs in hot water to keep warm. Have some rice ready boiled (according to any of the recipes on pp. 152–4), and put it in a warm place. Fry a teaspoonful of chopped onion in a tablespoonful of fat, till it is golden yellow. Have one tablespoonful of cornflour, with one dessertspoonful of curry powder, mixed smooth in a little cold milk (or water or stock), and add it to the onion in the saucepan; then add gradually three teacupfuls of milk or white stock. When the liquor thickens and clears, season with salt and pepper, and strain. It should be quite smooth, and golden yellow. Dry the eggs gently in a cloth, roll them in the sauce until they are completely coated; arrange the rice on a dish, like a deep nest, and put the eggs in. Carefully fill up the nest with the rest of the sauce.

310. CURRIED EGGS, No. IV

Cut up small one large onion and one apple. Put in a stewpan with one ounce of fat. Stir over a moderate fire till slightly browned. Add one tablespoonful of curry

powder and half a teaspoonful of flour. Mix well, and
add a pint of water. Simmer slowly for an hour, and then
add a little salt, and, if wished, a little lemon juice. Strain
and pour it over either hard-boiled eggs cut in halves or
lightly poached eggs. Serve with well-boiled rice.

311. DUCKS' EGGS

These are not only larger but richer than hens' eggs.
One duck's egg is equivalent to two ordinary eggs. They
are best when shirred (baked), scrambled, or made into
omelets, with a little seasoning of chopped parsley and onion.
They can also be hard-boiled and curried ; or fried and served
with tomato sauce. They need very little fat for frying,
being oily in themselves.

312. NORMANDY EGGS

Have half a pound of haricot beans soaked overnight,
and next day place them in a pan of cold water, with three
ounces of fat, and boil two hours or until tender. Drain, add
salt and pepper, and toss them in one ounce of fat. Meanwhile have six eggs hard-boiled, shelled, and halved, when
cold. Make a sauce with two ounces of fat and one ounce of
flour, and one pint of stock of any kind, vegetable or otherwise.
Season with salt and pepper, and carefully re-heat the eggs
in the sauce. Place the haricots on a hot dish, hollow the
centre of them, and arrange the eggs and sauce in the hollow.

313. PALESTINE EGGS

Trim and boil eight good-sized Jerusalem artichokes,
and set them to cool. Boil four eggs hard and let them
get cold (they can be plunged into a bowl of cold water),
then cut them up. Slice the artichokes, lay them in a greased
baking-dish ; strew the chopped eggs over them ; next,
put a layer of sliced tomatoes ; last, a layer of grated cheese.
Bake until lightly coloured, and serve very hot.

314. SAVOURY EGGS AND RICE

Take a pint of stock, and cook four ounces of Patna rice in it until tender. Colour it with a little strained tomato sauce; cut up two slices of fried bacon into little strips, and add these. Add salt and pepper to taste. Put the rice into a shallow greased pie-dish, and when it is well pressed and shaped, turn it out upon a heated dish. Have ready some eggs, either four (hot) hard-boiled, cut in halves, or five poached, and arrange these upon the rice. This is a nice dish, but must be served hot with care.

315. TRIPED EGGS

Have six eggs hard-boiled for fifteen minutes; place in cold water; subsequently shell, and slice them very thinly with a sharp knife. Melt three ounces of fat with about one ounce of flour in a saucepan; put in six small boiled finely minced onions, seasoned with salt and pepper; gradually add two tablespoonfuls of milk, and let simmer for ten minutes or so. Then add the sliced eggs, which must not be stirred; shake the pan gently to let them mix with the rest, and when they are heated through, in two or three minutes, pour off all upon a hot dish.

316. TURKISH EGGS

Put an onion cut into slices, with some fine herbs and butter, into a saucepan, adding a little flour, salt and pepper. When these have been on the fire a few minutes, add a glass of white French wine and the whites of six hard-boiled eggs cut into slices; when these ingredients are well united, add the yolks which had been previously set aside, and serve up very hot.

———

CHEESE must also be regarded as a very special article of food. It must never be served as a mere luxury course; nor should it be eaten *au naturel* with bread and salad. It should be reserved for addition to otherwise flavourless

I

articles, such as macaroni, or used along with potatoes or other vegetables *au gratin*, when a very nourishing and admirable dish is the result. In several recipes I have included grated cheese; not as a seasoning, but definitely to increase their food value. I believe that Parmesan cheese (the correct kind for grating, immensely hard and durable) is still obtainable at the big stores—at a very high price. So-called " cream " cheese (see recipes below) is available instead of butter, and is particularly wholesome, when you happen to have any sour milk. If cheese cannot be obtained, however, neither can it be replaced. There is, so far as I am aware, no known real substitute for cheese; you cannot imitate it either in flavour, texture, or peculiar food-value.

HOME-MADE CHEESE
317. I

Sour milk need not be wasted. Let it become quite thick, then stand it in a jar in a saucepan of hot water. It must heat slowly, but *not boil*, until the curd and whey are well separated. Then strain out all the whey through a cloth, pressing hard. Add a little salt, a morsel of dripping or margarine, and a very little fresh milk, to the curd, and blend them in thoroughly with a spoon until the mixture is quite smooth and fine. Shape into balls or cubes, and keep in a cool place.

318. II

Put one pint of milk in a warm place until it is sour and quite thick. Put it, loosely tied, into a piece of butter-muslin, and hang it up over a bowl for several hours to drain off all the whey. Then tighten the muslin as much as possible, and press for an hour between two plates.

319. III

Take some milk which has gone sour suddenly, and reduce it to curds and whey by boiling. Place the curd on (or in) a cloth to drain thoroughly, and when it is as dry as you can get it, press it down tightly in a small wooden box, with clean fresh hazel leaves in layers here and there. Keep a good weight on top of the curd, and turn it out when dry, which should be in two days.

In all these recipes, the milk must be *absolutely* sour, or the cheese will be tasteless.

320. BREAD AND CHEESE CUSTARD

Mix well eight ounces of soaked drained bread with eight ounces of grated cheese, salt and pepper to taste; pour in one pint of boiling milk, and let all cool; then stir in one beaten (dried) egg. Place in greased pie-dish and bake in a hot oven to a golden brown. This is extremely nutritive.

321. CELERY CHEESE

Take a sound head of celery, trim it, and place it in a saucepan containing macaroni which is nearly cooked, and add (if need be) enough *boiling* water to cover all. When the celery has cooked slowly until quite tender, remove it; strain off the water (which should be kept for stock), and replace it with a little milk; after a few minutes, mix one teaspoonful of flour smooth in a little water, and stir into the macaroni and milk (this makes it creamy), and just let it thicken. Then put the macaroni into a deep dish, chop up the celery very small and lay it on top; add a little grated cheese, a few little dabs of fat, and seasoning of salt and pepper. Place in a moderate oven and bake slowly to a golden brown.

322. CHEESE AND ONIONS

Have two pounds of parboiled English onions sliced, seasoned, and placed in a deep baking-dish. Cover them thickly with flaked, shredded, or thinly-sliced cheese—six to eight ounces will be required. Strew little dabs of fat—about two ounces altogether—on top; and bake for thirty minutes in a good oven. Serve immediately, before the cheese can harden.

323. CHEESE AND ONION PUDDING

Take a good-sized pie-dish, grease it, and place at the bottom a layer of sliced onions. Next put in a thin layer of grated cheese. Strew this with salt and pepper to taste, and a little pinch of dry mustard. Follow with a layer of onions, and so on till the dish is nearly full. Have a dried egg beaten with enough milk to fill up the dish, and bake until the onion is done, in a moderate oven.

324. CHEESE AND RICE PUDDING

Make a batter with a quarter of a pint of milk, one (dried) egg, and four ounces of flour. Beat it well, and let stand for at least half an hour. Have three ounces of rice boiled till tender, and well drained. Mix with it, one and a half ounces of grated cheese, half a teaspoonful of finely minced herbs, and seasoning of pepper and salt. Stir this into the batter; lastly, add a quarter-pint more milk, and half a teaspoonful of baking-powder. Blend thoroughly; pour into a greased pie-dish; bake about twenty-five minutes more or less in a hot oven.

325. CHEESE AND POTATOES

Cut some cold boiled potatoes in thin slices, and lay them in a greased pie-dish; over them lay cheese cut thin; then a little fat and a pinch of dry mustard, then more potatoes, and so on until the dish is full. Pour over all one pint of milk, and bake in a quick oven for one hour.

326. MOCK CRAB

Mix two tablespoonfuls grated cheese with one tablespoonful of margarine, one saltspoonful each of salt, pepper, and (dry) mustard, a little anchovy paste to taste, and a teaspoonful of vinegar. Blend thoroughly until you have got a smooth paste, and spread upon slices of bread.

CHAPTER VI

POTATOES AND OTHER VEGETABLES

THE cooking of potatoes is an immensely wide subject. Unluckily it is discounted by the dearth of fats. Potatoes are starchy foods, and without some sort of fat to accompany them, they are undoubtedly far from gay. They are eatable, but they are not interesting.

I therefore advise you to make potatoes one of your first considerations when you are salving fat of any sort. A steamed potato in its jacket is a fine wholesome sustaining thing; but a parboiled potato baked in a little fat is something to set before the king. Riced potatoes are an elegant dish in connection with gravy of some kind; but they have not the subtle appeal of mashed potatoes, which *must* have either milk, or fat, or both. As for "chips"—beloved of the working classes—these are, of necessity, almost things of the past.

Potatoes can be made presentable and delectable in so many different ways, that no other vegetable comes within a mile of them. In 1917, when we were practically potato-less, we realised how largely we depended upon that cheap and humble tuber. In vain to urge that we never had potatoes before the seventeenth century—that other nations don't bother about them; that hundreds of millions never see them; that rice, or haricots, or swedes do just as well. All these arguments may be true, yet they are not convincing. What we want is potatoes "every time." And we haven't yet used them for a fraction of their true value; no, not though potato-spirit is driving motors, impelling aeroplanes, and constituting a vital ingredient of high explosives.

You will find a lot of potato recipes here. But I have had to omit the most delectable. They simply couldn't be carried out in these days.

In this chapter potatoes are only treated as vegetables. For their use in puddings and pastry, *see* Chapter VIII. ; in bread and cakes, *see* Chapter IX.

For all ordinary purposes, it is necessary to have a good sieve or a potato ricer. Mashing with a rolling pin or any other implement never achieves the same result as one of the above, takes longer, and leaves hidden lumps. But whether you sieve, rice, or mash it, do so *while the potato is hot*. If you let it go cold first, it is much more difficult to deal with, and will make your dish heavy.

I need hardly say that potatoes should *never* be peeled before cooking. Peeling wastes not only the potato, and its flavour, but the mineral salts which lie next the skin, and 85 per cent. of all its most important qualities are literally *thrown away*. The potato must be boiled, or better, steamed, in its " jacket," after a good scrubbing.

The potato baked in its skin is a very appetising thing ; but this is a wasteful way of treating it, and I don't commend it, on that account.

To mash potatoes in the old way, with butter and milk, is undoubtedly too extravagant now. To sauter them is usually out of the question. Cooked potatoes, however, are an indispensable means of eking out one's meat, fish, bacon, or eggs ; a very little fat will do to heat them through, or they can be sieved for fish-cakes and rissoles.

As regards the *Other Vegetables*, please note that the most nourishing (after Potatoes, which are miles ahead) are Jerusalem Artichokes—(it is astounding how many folks are ignorant of these)—Parsnips, Carrots, Beet, and Onions ; the " pulse " vegetables, dried or fresh Peas, Beans, Runners, Haricots, Kidney Beans, etc. (dried are more nutritious than fresh) ; and then the rest in go-as-you-please order ; scientists never seem to agree about their respective degrees of nutriment. But beyond actual food-value, one must take into consideration the mineral salts supplied by vegetables, and by green saladings, which play a most important part in the purifying of the blood. I think it may fairly be stated that the vegetable of least value (for human beings), from any point of view, is the Turnip. But Turnip-*tops* are extremely useful and beneficial, so that it is hard to generalise.

A number of tasty recipes are set forth in the Ministry of Food vegetable leaflet—but as they nearly all involve the use of fat—our priceless fat !—or of cheese—that exceedingly rare article !—I do not quote them. An excellent piece of advice in the leaflet, however, is that with reference to cooking all vegetables "in very little water in closed vessels. Water is only used to prevent the vegetables from sticking to the pan and getting burnt ; so that the vegetables are really steamed." Half a teaspoonful of fat to one pound of vegetable has been stated as sufficient : this fat not only improves the flavour, but helps to cook the vegetable.

If cooked thus in an earthenware casserole, tightly covered, the flavour is all retained and there is no waste of anything. If you have no casserole, the vegetable can be put in a steamer. The old-fashioned plan of using quarts or gallons of water, is at once wasteful and insipid. All the mineral salts and true taste of the vegetable get washed away. You will be surprised at the difference when you have tried the little-water method.

If cereals are used as vegetables, soak them for twelve hours before cooking ; this includes rice, pearl barley, sago, tapioca, hominy, etc. Pulse (dried) vegetables such as haricots, dried peas, split peas, lentils, butter beans, etc., require twenty-four hours preliminary soaking. *Be sure to keep for stock the water in which any of the above has been boiled.* In these cases plenty of water is necessary, that the cereals or pulse may absorb it and thus swell out and become tender. Remember that if they don't swell out properly in the cooking, they will attempt to do so inside the human stomach ; a most unpleasant process.

A very important statement regarding pulse foods was recently made in *The Garden*, *i.e.*, that haricots, dried broad beans, dried peas, are much more digestible and nourishing if eaten as in Burmah—soaked for a day or two, then put, covered with a cloth, for forty-eight hours or so, in a warm place (sixty to seventy degrees Fahr.) such as a warm cupboard near the kitchen fire, and *allowed to sprout*. When little shoots about half an inch appear on them, as they should do in two days, the starch in the beans or peas is converted into maltose; the seeds have softened, the thick outer coat comes off. They require much less boiling, and are far more readily digested. This is a valuable "tip."

Pulse food should always be accompanied with fat in some form, however little; and bottled salad dressing, which contains oil, is a fine sauce for plain boiled haricots.

Further vegetable recipes may be found in the "Vegetable Book" of this series, and issued with a war-time supplement.

POTATOES

327. POTATO BALLS

Mix two ounces of flour with twelve to sixteen ounces of cooked sieved potatoes; add two teaspoonfuls of minced parsley, one teaspoonful of minced herbs, salt and pepper to taste. Moisten with one beaten (dried) egg. Make the mixture into balls. Have ready any odds and ends of meat, put through the mincer, and flavoured with a little tomato sauce or curry powder. Put a teaspoonful of meat into each ball, cover, and re-shape and bake in a greased tin in a hot oven until the potato is a golden brown.

328. POTATO CAKES, No. I

Have twelve ounces of potatoes (boiled in their skins and sieved) mixed with two ounces of flour (any sort); add half a teaspoonful of salt and one teaspoonful of fat. Bind with a dried egg; roll out to desired thickness, cut into small

rounds, and bake or fry to a golden brown. Serve at once
as a vegetable.

329. POTATO CAKES, No. II

Take one breakfastcupful of cold sieved or mashed potatoes ;
one tablespoonful of self-raising flour, mix thoroughly with
the fingers ; season with salt and pepper, and moisten with
enough milk to make a stiff dough. Roll out a quarter of an
inch thick, cut into rounds, and fry. Serve as a vegetable.

330. POTATOES, CURRIED

Fry in dripping an onion, cut into thin slices. Cut up
some boiled potatoes, and fry with the onion, dredge them
with curry-powder, and add a little gravy, salt and some
lemon juice, if you have it. Allow this to stew for a quarter
of an hour, and serve.

331. POTATO CUSTARD

Peel some potatoes as thinly as you can, slice them very
finely, and lay them in overlapping scales in a deep fireproof
earthen pie-dish. Make a custard with dried eggs or custard
powder, and a little milk and stock or water. Pour a little
meat extract over the potatoes, just enough to moisten them ;
sprinkle them with a very little finely minced parsley and
onion. Season the custard, pour it over the potatoes, and
bake in a hot oven for thirty-eight to forty minutes.

332. POTATOES, DELMONICO

Chop cold, boiled potatoes into bits the size of peas ; make
a white sauce and stir the chopped potato into it, using a
generous cupful of potato to each cup of sauce. Pour in to a
greased pudding-dish, cover the top with bits of fat and
crumbs, and bake about fifteen minutes in a hot oven.

333. POTATOES, DUCHESSE, No. I

Take ten ounces of mashed potatoes, and beat up with
them, while still hot, three ounces of Spanish onions boiled

very soft. Add one and a half ounces of fat, one tablespoonful of milk, one dessertspoonful of grated cheese, one beaten
egg (dried). Mix all these well while hot. When the mixture
is cold, roll it out on a floured pasteboard, to about one
inch thick; cut it into rounds or ovals; dredge these, and
fry them a golden brown, in dripping, over a low fire.

334. POTATOES, DUCHESSE, No. II

Prepare a potato purée. Divide into six equal parts.
Spread a little flour on a corner of a table, roll each piece
of potato in the flour, then give to each a nice heart-shaped
form; nicely criss-cross their surfaces with a knife. Butter
a small pastry-pan with a teaspoonful of fat, arrange the
potatoes over, and lightly grease their surface. Place the
pan in a hot oven and bake for ten minutes, or until of a fine
golden colour. Remove from the oven, and with a skimmer
lift them up and place on a heated dish, and serve.

335. POTATO DUMPLING

Beat up some dry floury cooked potatoes until they are
perfectly smooth, then mix with them one quarter of their
weight in fine flour, season with salt, and form into a moderately firm paste with an ounce of fat, melted in a little warm
water or stock. Put the mixture into a greased basin and
steam over plenty of boiling water until the dumpling is
quite firm and light, then turn it out carefully on to a hot
dish, garnish it with sprigs of parsley, and send to table
very hot, with some pleasantly flavoured sauce or gravy
as an accompaniment. Or, if preferred, instead of sauce or
gravy, some stewed mushrooms, baked tomatoes, or fried
onions, etc., may be served with the dumpling.

336. POTATO DUMPLINGS, No. I

Mash one pound of steamed potatoes, keep them hot in a
saucepan, stir in one well-beaten dried egg and one tablespoonful of milk. Then mix in thoroughly one breakfast-

cupful of flour and one teaspoonful of baking-powder, and leave the mixture to cool. Make it into small dumplings. Put the dumplings for fifteen minutes in (slightly salted) boiling water, drain, and serve them. A sharp sauce is an excellent addition.

337. POTATO DUMPLINGS, No. II

Have eight large potatoes steamed in their jackets, peeled, and rubbed through a sieve while warm. Let them grow cold, then add three ounces of flour, and one ounce of fat, melted till soft but not oiled. Add one beaten (dried) egg, salt, pepper, and nutmeg to taste; beat well; then stir in one teaspoonful of baking-powder. Form the dumplings into small balls, and place them in boiling stock or water. They must boil fast for twenty minutes or so. Lift out and drain, and serve at once, with a good gravy or sauce.

338. POTATO FRITTERS

Take one pound of hot sieved potatoes, and work into it one beaten (dried) egg, three ounces of flour, pepper, and salt, and nutmeg to taste. Form into fingers about one inch wide by three inches long; fry in boiling fat, drain, and serve.

339. POTATOES HASHED

Grease an omelet pan and put into it cold boiled potatoes chopped rather fine; sprinkle with a little salt, scatter bits of fat over the top, and pour over a little white stock or hot water. Cover and cook slowly until thoroughly heated through. Turn out carefully into a hot dish without stirring. Care needs be taken that the potato be not browned, but the stock and fat absorbed.

340. POTATOES WITH HERRINGS

Well wash and boil some potatoes, taking care not to let them break or get too soft; then drain off the water, peel and slice them fairly thickly, and keep them hot. In the meantime put a chopped onion into a stewpan with an ounce of fat, and fry until lightly browned ; then dust in some flour, add three tablespoonfuls of vinegar, a bay leaf, and rather under a pint of water ; season with salt and pepper, draw the pan to the side of the stove, and let simmer for a little.   Well wash two red herrings, cut them down length-ways, remove the bones, cut up the flesh small, put it into the sauce, and let it cook in this for a few minutes ; now put in the potatoes, and stir them gently, being careful not to break them.   Next add two ounces of fat and a gill of milk, and stir over the fire until it reaches boiling point.   When cooked, turn out on to a hot dish, and serve.

341. POTATO MIROTON

Boil or steam twelve fair-sized potatoes in their skins. Skin, mash, and season them with salt and pepper.   Mince up a small onion, and fry it in two tablespoonfuls of fat. When the onion is light brown, add in the mashed potatoes, stir all well, and put in a tablespoonful of mushroom ketchup or some similar flavouring, and two dried eggs well beaten. Sprinkle a greased mould with breadcrumbs, and bake the mixture in it for half an hour.   Moderate oven.

342. POTATO PANCAKES

Have six ounces of G.R. flour in a bowl, make a hollow in the middle, and pour into it one and a half breakfast-cupfuls of water.   Beat well until you have a smooth batter. Then add six ounces of grated raw potato, one ounce of grated or minced onion, salt and pepper to taste ; mix thoroughly. Let stand for an hour, mix in one teaspoonful of baking powder, and cook as for other pancakes.

343. POTATO SAVOURIES

Boil and mash some potatoes ; moisten with milk or white stock ; add a seasoning of salt, pepper, chopped herbs, and grated lemon-rind.   Have some small patty-pans greased and dusted with fine crumbs ; fill these with the potato mixture, lay a little bit of fat on the top of each, and brown them in a moderate oven.

344. POTATOES STEWED IN MILK

Slice some waxy potatoes. Melt two ounces of fat in a pan, add to this gradually one ounce of flour, and stir gently without allowing the flour to colour; then add by degrees one pint of cold milk, stirring all the time; directly this reaches the boil, put in the potatoes, which must be well covered by the liquid; add salt, and put on the lid tightly; then let the whole simmer gently at the side of the fire till the potatoes are cooked; this will take about half an hour. Five minutes before serving, sprinkle in some finely minced parsley, and serve.

345. POTATOES WITH WHITE SAUCE

Put into a saucepan a small piece of fat, with a little flour, diluted with a little stock; to which add some salt and pepper, and thicken it over the fire; having boiled the potatoes, peeled them, and cut them into slices, pour this sauce over them, and serve hot. To vary the flavour, some minced capers or a little chopped parsley may be added to the sauce.

OTHER VEGETABLES

346. ARTICHOKES, CHINESE (OR JAPANESE)

For a pound of the vegetables, put one pint of water into a stewpan with a saltspoonful of salt, a dessertspoonful of vinegar, a teaspoonful of flour, and an ounce of fat; stir these all over the fire till boiling then put in the artichokes, which should have been washed and scraped, and simmer slowly for fifteen minutes with the stewpan not quite covered down. Then drain, and serve with any sauces suitable for celery.

347. ARTICHOKES (JERUSALEM) AND ONIONS

Boil two pounds of Jerusalem artichokes, drain, and sieve; add one gill of stock (any sort), and season to taste. Mix with them two large Spanish onions, well boiled and finely chopped. Pour the mixture into a greased baking-dish, dust the top with grated cheese, and bake a light brown. A little thickening of cornflour can be added at pleasure.

348. BEANS AND CARROTS

Soak eight ounces of butter beans in four pints of cold water for a day and a night. Boil them in the same water ; add salt and pepper, mixed spice and herbs to taste, and two onions and six carrots sliced small ; also any other vegetables, cut up small ; place all in a casserole, cover, and let simmer slowly for two hours. Towards the last, put in a small teaspoonful of curry powder, and the same of minced parsley.

349. BEANS AND RICE

Soak half a pound of butter beans overnight—next day cook them for two hours, or until tender. Have one ounce of rice boiled in vegetable stock, add salt and pepper. Place half a pound tin of tomatoes in a stewpan, with one ounce of fat and a muslin bag of minced herbs and parsley (a teaspoonful will suffice). Cook until the tomato can be sieved. Blend it with the rice and butter beans, and serve very hot.

350. BEAN ROAST

Soak half a pound of butter beans overnight ; next day cook gently for three hours, or until soft enough to sieve. Have eight ounces of rice boiled for a quarter of an hour, and two minced onions lightly browned in about an ounce of fat. Add these to the sieved butter beans, along with a teaspoonful of minced parsley, an ounce of minced bacon, and pepper and salt to taste. Some people put in a pinch of dried herbs. Mix well, and to moisten the mixture use the following : Have two ounces of flour mixed smooth in a little of the (cold) stock from the butter beans. Boil enough additional stock to make a breakfastcupful altogether, and add it to the paste, stirring until all is smooth. Season, and add a tablespoonful of tomato ketchup. Boil up, and simmer from eight to ten minutes ; add to the beans, etc. Shape the whole mixture into a roll, dredge it with oatmeal, sprinkle with little bits of fat, bake on a floured tin in a hot oven for thirty minutes.

351. BEETROOT, BAKED

Put the beetroot without washing it into a slack oven, and bake for eight hours. When cold, peel and serve.

352. BEETROOT, FRIED

Cut up a boiled beetroot in thin slices, also one onion ; fry both in dripping, add pepper and salt, drain, and serve very hot.

353. BEETROOT MOULD

Boil a large beetroot, and while hot pass it through the masher ; mince a raw onion ; add it to the beet with pepper, salt, and one ounce of fat. Place in a greased basin or mould with a cover over, and bake for one hour.

354. BEETROOT RAGOÛT

Boil a good-sized beetroot ; fry an onion, and season with salt, pepper, and a teaspoonful of vinegar ; add the beetroot cut into small pieces and one cupful of milk or stock, thicken with flour, and serve very hot.

355. BEETROOT SAVOURY

Fry a large onion in rings ; cut up a boiled beetroot in large dice. When the onion begins to colour, add the beetroot, pepper and salt, and three tablespoonfuls of tarragon vinegar. Serve very hot.

356. BEETROOT STEWED, No. I

Make some thickened stock very hot on the fire ; add a small parboiled and skinned beetroot cut in thin slices, a spoonful of vinegar, and some pepper and salt. Let all boil until the beet is tender, but not mashed at all—about one hour. Serve very hot.

357. BEETROOT, STEWED, No. II

Take two medium-sized cooked beetroots ; peel and cut them into dice. Put them in a saucepan with just enough hot water to cover them (about one pint), add a little salt and pepper ; let them stew slowly for fifteen minutes. Mix one tablespoonful of cornflour smooth in a little cold water, and put this, with one ounce of fat, to the beetroot, stirring well until the cornflour thickens. Serve it in a heated vegetable-dish, and sprinkle over it one teaspoonful of chopped parsley.

358. BRUSSELS SPROUTS, LYONS

Cook and well drain one pound of Brussels sprouts. Fry one tablespoonful of minced Spanish onions in one ounce fat ; when this is a golden colour, add the sprouts ; toss them in the pan for three minutes, and serve very hot.

359. CABBAGE, PIEDMONT

Boil or steam one pound of cabbage. Drain, press, and let it get cold. Cook, separately from this, eight ounces of mild onions ; let them get cold. Grease a baking-dish, sprinkle it with minced parsley. Shred in the cabbage and onions in alternate layers of each, with a seasoning of salt and pepper to each layer, a few little bits of fat here and there, and a thin layer of grated cheese. When the dish is nearly full, moisten the mixture with stock (taking care not to make it too wet) till it is level with the top of dish. Brush the top with a little melted fat, cook in moderate oven for about half an hour, and serve when thoroughly hot.

360. CABBAGE (RED) FLEMISH, No. I

Shred the cabbage very finely, put into a saucepan with a piece of dripping for each cabbage, two large onions, two apples cut in slices, a spoonful of stock or water, a spoonful of vinegar, pepper, salt, and Demerara sugar. Cover and well boil at least three hours. When the cabbage is soft, stir with a wooden spoon ; mix well ; if necessary, add more sugar. Strain before serving.

361. CABBAGE (RED FLEMISH), No. II

Cut one large or two small red cabbage in quarters; boil
them with an onion cut up, two cloves, salt, pepper, and a
bay leaf for an hour and a half. Strain the cabbage, and
place with some fat in a casserole in the oven for five
minutes. Serve very hot.

362. CABBAGE (RED) FRICASSEE

Stew a large red cabbage in some stock until nearly done;
there must only be enough stock to keep it from burning.
Drain it, cut the cabbage in thick slices, and fry with two
onions cut in rings, and either two tomatoes or a tablespoonful
of tomato sauce.

363. CARROT PATTIES

Clean, slice, and boil three medium carrots in slightly
salted water until soft enough to mince. Have ready two
ounces of (hot) boiled rice, add salt, pepper, and nutmeg
to taste, and half a teaspoonful each of curry powder and of
meat extract. Blend thoroughly and heat up gently. Meanwhile prepare some potato shortcrust (see p. 162), roll out
nearly an inch thick, and line some greased patty-pans.
The crust should be pricked with a fork before you put in the
carrot mixture. Sprinkle each patty with a very little grated
cheese, and place in a hottish oven for twenty minutes or so.

364. CARROTS, STEWED

Slice the carrots in rings thinly, simmer in weak stock or
water; when nearly soft, shake in one tablespoonful of flour,
add a chopped onion, one tablespoonful of chopped parsley,
salt to taste, and a very small piece of fat; simmer together
till it thickens, pour in a vegetable dish and serve. The
water or stock should only be sufficient just to cover the
carrots.

365. CARROTS À LA VICHY

Take some young carrots (or if old ones be used they must
first be parboiled) and slice them, then put them in a pan

K

with sufficient water to cover them, allowing half an ounce
of salt, one ounce of sugar, and two ounces of fat to the pint
of water, and let them boil up sharply till the water has
almost entirely evaporated, then serve sprinkled with chopped
parsley.

366. CELERY FRITTERS

This is a method of using the green parts of celery—young
leaves and green stalks—which are generally discarded as
uneatable. Wash them and mince them very finely ; about
a breakfastcupful of chopped celery will be enough. Make a
thick batter with one egg, one pint of flour, one teaspoonful
of baking-powder, salt and pepper to taste, and enough milk
to moisten the mixture ; add in the celery, and put large
tablespoonfuls of the batter into boiling fat. Fry a golden
brown, drain, and serve.

367. COLCANNON

Boil separately an equal amount of potatoes, of fresh
cabbage, and about half the amount of onion. Mash all very
finely, mix well together, with a little butter or dripping,
salt, and pepper, put in a buttered bowl and bake, well covered
up. Serve very hot.

368. COLD SLAW

This is a very popular American dish. Take half an ounce
of fat and half a tumblerful of vinegar ; warm them in a lined
pan, and shred in a tender cabbage, only using the heart.
Add a pinch of salt, two pinches of celery seed, and two
dessertspoonfuls of flour. Let the slaw simmer for a few
minutes, then add a lightly beaten egg and stir it well in.
When the mixture has cooked about five minutes longer,
take it off. To be eaten cold.

369. DARIOLES, SAVOURY

Take one breakfastcupful of soaked and drained bread-
scraps, and mix well with the following ; one medium boiled
onion finely minced or grated, one teaspoonful finely-minced

parsley, pepper and salt to taste, two (dried) beaten eggs, a little fat of some sort, and a little milk to moisten. Have ready some greased dariole tins; half fill with the mixture; place in good oven for about twenty-five minutes.

370. GIPSY PIE

Cut some cold boiled potatoes in slices about a quarter of an inch thick and arrange these in layers in a well-greased pie-dish with a little salt, pepper, finely minced parsley, boiled onion chopped small, and tiny bits of fat, between each layer. When the dish is sufficiently full, and the potatoes on top arranged as evenly as possible, brush over the surface with dripping, and bake in a moderate oven until the pie is bubbling hot and well browned. If you have it, a little finely chopped meat of some kind, pleasantly seasoned and moistened with good gravy or sauce, may be placed between the layers of potatoes, and the whole covered in the usual way with crust of well-made potato pastry. Some brown gravy, or a well-flavoured sauce is a great improvement to a gipsy pie, in the opinion of some people, while others prefer it without.

371. HARICOTS, BOILED

Soak one pound of haricots overnight. Have two good-sized onions cut up in rings, and browned in one teaspoonful of fat. Put the haricots to this; add enough cold water to cover them, and let them simmer slowly for two and a half hours, or until tender. Season with pepper and salt and pour into a hot dish.

372. HARICOT MINCE

Soak half a pint of haricots overnight. Boil with a little chopped onion, until quite tender; drain. Add to these any scraps you have got; odds and ends of cooked vegetables, of crusts, etc.; and seasoning of pepper, salt, nutmeg, sage, parsley, etc. Mix well, and put the whole lot through the mincer. Then place in a greased pie-dish and bake. The more scraps you put into this, the better it will be. A few little bits of fat should be strewn on the top. If cocoa butter be used, the seasoning employed should disguise its flavour.

373. HARICOT MOULD

Soak half a pint of haricots overnight; place in salted boiling water, let boil two and a half hours; drain. Have ready in a frying pan half an ounce of minced onion, and a teaspoonful of minced mixed herbs, browned in one ounce of fat, to this add the haricots, with half an ounce of maize flour, pepper and salt to taste, one tablespoonful of minced chutney (any sort) and half a gill of stock (any sort, but preferably meat stock). Let simmer twenty minutes; then put in half a gill more stock, and continue to simmer till it is absorbed. Add half an ounce of fat and half a teaspoonful of mixed spice. Blend thoroughly, and rub all through a sieve. Place in a mould that has been rinsed with cold water, pressing the mixture well in. When cold, unmould and serve.

374. HARICOT STEW

Soak half a pound of haricots overnight; drain, and boil. They should be done in about one and a half hours. Drain and cool. Have one ounce of fat browned in a pan, with a little minced parsley. Add the beans, let cook a quarter of an hour. Put in one tablespoonful of tomato sauce, pepper and salt to taste, and a glass of white wine. Mix well, simmer for five minutes; serve at once.

375. IRISH HOT POT

One pound of potatoes, one pound of onions, half a pound of good cheese. Slice potatoes, ditto onions, ditto cheese, and fry them separately. Then line a dish with potato and fill it with onions mixed with cheese, pepper, salt and sage. Cover with the potato to form crust. Bake. To be eaten very hot. If left, the cheese will get hard.

376. LENTILS, BOILED

Soak a pint of lentils overnight in slightly salted water; leave them soaking till wanted, then place them in slightly

salted boiling water, and let cook until tender but not broken.
Fry a good-sized onion brown in a little salad oil, in a stewpan,
add a teaspoonful of flour, then put in a breakfastcupful of
stock (any sort). Boil slowly, stirring well. Then strain the
lentils (keep the water they were cooked in, for stock), and
put them in the pan, with a little salt and pepper. Let cook
gently for three or four minutes ; serve on a hot dish at once.

377. LENTILS, CURRIED

Soak half a pound of lentils overnight (twenty-four hours
is not too long) in a pint of water. Place them, water and
all, in a saucepan ; when they boil, take out half a teacupful
or so of the liquor, and mix smooth a thin paste, with a
dessertspoonful each of curry powder and of flour, and one
cube of Oxo or similar meat extract. Put this mixture back
to the lentils, mix well, and let simmer until thoroughly tender.
Serve with plain boiled rice.

378. LENTIL CUTLETS

Have one pound of lentils soaked overnight, and gently
stewed next day until tender, with just enough water to
cover them. Have a beetroot minced very small, a large
onion chopped and fried, one tablespoonful of minced parsley,
one teaspoonful of minced thyme ; pepper and salt to taste ;
two tablespoonfuls of ketchup (any kind), one ounce of dripping or other fat. Mix all above thoroughly well, bind
with one and a half (dried) beaten eggs, set aside to cool.
Shape into cutlets ; egg and flour ; fry in boiling fat or oil.

379. LENTIL MOUSSE

Soak half a pint of lentils overnight ; place in boiling salted
water, enough to cover them ; add two cloves. Boil until
tender enough to sieve, first draining off the water. When
cool, add one and a half dried eggs, a little salt and pepper,
a pinch of curry powder, and a gill of milk. Blend thoroughly,
place in a greased mould, put a greased paper on top, and
steam for an hour.

Minced onion and parsley can be added if liked.

380. LENTILS AND RICE FRITTERS

Soak half a pound of rice and half a pound of lentils over·
night. Tie up loosely in butter-muslin, and place in salted
boiling water. The cloth will have to be tied higher up
as the rice and lentils swell.   When they cease to expand,
remove them and leave them to cool, still tied up.   In about
two hours they should be cold. Take them from the cloth,
when a solid mass will be found. Cut this into thin slices,
which should be dusted with pepper, salt, and powdered
herbs, and fry.

381. LENTIL AND POTATO PATTIES

Make half a pint of onion sauce (using stock in which
macaroni or rice has been boiled, instead of milk), and mix
with it one breakfastcupful of cooked lentils, one teaspoonful
of finely minced parsley, salt and pepper to taste. Make
a potato shortcrust (see pp. 162–3) and line some patty-tins ;
bake, and fill with the hot lentil mixture. Serve at once.

382. LENTILS, POTTED

Take about half a pound of lentils, rather more than less.
Simmer them in a muslin bag until tender, in stock or water.
When they are soft, beat them to a pulp in a basin, or pulp
them through a sieve ; and while they are hot, add one
tablespoonful of fat, half a teaspoonful of powdered or finely
chopped sage, a piled tablespoonful of drained soaked bread,
salt and pepper. Mix thoroughly well and bake slowly
for about an hour in a greased pie-dish. Keep the water for
stock.

383. LENTIL PURÉE

Soak one pound of lentils overnight. Drain them, and
place in salted boiling water or stock, with a sliced onion,
four or five cloves, and one ounce of fat bacon. In an hour
and a half they should be tender enough to serve. Add
pepper and salt, and dilute with stock of any sort to the
consistency desired. Re-heat and serve.

384. LENTIL SAUSAGES

Soak eight ounces of lentils overnight; next day boil till tender enough to mash. Add three pounds of boiled and mashed potatoes, one onion chopped (and fried, if possible), pepper and salt to taste. Let the mixture cool; shape into sausages, drop into milk and flour or oatmeal; fry.

385. LENTILS, STEWED

Soak one pound of lentils overnight; place them in one quart of salted boiling water. Boil quietly until nearly tender. Have ready a little chopped onion and parsley, brown them in a saucepan with one ounce of fat and a tea-spoonful of anchovy essence. Add the lentils, pour in enough stock to cover them, and stew until the lentils are quite done.

MAIZE OR SWEET CORN, GREEN

Even as its grains are much larger and of a different forma-tion to those of other cereals, so, when cooked green, the taste of maize is of a pleasant sweetness, quite unlike any other flavour one can recall.

Strip off the husk to the inner layer, and remove the " silk "; then replace the inner layer, and tie it at the top end. In some cases, separate the grains from the cob; but this is only necessary where indicated. Short thick ears are the best.

386. MAIZE, BAKED

Prepare as above; smear the cobs with softened fat, dust them with pepper and salt, place them in a baking-dish in a hot oven, turning and basting them so that they may brown all over.

387. MAIZE, BOILED, No. I

Prepare as above, and place in boiling water, *not* salted. Boil fast for at least fifteen minutes. Serve with fat, salt, and pepper, or with white sauce or Sauce Hollandaise.

388. MAIZE, BOILED, No. II

Pare off stems, remove leaves and silk from six sound, tender ears of green corn.   Boil in a saucepan three quarts of water, one gill of milk, one tablespoonful of salt, and half an ounce of fat, then plunge in the corn and boil twenty-five minutes.   Lift up, thoroughly drain, dress on a hot dish and serve, enveloped in a napkin, with a little melted butter separately.

389. MAIZE, ROASTED

Cut off the stalks, remove the leaves and silk from six ears of fresh, sound, green corn, place them in a saucepan with two quarts of water, one gill of milk, and a teaspoonful of salt, and boil for twenty minutes only.   Lift up with a skimmer, drain on a cloth, then place them on a tin ; lightly baste with a little melted fat ; then set them in a brisk oven until a nice golden colour, being careful to turn them once in a while.   Remove, dress on a hot dish, envelop in a napkin, and serve.

390. MAIZE SAUTÉ (CRÉOLE)

Cut away stalks, remove leaves and silk from six fresh, sound, white ears of green corn, then with back of a knife-blade detach from the cobs.   Heat a tablespoonful of oil in a frying-pan, add one finely chopped small white onion. Nicely brown three minutes, add corn, and fry eight minutes, occasionally tossing meanwhile ; add two finely chopped, peeled, red tomatoes.   Season with half a teaspoonful of salt and half a teaspoonful of sugar ; toss well, and cook eight minutes, lightly mixing meanwhile.   Dress on a vegetable dish, and serve.

391. MAIZE, STEWED

Thoroughly drain a pint tin of corn, then place in a small frying-pan with a gill of milk and half an ounce of fat, season with half a teaspoonful of salt, two saltspoonfuls of white pepper, and half a saltspoonful of grated nutmeg.

Gently mix, and let slowly cook for eight minutes. Remove, pour into a vegetable dish, and serve.

392. NETTLES, BOILED

Take young nettle shoots, wash and drain well, place in boiling salted water. Boil twenty to twenty-five minutes. Drain and chop; return to pan and thicken with a little fat, a little flour (two teaspoonfuls to the pound) and stock; season with salt and pepper; serve very hot.

393. NETTLES, FRIED

Wash the young nettle-tops thoroughly in salted water. Put into a very little boiling water, salted; some people add a pinch of soda bicarbonate. Boil fast for thirty minutes; then squeeze dry, chop, season, and make into small flat cakes (using a little sieved potato to bind the nettles if need be). Fry, and serve with fried eggs.

394. NETTLE PUDDING

Take half a gallon of young nettle-tops, wash them thoroughly. Clean, prepare, and chop one good-sized onion or leek, one broccoli head, or the same bulk in Brussels sprouts, and two ounces of rice. Mix all well with the nettles, season, tie them up in a muslin bag, and place in salted boiling water. Boil till all is thoroughly cooked, and serve with a little good gravy.

395. NETTLES, STEWED

(Only very young nettle-tops must be used.) Wash one pound of nettle-tops very thoroughly; boil and chop them up. Place in a stewpan in which one tablespoonful of barley flour has been browned in two ounces of fat, and a teacupful of stock added. Mix well, stew till re-heated, and serve.

Nettles may also be cooked exactly like spinach. They should be picked first thing in the morning.

396. ONION PIE

Take four Spanish onions, peel and slice; boil in salted water for five minutes; place in a casserole with two ounces of fat. When they are nearly soft, take them out; have ready sufficient sliced parboiled potatoes to fill the casserole in alternate layers with the onions. You must begin with potatoes at the bottom, and end with potatoes at the top. Season each layer well with salt and pepper, cover, and bake for an hour or so in a moderate oven.

397. ONIONS, SAVOURY

Put four peeled Spanish onions into salted boiling water; cook for five minutes; then put into a casserole, with one ounce of fat, and let cook slowly until quite soft. Take out the inside of each onion so as to leave a firm outer shell, and mince finely what you have removed; then mix it well with two ounces of either mashed potato, boiled rice, cooked porridge, or semolina—one ounce each of fat and of grated cheese, salt and pepper to taste. Moisten with a little stock. Fill the onion shells with this mixture, replace them in the casserole, and reheat through. Serve at once.

398. ONIONS, SUPPER

Peel and wash eight or ten large onions, throw them into a large saucepan of boiling water with two ounces of salt; let the onions boil one hour exactly—take them up with a wooden spoon on to a flat dish, put an inverted pie-dish over, and drain the water away. Serve with potatoes baked in their skins.

399. PARSNIP PIE

Take cooked parsnips (hot) and mash them up with a little fat, pepper and salt. Let them go cold; then mix with minced parsley to taste, and cold cooked rice, and any vegetables (chopped or sieved) left over; place in a pie-dish, moisten with stock or gravy, and cover with a potato crust.

400. PEAS, GREEN, À LA FRANCAISE

Put one pint of shelled green peas into a casserole or pan containing half a pint of boiling water; add one teaspoonful of sugar, and pepper and salt to taste; a head of cabbage

lettuce, a spray of parsley, and four or five tiny onions.   Let
boil for thirty minnutes ; remove the lettuce and parsley
(which can be used for some other dish, such as Haricot
Stew, or Parsnip Pie, or for soup), and put half an ounce of
fat to the peas.   Let simmer slowly for five minutes ; pour
off contents of pan into heated vegetable dish, and serve
immediately.

401. PEAS, JUGGED

This is one of the best ways to cook peas, whether fresh,
dried green, tinned, or bottled.   Shell a pint of peas, put
them into a clean two-pound pickle-bottle or any jar with
a closely fitting top, adding a tablespoonful of fat, a teaspoonful of powdered sugar, a saltspoonful of salt, a dozen mint
leaves, and, at discretion, a very little black pepper.   Cover
the vessel tightly, and immerse it, to the extent of half its
depth, in a pan of boiling water.   Set the latter on the fire
and boil briskly.   Examine in half an hour ; the peas, if
very young, should be done by then ; if old, they will of
course take longer.

402. GREEN PEAS PUDDING, No. I

Have half a pint of shelled peas boiled and sieved, and
mixed with four ounces of sieved cooked potato.   Add salt
and pepper to taste, a teaspoonful of finely-minced onion,
and one ounce of fat.   Mix thoroughly ; bind with a dried
egg ; place in a greased pie-dish, and bake for thirty minutes.

403. GREEN PEAS PUDDING, No. II

Make a batter with a breakfastcupful of flour, two breakfastcupfuls of milk, one (dried) egg, salt and pepper, a pinch
of powdered mint, and one teaspoonful baking-powder)
Add to this, half a pint of cooked peas (either fresh or tinned.
pour into a greased pie-dish, and bake until well set and
slightly browned.

404. PEAS PUDDING

Soak for twenty-four hours a quart of dried peas, tie them
rather loosely into a cloth, put them down in cold water to

boil slowly till tender—good peas will take at least two hours and a half. Rub through a sieve, adding a dried egg, an ounce of fat, some pepper and salt, and beat them well for about ten minutes. Flour the cloth, and tie the pudding tight as possible, and boil an hour longer.

SALADS

405. APPLE SALAD

Two cupfuls of sour apple, half a cupful of celery, half a cupful of blanched walnuts, four tablespoonfuls of salad dressing, one teaspoonful of sugar. Salt and pepper on nuts.

406. DANDELION SALAD

Very young dandelion shoots should be used. Wash well and shred finely; add a very little finely-minced onion and mint. Mix a little brown sugar with vinegar containing a pinch of raw mustard; pour some of the liquor over the dandelions, enough to moisten; serve immediately.

407. HARICOT SALAD

One pint of white haricots, well boiled. Sprinkle over them one teaspoonful of salt and half a teaspoonful of pepper; add a very finely chopped onion or a few drops of shallot vinegar, one tablespoonful of vinegar, two tablespoonfuls of oil, and a sprinkling of very finely chopped parsley.

408. NUT, CRESS, AND CELERY SALAD

Take a shallow bowl, and arrange watercress in a wreath around the centre. Put inside this some finely sliced celery, and in the very middle put some skinned and thinly cut walnuts. Pour over this a salad dressing. Thin slices or cubes of apple may be added at discretion. Lemon juice should be squeezed on apple to keep it white.

409. TOMATO SALAD

Take some good ripe tomatoes, cut them into slices with a sharp knife, lay them in a salad bowl with a few finely sliced rings of Spanish onion or a dozen young spring onions. Season with pepper and salt and a pinch of sugar, sprinkle with chopped parsley, and pour a salad dressing over.

Add, at pleasure, thin slices of cold cooked potato, a few chopped capers, or a little grated cheese.

410. VEGETABLE SALAD, MIXED

Take half a pint each of shelled broad beans and of peas, cook, and drain, and add to them one breakfastcupful of parsley sauce, well seasoned. Let the whole go cold. Have a glass bowl lined with very thinly sliced alternate cucumber and beetroot ; put in a few spring onions very finely minced. Add the beans, etc., and (at pleasure) use radishes, mustard and cress, for garnishing.

411. VEGETABLE SALAD, COLD COOKED

The remains of a cold cauliflower, pulled into small heads ; a small carrot sliced finely ; a teacupful of haricot beans or green peas ; thin slices of cold potato ; any scraps of cheese which can be grated. Arrange symmetrically and pour a dressing over.

412. WINTER SALAD, No I

Take some white haricot beans, French beans, potatoes, beetroot, and onions. Blanch all the vegetables separately, cool, and drain them. Chop the onions, and put them in the corner of a cloth ; dip this in cold water, and press the water out of the onion. Do this two or three times, which will render the onion more digestible. Cut the potatoes and beetroots in half-inch discs. Put all into a salad-bowl, adding some chopped chervil ; season with salt, pepper, oil, and vinegar, and mix the whole well.

413. WINTER SALAD, No. II

Take a stick of celery and a little endive, cut and shred them up in short pieces ; mix in two tablespoonfuls of russet apples cut in dice after peeling and coring. Cover these with half a pound of grated nuts of any kind, and pour a thick dressing over all.

NOTE.—A large number of other salads will be found in the "Vegetable Book" of this series.

414. SIMPLE SALAD DRESSING

Blend equal quantities (say a quarter of a teaspoonful each) of salt, pepper, and dry mustard. Add one dessertspoonful each of oil and of vinegar, and one tablespoonful of milk. When these are thoroughly mixed, stir in one tablespoonful of honey.

415. SWEDES, MASHED

Take two pound of swedes; wash and peel them, and slice. Boil for an hour; then drain, mash and season with salt and pepper, and add two teaspoonfuls of fat and a teacupful of milk (or any sort of stock). Beat thoroughly, heat up again; serve at once.

416. SUCCOTASH, No. I

Have green maize freshly cut, and take the cobs cleanly out of the outer leaves, etc.; add an equal quantity of soaked butter or haricot beans. Put them into a saucepan with only just enough water to cover them; let them stew till perfectly tender, then pour off the water, and pour in the same amount of milk. Let the vegetables stew a little more, then add pepper and salt and a teaspoonful of cornflour mixed smooth in a little cold milk, and a lump of fat about as big as a large walnut. Mix well, let all boil up once, and serve very hot.

417. SUCCOTASH, No. II

Scrape, wash, and score in quarter-inch slices a quarter of a pound of salt pork. Cover with boiling water, and let simmer five or six hours, or until nearly tender; add one pint of freshly shelled Lima beans, and more water, if needed. When the beans become tender, add one pint of grated (green) maize pulp. Cook about fifteen minutes, and add two tablespoonfuls of fat, and salt if needed. Pour the succotash into the serving-dish, slice the pork according to its scorings, and serve at once. This dish is particularly good prepared with dried beans and either dried or tinned corn. If dried vegetables be used, let soak overnight in cold water. To remove the pulp from the ears of corn without the hull, with a sharp knife cut down through the centre of each row of kernels, then with the back of the knife press out the pulp, leaving the husk on the cob. For a change, add a cup of reduced tomato pulp, seasoning accordingly; or an onion may be cooked with the beans, and removed before the dish is sent to table.

418. TOMATOES WITH SAVOURY CUSTARD

Mix together one pint of tomatoes (tinned), one-fourth of a cup of soaked drained bread, one tablespoonful of finely-chopped onion, one teaspoonful of sugar, and salt and pepper to taste; pour into a greased baking-dish. Beat two dried eggs, add half a teaspoonful of salt, a teaspoonful of sugar, and a cup and a half of milk; pour over the tomato mixture, and bake in a slow oven until set (about three-quarters of an hour).

419. VEGETABLE CURRY, No. I

Take some boiled and sliced carrots and turnips, some cooked peas, French beans, little squares of cooked vegetable marrow, some cauliflower or broccoli—in fact, any cold cooked vegetables which may be to hand. Place them in a stewpan with a little dripping, and put on the edge of the stove, so that the dripping may be melting and the vegetables warming, while the curry sauce is prepared. For the sauce, fry two sliced onions, then mix with them one dessertspoonful of curry-powder, and fry for two minutes. Pour into the stewpan three-quarters of a pint of stock and cook until the onion is quite tender. Mix one dessertspoonful of arrow-root with some water to a paste; stir into the sauce, and simmer for eight to ten minutes. Add five or six drops of lemon juice. Pour on to the vegetables, stir gently, make thoroughly hot, and serve in the centre of a wall of boiled rice.

420. VEGETABLE CURRY, No. II

Cut onions into thin slices, and fry a good brown; add breakfastcupful of stock in which a teaspoonful of curry has been mixed. Let all boil together for twenty minutes, stirring the whole time; then add the vegetables—previously parboiled—and let all simmer for an hour. Potatoes, peas, beans, carrots, and turnips may be used. Broad beans alone make a delicious curry.

421. VEGETABLE FISH, No. I

Boil one breakfastcupful of milk; thicken it with two ounces of ground rice. Add salt, pepper, a pinch of mace, one small minced or grated onion, and a little fat of some sort. Mix well, and let cook, stirring often, for ten minutes. Have ready three boiled potatoes, pass them through ricer, stir them at once into rice, turn out the mixture on a dish to set cold. Then cut in slices, egg and flour them, fry. Serve with anchovy sauce, parsley sauce, or sauce piquante.

422. VEGETABLE FISH, No II

Boil a quarter of a pound of ground rice in one pint of mixed milk and water; then add two potatoes boiled and mashed, one saltspoonful of mace, about one teaspoonful of pulped onion or onion juice. Mix all pretty stiff, and spread it out to cool, about one inch thick. When cold, cut it in slices, breadcrumb and fry it, and serve with a sharp sauce.

423. VEGETABLE GOOSE

Soak and well drain any scraps of bread. Season with salt and pepper and one teaspoonful of powdered, or finely-minced fresh sage. Add one tablespoonful of barley flour, and mix all well with two tablespoonfuls of milk. Put into a greased baking-tin, strew plentifully with shredded dripping or other fat; place in good oven for twenty minutes or so. Remove from tin, cut into squares, pile on a hot dish; serve with onions or leeks, or with apple sauce.

424. VEGETABLE RAGOÛT

Take the remains of cooked vegetables, the larger the variety the better, and cut them into small pieces, then season these pleasantly with salt and pepper and put them in a well-greased stewpan; toss them over the fire for a minute or two, after which moisten them with a little gravy, or some suitable sauce, and allow them to get thoroughly hot, giving the pan a gentle shake every now and then to prevent them burning or sticking to the bottom. Do not stir during the process of reheating, as the ragoût presents a much more dainty appearance if the vegetables are kept unbroken. When thoroughly hot, pile up the ragoût in the centre of a well-heated dish, and serve at once.

425. VEGETABLE TURKEY

Have one pound of lentils soaked overnight, and boiled next day until tender. Grease a pie-dish, and line it throughout with lentils. Have ready a turkey stuffing, which can have dried eggs substituted for fresh ones, and any other fat for suet. Place it so as to fill the rest of the dish, and put the remainder of the lentils on top. Strew with a few bits of fat, and bake three-quarters of an hour or longer. To be served at once.

426. VEGETABLE MARROW, STUFFED

Cut off a thick slice from the top of a young marrow, and scoop out the seeds; stuff the inside with any forcemeat most convenient or merely breadcrumbs and herbs. Rub a saucepan or casserole with a blade of garlic, and, when you have put on the top which was cut off the marrow, lay it carefully in the pan (it should only just fit), pour upon it half a pint of stock, and add herbs, pepper, salt, and a little bit of onion or a clove of garlic; lastly, a tablespoonful of

L

vinegar. Cover the pan closely, and let the marrow simmer slowly for two hours. Dish up carefully, and pour the sauce through a strainer over the marrow.

427. VEGETABLE MARROW MOCK WHITEBAIT

Parboil a medium-sized vegetable marrow; cut it up into slices about the size of whitebait; roll these on a floured cloth; get them as dry as possible. Have ready a pan of boiling fat, deep enough to cover the slices completely; fry them a golden brown. Drain them, pile them on a paper serviette. Serve with sliced lemon (or salad dressing).

CHAPTER VII

CEREALS

UNDER this heading are included those invaluable articles of food, most of which are the staple diet—sometimes almost the only diet—of whole nations.

Maize or Indian corn, with its preparations, hominy, semolina, maize-meal, flaked maize, etc.; wheaten preparations, such as macaroni, vermicelli, wheat semolina, etc.; oaten preparations, oatmeal, oatflour, rolled oats, etc.; rice, rice flour, flaked rice, etc.; barley preparations; and for purposes of convenience I will add sago and tapioca (although as a matter of fact, sago is the pith of a palm, and tapioca is the hardened juice of the cassava tree). There are also Force, Grapenuts, and a variety of similar proprietary articles.

In these islands we have never used cereals to a thousandth part of their food value; partly, I think, because they require a little more trouble in cooking successfully than the average person cares to give. But now we shall be only too glad to fall back on them. The bother is, so many of them come from overseas. The beautiful macaroni and spaghetti that we used to buy so cheaply, we shall very likely never see again. It was made of Rumanian wheat from the Danubian provinces, which has a peculiarly glutinous quality. We are now having to make shift with Canadian and Japanese macaroni, spaghetti, vermicelli, etc.; " and good they are, but not the best."

The main value of cereals lies in their starch and fat. One does not associate fat with these dry things, but it is present, especially in maize and oatmeal.

As the food value of bread and of potatoes mainly consists

in starch, it is as well to know what excellent substitutes for bread and potatoes can be provided, if need be, by other materials.

	Per cent. starch.		Per cent. starch.		Per cent. starch.
Sugar	.. 98	Oatmeal ..	60	Green Fruit	
Tapioca, Sago,		Peas, Beans,		and Beans	17
Arrowroot	85	Lentils (dried)	60	Bananas	14
Rice	.. 79	Dried Fruits	60	Fresh Fruit	12
Flour	.. 75	Treacle ..	55	Milk ..	5
Barley Meal	73	Bread ..	57	Nuts ..	5
Maize	.. 66	Potatoes ..	21		

So, you see, three pounds of potatoes are equivalent in starch food value to one pound of bread.

But three-quarters of a pound of tapioca, sago, arrowroot, or rice; or one pound of oatmeal, beans, peas, or lentils, are equivalent in starch food value to one pound of bread.

And you can get the equivalent of one pound of potatoes in four ounces each of either rice, sago, tapioca, or arrowroot; or in five ounces each of either maize, barley meal, oatmeal, beans, peas or lentils.

Add to this, the amazing increase in bulk and weight of *cooked* cereals (three ounces of rice, for instance, will expand to one pound by the time it has absorbed enough water to cook it. See " Mixture Breads " in Chapter IX.), and you will perceive how enormously valuable cereals are.

But they *must* be well soaked and cooked to be digestible, and well seasoned and flavoured to be palatable.

In the case of hominy, soaking overnight is necessary; pearl barley should also be soaked (boiling water poured on it) for at least two hours before cooking. The actual boiling should not be scamped; and in every instance, you should use a double-boiler or its equivalent—a jam-pot standing in a pan of boiling water—unless you are prepared to stir all the time, or risk having your preparation stuck to the pan and burned,

Cereals are the only valid substitute—of sorts—for bread and for potatoes. There are many which we hardly know in England, such as millet, buckwheat, and rye (the latter is very little used), but which might well be included in our bills of fare. The recipes in this chapter only refer to cereals used in *salt* or savoury form. You will find them in *sweet* form in the chapter on puddings (No. VIII.) and on Bread and Cakes (No. IX.). Porridge, which is eaten by some with salt and by others with sweetening, figures here in considerable variety.

Vermicelli is like a baby macaroni—very minute tubes. It may be used for anything for which one uses macaroni.

Semolina is employed very largely for that popular Italian and Spanish dish, polenta. It is highly nourishing and (properly flavoured) most palatable. We mostly are acquainted with it only as a nursery pudding.

For further particulars and recipes regarding cereals, I will refer you to Chaps. VIII. and IX.; I advise you to do all you can with these cheap and invaluable foods.

PORRIDGES

Note.—Porridge, for many, is an indispensable article of breakfast. Many others take it for lunch, and in the country it is frequently a supper dish. The above usually means oatmeal porridge, or rolled oats in one of the proprietary forms.

Oatmeal porridge is very nutritious; slightly too blood-heating for some people; can be eaten with either sugar (or treacle) or salt, the latter being the Irish method; and, when milk is plentiful, can be made with milk instead of water, which of course doubles its nutritive quality. It has two drawbacks:

(*a*) That it really requires *some* milk along with it; and milk is so very scarce just now.

(*b*) That it often "stodges you" at the time of eating,

and leaves an amazing void about two hours later, so that you feel as if you had had no breakfast.

I don't know how to remedy these disqualifications.

However, remember, in making porridge :

(1) That it is best to use a double saucepan, or else a big jam-pot placed in a saucepan of boiling water, with two pieces of wood to rest the pot on, so that the water can get all round it, otherwise you will have to keep on stirring all the time.

(2) That the water must be boiling fast before the meal (whatever it is) goes in.

(3) That the meal should not be shoved or shot in *en masse*, but gradually sprinkled in, a very little at a time.

(4) That a pinch of salt improves the flavour of anything and—I may say—everything.

(5) That unless the porridge is properly cooked enough, it is worse than useless—because it will disagree with you vilely.

(6) That unless you serve it very hot, it is a most unappetising affair.

This last clause particularly refers to oatmeal porridge which has been cooked overnight and re-heated. Rolled oats are much more quickly prepared.

There are, however, a number of other porridges, including the "corn-mush" or maize-meal porridge so popular in Canada and the U.S.A. I give recipes for some of these.

428. SCOTCH OATMEAL PORRIDGE

Put three breakfastcupfuls (one and a half pints) of boiling water into a double saucepan, with half a teaspoonful of salt. Let it boil again, then sprinkle in one breakfastcupful of coarse oatmeal very gradually. Do this with your *left* hand, so that you may stir continually with your right ; the handle not the bowl of a wooden spoon should be used. Be sure to get the mixture quite smooth by stirring well and brushing out lumps. When the porridge boils, cover it up and let it boil gently for two hours. It may require more (boiling) water.

NOTE.—Any cold cooked porridge can be utilised for stuffing or forcemeat (instead of breadcrumbs) for cakes (mixed with barley flour enough to stiffen), and for " cutlets." Maizemeal porridge is practically the same as polenta.

429. BARLEY PORRIDGE

Have ready one pint of salted boiling water ; throw in two tablespoonfuls of pearl barley and one of oatmeal, and boil for one hour. Then mix into this four tablespoonfuls of barley kernels, and let cook at least twenty minutes.

430. HOMINY PORRIDGE, No. I

Put eight ounces of hominy to soak overnight in half a pint of water. Next morning, place in a double-boiler with the water it was in, half a pint of milk, and a pinch of salt. It will take about one and a half hours to cook ; so must be used for lunch, not for breakfast. Once cooked, it can be (1) re-heated, (2) sliced and fried, (3) made into puddings, (4) or cakes.

431. HOMINY PORRIDGE, No. II

Soak a teacupful of hominy overnight in a breakfastcupful of cold water. Next day, put on to boil with two break-fastcupfuls of cold water, slightly salted, and boil for one hour.

432. MAIZE (OR INDIAN) MEAL PORRIDGE, No. I (ALSO KNOWN AS CORN-MEAL MUSH)

Put two and a half pints of water into a double-boiler, add one dessertspoonful of salt. When it boils, gradually stir in three teacupfuls of maize-meal, and mix it very smooth. Let it cook for three hours. If to be served for breakfast re-heat next day for half an hour. This porridge, like hominy porridge, can be re-heated in different ways.

It is usually served with syrup or treacle.

433. MAIZE-MEAL PORRIDGE (CORN-MUSH), No. II

Have ready one pint (two breakfastcupfuls) of boiling water, put in a small teaspoonful of salt; sprinkle in, very gradually, two tablespoonfuls of maize-meal. Stir with a wooden spoon while you put the meal in, and continue to boil and stir for half an hour. Unless the mush is in a double-boiler, you will not be able to leave it until the half hour is up, when the pan must be moved to the side of the range for another half hour, but must continue to simmer and move, and will want occasional stirring.

434. MAIZE-MEAL PORRIDGE (CORN-MUSH), No. III

Have ready one pint of fast-boiling water; stir into it four to six tablespoonfuls of maize-meal. Add one tea-cupful of milk, and salt to taste. Boil until the maize is thoroughly cooked, which should be in about half an hour, but may take an hour.

435. FLAKED MAIZE PORRIDGE

Boil one pint of milk with one tablespoonful of sugar. Sprinkle in three heaped tablespoonfuls of flaked maize, stirring gently all the time, and let boil quietly for twenty minutes.

436. PEASE PORRIDGE

Have one pint of fast-boiling water, sprinkle in two heaped tablespoonfuls of pea-flour; stir well and quickly, get it perfectly smooth. Boil for an hour or more, and season with salt. A lump of dripping or margarine improves it.

437. RICE FLOUR PORRIDGE

Mix two tablespoonfuls of rice flour with half a teacupful of milk-and-water, and pour it into one pint of slightly salted boiling water. Boil for a quarter of an hour, stirring well. A bit of margarine will improve this.

438. ROLLED OATS PORRIDGE

Have ready one pint (two breakfastcupfuls) of boiling water; salt it and sprinkle in 1 breakfastcupful of rolled oats. Stir well, and let boil fast for twenty minutes. More (boiling) water can be added if the porridge gets too thick.

439. SAVOURY PORRIDGE

Have ready one pint of boiling salted water, sprinkle into it three tablespoonfuls of rolled oats ; let boil for twenty minutes, stirring now and then. Add a walnut-sized lump of margarine or other fat, and one teaspoonful of any good vegetable extract. Continue to boil and stir for five minutes ; season, and serve. A little very finely minced parsley may be added at pleasure.

440. SEMOLINA PORRIDGE

Put two piled tablespoonfuls of fine semolina to soak overnight in one teacupful of water. Next morning, put the semolina into three teacupfuls of cold milk-and-water, and boil for twenty minutes, adding a small pinch of salt.

HOMINY

-NOTE.—Hominy is the coarsest-ground form of maize, as cornflour is the finest, and semolina the medium. Flaked maize (which I have found admirable as a substitute for flour in puddings) is differently prepared, and easier to cook than hominy, etc., it needs no soaking. But hominy must be well soaked overnight before cooking, and well cooked before you can make any use of it. It is very nice for a change.

See previous directions for hominy porridge, which is the basis of the following dishes.

441. HOMINY SAVOURY BALLS

Take a quart of well-boiled hominy while hot, and make it into balls about the size of an orange ; roll them in breadcrumbs, then in a beaten dried egg mixed with two tablespoonfuls of cold water. Crumb them again and fry in deep fat and drain well ; then roll them in grated cheese, and serve in a hot vegetable dish. Salt and pepper to taste may be added before shaping the balls.

442. HOMINY CHEESE

Stir four ounces of grated cheese into eight ounces of cooked hominy; season with salt and pepper; add minced parsley and minced parboiled onion to taste, and a teaspoonful of fat. Mix thoroughly, place in greased pie-dish, bake for twenty minutes in good oven.

443. HOMINY CUTLETS

Take one breakfastcupful of cooked hominy, with pepper, salt, minced parsley, and a teacupful of drained soaked crusts; add one ounce of creamed fat, and a beaten dried egg. Mix thoroughly, shape into cutlets, dip in milk or stock, dredge with fine oatmeal, fry.

MACARONI

Note.—There is not very much variety about the salt and savoury dishes to be made with macaroni. But they are very nourishing, comparatively cheap, and as a rule most easily digested. Of course cheese is an almost invariable ingredient; but a little tomato sauce makes the macaroni appetising, if you have no cheese. Breadcrumbs are often strewed on top; but this is unnecessary. Butter can be done without; so can milk. The macaroni will still be quite nice. Fried chopped bacon is an admirable addition.

444. HOME-MADE MACARONI, No. I

(Macaroni made as below will not keep beyond three or four days.)

Put one pound of barley flour in a basin, make a "well" in it, and put in three beaten eggs, a pinch of salt, and a little tepid water (about three tablespoonfuls), enough to moisten into a dough. Work this well, let stand for five minutes, and cut in half. Roll each half until it is very fine, soft, and pliable; do not roll heavily. Roll out very thin, dust it with flour, and cut with a sharp knife into fine strips. Lay these separately to dry for fifteen minutes. Any other kind of flour can be used if preferred.

445. HOME-MADE MACARONI, No. II

Proceed as above, but when the dough is well worked, cover it up with a cloth, and leave it for about a quarter of an hour ; next, roll out very thin, and place to dry on a cloth for another quarter of an hour. Then dust it with a little semolina, and cut into thin strips. Have boiling salted water ready, and boil twenty-five minutes.

446. MACARONI AND CHEESE

Boil three-quarters of a pound of best macaroni in three quarts of water, with a teaspoonful of salt, for forty minutes. Drain on a sieve, return to the saucepan, season with half a teaspoonful of salt, half a teaspoonful of white pepper, and a saltspoonful of grated nutmeg, adding one ounce of good fat and two ounces of grated cheese ; carefully mix with a fork until well amalgamated, and transfer to a deep dish. Nicely brown a very finely chopped white onion in a frying-pan, with a tablespoonful of butter, for eight minutes, frequently mixing meanwhile ; then pour over macaroni, and serve.

447. MACARONI CURRY

Melt two tablespoonfuls of fat in a lined pan ; cook two slices of onion in it to a light straw colour ; mix in two table spoonfuls of flour, one tablespoonful of curry-powder, a little pepper and salt, and last, very gradually, stir in a breakfast-cupful of milk. When all is boiling smoothly, pour it over one breakfastcupful of macaroni which has been cooked till tender in (salted) boiling water, and afterwards rinsed in cold water. Heat up all again in the pan, and add two tablespoon-fuls of tomato pulp.

448. MACARONI MILANESI

Put one-fourth of a cup of dripping into the frying-pan, and, when melted, sauté in it an onion sliced thin, a stalk of celery cut in cubes, and a sprig of parsley; stir to keep from burning, and when of a golden brown, add a tin of tomato; season with salt and pepper, and let simmer about half an hour, or until the watery juice is evaporated. Meanwhile cook half a pound of macaroni in boiling salted water; let boil about twenty minutes or until tender, but in perfect shape; drain and rinse in cold water, then set in a hot place. Press the tomato sauce through a sieve fine enough to keep back the seeds, but coarse enough to let the pulp pass through (it should be of the consistency of thick cream). Dust a hot platter with Parmesan cheese, cover with macaroni, pour over sauce; add grated cheese, then more macaroni, sauce, and cheese, until all is used; then with a spoon and fork gently turn the macaroni over and over until it is thoroughly mixed with the sauce; add a generous sprinkling of cheese to the top, and serve. Mix quickly, so that the macaroni may be served hot.

449. MACARONI MOCK TRIPE

Put half a pound of macaroni, broken up small, into a saucepan full of boiling water. Let simmer till it is fully swelled and quite tender, which may take one and a half hours. Have ready a Spanish onion, sliced and cooked (in as little water as possible), and kept hot. Boil half a pint of milk and water (in equal parts), put in a walnut-sized lump of fat, and one dessertspoonful of cornflour mixed smooth with a little cold water. Let this thicken for five minutes; add salt and pepper; stir the macaroni and onion into it, and serve at once.

450. MACARONI AND MUSHROOM SAVOURY

Put half a pound of macaroni into boiling salted water, let cook for half an hour. Have ready four ounces of well-cleaned mushrooms, simmered with one ounce of fat and just enough water to cover them, in a casserole for a quarter of an hour. Take half a pint of milk, and take out two tablespoonfuls, which must be mixed smooth with half an ounce of cornflour. Remove the mushrooms from the casserole, and keep them warm ; meanwhile add the milk and the cornflour paste to the liquor in the casserole ; let it boil, and then simmer for five minutes. Have a small onion finely minced, and a rasher of bacon chopped small ; fry them. Grease a deep basin, line it with the macaroni ; put in the mushrooms, bacon, onion, and sauce from the casserole, all thoroughly mixed ; cover with the rest of the macaroni and with a greased paper. Steam for one hour, and serve in the sauce basin. This dish is well worth the extra trouble entailed in making it.

451. MACARONI QUENELLE

One ounce macaroni, four ounces breadcrumbs, two beaten dried eggs, half a pint of milk, one teaspoonful of minced parsley, salt and pepper to taste ; two ounces of fat melted, two tablespoonfuls of minced ham. Boil the macaroni till cooked, cut into small pieces, boil the milk and pour in the breadcrumbs, soak five minutes, then mix all the other ingredients into it. Steam in a well-greased mould for one hour, turn out and serve with either mushroom or caper sauce.

452. MACARONI AND VEGETABLES

Boil four ounces of macaroni in water till tender ; drain and cut into convenient lengths. Boil eight ounces of onions till rather more than three-parts cooked ; drain and slice them. Take eight ounces of tomatoes, dip them a minute into boiling water, then skin and slice them. Butter a pie-dish, dust it with fine breadcrumbs and grated cheese, with a sprinkling of finely minced parsley ; put a bottom layer of the macaroni, moistened with a little milk, and dusted with a little cheese and parsley ; then a layer of onions, and a layer of tomatoes, each similarly moistened and flavoured ; finish up with a layer of macaroni. Stew this with four ounces of grated cheese, three ounces of breadcrumbs, a little minced parsley, and about one ounce of fat broken up small. Put into a hot oven for twenty minutes or so, to become nicely and evenly browned.

453. OATMEAL DUMPLINGS

Mix four ounces of grated suet with one breakfastcupful of fine oatmeal, one minced onion, one dessertspoonful of minced parsley, salt and pepper to taste. Blend thoroughly with the fingers ; moisten with cold water until a stiff dough is obtained. Scald a pudding-cloth, dredge with fine oatmeal, and put in the dumpling, giving plenty of room for it to expand to almost twice its size. Place it in a pan of boiling water and let boil fast for nearly two hours. Serve at once.

454. POLENTA

Boil one quart of fresh milk in an enamelled saucepan ; add a pinch of salt, and stir in very gradually five or six ounces of fine semolina. Let boil very gently for about fifteen minutes, stirring well (or it will stick), till it becomes a thick paste. Pour this into a greased baking-tin, let it get cold, then cut it up in fingers ; pile them neatly in a baking-dish. Pour a little melted fat over, so as to cover each piece, then cover all with a thin layer of grated cheese, and bake a golden brown.

455. SEMOLINA CREAM

Have a pint of boiling milk ; add four ounces of semolina, slightly flavoured with nutmeg ; stir well till it thickens ; add three ounces of grated cheese, and continue to stir. When it is very thick, take it off the fire, stir in one beaten egg, and place it on a dish till cold ; then cut it in slices, pile it in a baking-dish, cover with grated cheese, sprinkle with fine crumbs, strew with little bits of fat, and bake to a light golden brown.

456. SPAGHETTI À L'ITALIENNE

Have ready boiling a pan of three quarts of water, to which has been added one tablespoonful of salt. Put in, stirring it gently so as not to break it, one ounce of Italian sphaghetti. Boil twenty-five minutes, and thoroughly drain off the water. Place the spaghetti in a frying-pan, with a full tablespoonful of fat, and one tablespoonful each of salt, pepper, and grated nutmeg. Shuffle and toss gently over the fire for four minutes. Add a bare half pint of hot tomato sauce, mix gently with a fork and add two ounces of grated Parmesan cheese, mix for a minute more, and pour upon a hot dish. Serve at once.

457. VERMICELLI RISSOLES

Boil half a pound of vermicelli in one pint of milk till tender. Mix into this one hard-boiled egg pounded small, two ounces of grated cheese, a little salt, pepper, and nutmeg. Place the mixture on a dish to cool, and subsequently shape it into rissoles ; flour, or egg and breadcrumb them, and fry in boiling fat.

RICE

NOTE.—Boiled rice, properly cooked, is a thing one very rarely meets. A stodgy unappetising cannon ball of wet pulp, *tied up in a cloth*, is what the working classes indulge in. I have therefore given a large number of recipes, which vary considerably in detail, but should not vary in result.

Once you have got the well-boiled rice, any rice left over can be used in a number of little ways, to impart variety to other dishes. Mixed with sieved boiled potato, made into balls and fried ; with a little minced parsley and onion, pepper and salt, at discretion. Or, flavoured with celery salt, made into potato shapes and served as a vegetable. Or, mixed with slices of hard-boiled egg, and moistened with milk, and flavoured with a hint of anchovy or of grated cheese, baked *au gratin*. There need not be any waste of rice that is properly cooked. It is only the miserable wet stuff that requires to be disguised in various half-hearted ways.

There are several ways of cooking rice, each of which has its own points of merit. " As a rule rice-growing people prefer the rice-grains less tender than do those of Northern climes, just as the Italians prefer macaroni in a state which by many would be called an under-done condition." But soft or not, all wish rice dry. The quantity of liquid that the grain will absorb depends upon the variety of the rice, the season in which it was grown, the time it has been kept, and the liquid used. These things affect, also, the time of cooking. Rice will absorb in cooking from two and a half to four times its bulk of liquid. When three cups of water or thin stock would suffice, three and a half or four cups of milk are required.

Rice must be thoroughly cleaned before cooking. It may be washed in several waters, being rubbed, meanwhile, between the hands, but one of the most satisfactory ways is to blanch rice. Put the rice over a hot fire in a large saucepan of cold water, and stir, occasionally, while it is heating ; let it boil five minutes, then drain on a sieve and pass cold water from the top through it. The rice is now beautifully white and clean and the grains do not adhere to each other. To cook, return to the fire, covered with the hot liquid, whatever this be, in which it is to be cooked, let cook rapidly, until nearly all the liquid is absorbed, then finish cooking over hot water. If the liquid be milk, cook from the first (after blanching) in the double boiler.

458. TO COOK RICE, No. I

Give the rice a thorough good washing in four or five waters ; then place in a pan, allowing to each breakfastcupful of rice one pint of water and half a teaspoonful of salt. Cover it, and let boil till all the water has boiled away. Then stand it on the side of the range, move the cover ajar, and let it steam till it becomes quite dry.

459. TO COOK RICE, No. II

Have a pan of fast-boiling water, say one quart. Put one breakfastcupful of rice into it ; leave the lid off, and continue to boil till the water has boiled away. Then steam at the side of the stove.

460. TO COOK RICE, No. III

Wash the rice well, throw it into plenty of boiling water, adding a teaspoonful of salt. Boil it fast until tender but not broken; drain through a colander, run cold water through it to separate the grains and heat it again in the oven.

461. TO COOK RICE, No. IV

Put half a pound of rice into one quart of cold water; when it has boiled for twenty minutes, put it to drain in a sieve, after which dry it before the fire to get rid of all superfluous moisture, stirring from time to time, and serve very hot.

462. TO COOK RICE, No. V

Wash the rice thoroughly, cook, in four times as much water, directly over the fire. Use a tightly covered saucepan, that the steam may be absorbed by the rice. Have the fire less brisk at the last part of the cooking than at first.

463. TO COOK RICE, No. VI

Cover the blanched rice with a relatively large quantity of salted boiling water and let cook rapidly in an uncovered saucepan until the grains are tender; drain off the water, cover the saucepan with a cloth and let stand on the back of the range to dry. Serve in a hot dish.

464. TO COOK RICE, No. VII

Put one gill (half a breakfastcupful) of rice, well washed, in a clean tin canister with a lid that fits tight. Add to the rice a pinch of salt and half a breakfastcupful of cold water. Fix the lid on, and stand the tin in a pan of boiling water. In half an hour the rice ought to have absorbed the water in the tin, and to be nicely cooked with the grains all separate. (A pound canister would probably be best, to leave ample room for the rice to expand.)

M

465. TO COOK RICE, No. VIII

Put one teacupful of well washed rice into two teacupfuls of cold water. Boil until the water is absorbed, then let the rice steam until quite dry.

466. TO COOK RICE, No. IX

Take half a pound of rice, wash it in cold water in a colander, put it into two quarts of salted boiling water. Let cook quickly with the lid off, removing any scum that rises, until the rice is tender—a quarter of an hour or so. Drain, and dry the rice in gentle heat, until the grains are well separated.

467. RICE AND CABBAGE

Boil a large cabbage; drain it; place it in a hot clean saucepan; add one teacupful of hot, boiled rice, pepper, salt, and a large piece of dripping; mix and stir well on the fire, and serve very hot.

NOTE.—This is very economical, as the remains of either cold cabbage or cold rice can be used. It is best to cut the cabbage quite small before adding the rice.

468. RICE CHEESE

Have four ounces of rice boiled in some vegetable stock till it is tender but not broken. Drain it well, and of course save the stock for future use. Add one and a half ounces of dripping, three ounces of grated cheese, and salt and pepper to taste. Serve very hot, heaped on a hot dish.

469. RICE (CRÉOLE), No. I

Place in a saucepan one medium, chopped onion; pour in one tablespoonful of melted fat, and fry six minutes, stirring meanwhile; add six ounces of raw rice, and cook on range five minutes, stirring meanwhile; add three peeled and finely chopped red tomatoes and one pint of stock. Season with a teaspoonful of salt; mix well. Cover pan, and as soon as it comes to a boil, set in oven thirty-five minutes. Remove, dress rice on a hot dish, and serve.

470. RICE (CRÉOLE), No. II

Chop fine a white onion; sauté with half a cupful of raw ham, shredded rather fine, in one-fourth of a cup of fat; cook about ten minutes, then add a cup of blanched rice and three cupfuls of stock; simmer twenty minutes, then add four tomatoes, peeled and cut in slices, and one teaspoonful of salt. Cover, and finish cooking in the oven or in a double-boiler.

471. RICE CROQUETTES, PLAIN

Half a cupful of rice, half a teaspoonful of salt, one cup of boiling water, one dried egg, one cupful of hot milk, two tablespoonfuls of fat.

Blanch the rice as on p. 152, cook in a double-boiler, with the water, milk, and salt, until the rice is tender and the liquid is absorbed; stir in the beaten egg and the fat; let cool, and finish as usual.

472. RICE CROQUETTES, SAVOURY

Half a cupful of rice, one cupful of stock, one egg, two cups of tomatoes, half a cupful of grated cheese, a slice of onion, one tablespoonful of fat, a sprig of parsley, quarter of a teaspoonful of pepper, two cloves, quarter of a teaspoonful of salt.

Cover the rice with cold water and bring quickly to the boiling-point; let boil for five minutes, then drain, rinse in cold water, and drain again. Cook the tomatoes with the onion, parsley, and cloves fifteen minutes, and pass through a sieve; add to the rice with the stock, pepper, and salt, and cook over hot water until the rice is tender and the liquid absorbed, then add the cheese, fat, and beaten egg. Spread on a dish to *cool* (do not let it become too cold,) then shape and finish as any croquettes.

473. RICE, CURRIED

Take two breakfastcupfuls of rice, put into a saucepan in three pints of cold water, and set over a hot fire to boil quickly. When the water boils, let it continue five minutes ; then drain the rice through a colander, rinse it with cold water, and put it back into another pan, which must contain three pints of boiling water, one teaspoonful of salt, and juice of half a lemon. Stir occasionally, and add more hot water if it boils away. Let it boil fast till the rice is tender, then stir in three tablespoonfuls of creamed fat and one tablespoonful of curry-powder. Serve at once.

474. RICE WITH EGGS, SAVOURY

Boil a quarter of a pound of Patna rice in one pint of good stock. Mix with it sufficient tomato sauce to colour it, two tablespoonfuls of grated cheese, and salt to taste. Reheat until it is sufficiently reduced to take a shape. Meanwhile put one ounce of fat in a frying-pan, and fry four good eggs in it ; trim each into a nice round. Press the rice in a shallow buttered mould, as firmly as possible, and quickly unmould it in a heated dish. Arrange the eggs on top of it, garnish with bits of parsley, and serve at once.

475. RICE WITH FRENCH BEANS.

Having boiled a breakfastcupful or so of rice, and got all the grains clear and separate, fry it lightly in a little fat, add enough tomato sauce to moisten it with the beaten yolk of one egg and two good tablespoonfuls of grated cheese, Mix thoroughly and set this rice as a wall round the centre of a hot dish. Place in the middle some French beans, boiled, drained, and seasoned with fat, pepper, and salt.

476. RICE, GOLDEN

Put one quart of water in a pan, with the following seasoning : one small whole onion, one bayleaf, one head of garlic, ten cloves, five cardamoms, half a teaspoonful each of cinnamon, mace, and salt, and saffron sufficient to colour all. When the water boils, add six ounces of rice ; let it boil till tender ; drain it, steam it, and serve it piled upon a hot dish, garnished with fried onions, and fried almonds, at discretion.

477. RICE, ITALIAN

Melt one ounce of fat, in a stew-pan. Take one onion about the size of a golf ball, mince it very finely, and fry it. When it is a golden yellow, stir in four ounces of hot, well-boiled rice. Work it well with a fork, at the same time shaking in two heaped tablespoonfuls of grated cheese. Serve it piled on a flat dish, garnished with sliced hard-boiled eggs.

478. RICE, MILANESE

Take half a medium-sized onion, chop it small, and cook it in two tablespoonfuls of fat in a hot stew-pan; don't let it get brown. Then add half a breakfastcupful of rice and about one quart of hot water (or white stock). When the rice has soaked up all the liquid, and is cooked quite tender, add a little salt and pepper, and two tablespoonfuls of grated cheese; mix this in gently with a fork, and serve it as a vegetable, with a little more grated cheese on top. A sauce may be served with it.

479. RICE PILAF

Mix one cupful and a half of stock, with one cupful of stewed and strained tomato. When boiling, add one cupful of well-washed or blanched rice and half a teaspoonful of salt; stir lightly with a fork occasionally, until the liquor is absorbed, then add half a cupful of fat and cook over hot water until tender; remove, cover, and stir with a fork before serving.

480. RICE, WITH PARSLEY OR CHIVES

Cook half a cup of blanched rice in boiling salted water until tender (an aluminoid dish will be found useful for this purpose); add two tablespoonfuls of fat and one teaspoonful of finely chopped parsley or chives; mix gently so as to avoid breaking the grains. Serve as a vegetable.

481. RICE SAVOURY, No. I

Take about four ounces of rice, and place in about one pint and a half of salted cold water along with three large

Spanish onions finely chopped. Let it stew quietly for at least two hours; if the water boils away, so that the rice is in danger of burning, add a little more hot water. When the rice is quite tender, stir in two ounces of fat, and serve very hot.

482. RICE SAVOURY, No. II

Set a cupful of rice over the fire in three pints of cold water; let come quickly to the boiling-point, and boil five minutes; then drain through a colander, rinsing with cold water. Return to the fire with a quart of boiling water, one teaspoonful of salt, and the juice of half a lemon; shake the pan occasionally, lest the rice burn, and add a little more water if necessary, or set on an asbestos mat or in a pan of cold water. When tender, stir in very carefully one-fourth of a cup of fat, creamed with a tablespoonful of curry-powder.

483. RICE AND SHRIMPS

Chop finely enough onion to make half a tablespoonful and fry it in three tablespoonfuls of fat. Add one and a half tablespoonfuls of cornflour, mixed with two teaspoonfuls of curry powder, salt and pepper. Stir till all is thoroughly mixed. Continue to stir, and gradually add two breakfast-cupfuls of milk. Let boil; then add one breakfastcupful of warm boiled rice, and nearly twice as much of shelled shrimps. When all is well heated through, serve at once.

484. RICE VALENCIENNES

Finely chop a medium white onion, and lightly brown in a saucepan with two tablespoonfuls of oil for five minutes; add six ounces of raw rice, and brown eight minutes, frequently stirring meanwhile. Moisten with a pint of stock and two gills of tomato sauce, add three tablespoonfuls of cooked green peas, half a teaspoonful of salt, three saltspoonfuls of white pepper, and a saltspoonful of Spanish saffron. Mix well, cover pan, and set in oven forty-five minutes; remove, dress on a vegetable dish, and serve.

CHAPTER VIII

PUDDINGS, PASTRY, AND SWEET DISHES

THEY are indispensable in every decent English household. The question arises, of what shall we make them ? Milk is scarce and dear; suet ditto; dried fruits are almost non-existent; pastry of the good old sorts is practically *hors de combat ;* we ought not to use wheat flour more than we can possibly help.

Well, you can still have *some* milk puddings; cocoa-butter can replace suet for boiled or steamed ones ; rhubarb and fresh fruits must be largely used; and potato-paste, though only a makeshift, is much better than no paste at all. Dried eggs and egg-powders are invaluable ; jam still is made and sold. And there are plenty of bottled fruits, which even if rather acid in themselves, are very good when accompanied with a custard-powder custard. Sweetness can be imparted, as I have already pointed out, by various means (see pp. 9–11). Dates, when procurable, stoned and chopped, do very well instead of raisins. Soaked drained crusts or stale bread make a quite satisfactory basis for a vast number of dishes. And potatoes are an invaluable stand-by in emergencies.

Amongst the following recipes you will find a considerable variety of puddingified concoctions. Sometimes, I allow, looking round on a depleted larder, one is tempted to tear one's hair above a reeling brain. But a few moments' calm reflection will convince one of the folly of such a proceeding ; at the same time such reflection may provide one with a pudding.

Let milk (baked) puddings cook very slowly; to ensure

their being properly done, to retain as much as possible of the milk (which evaporates if cooked too fast), and to preserve the flavour. See "Rice Pudding, Economical," No. 538.

"Barley-kernels," sold in packets, are a pleasing variety from the hackneyed rice, semolina, sago, etc., and are particularly wholesome. So (properly soaked) is pearl barley.

Fruit can be sweetened by honey, or treacle, or any of the substitutes now being sold. Saccharin has a peculiarly nasty effect on fruit. In the case of rhubarb and gooseberries, chopped dates are a good sweetener. A pinch of bicarbonate of soda, or a pinch of salt, helps to lessen the acidity of the fruit. So does cooked sago. A (dried) egg or (powder) custard is invaluable in this respect.

Except for special dishes, it is *extremely wasteful to peel apples*. With them, as with potatoes, the most valuable properties lie next the skin. Their beauty, in fact, is skin-deep; and then their utility begins. They should be either *very* thinly sliced, peel and all, and the core removed; or they should be stewed in a little water until tender enough to rub through a sieve. By this means you waste nothing except the cores and pips, and save the flavour of the skin, besides all that would have been wasted in parings. If, however, for some special dish it be absolutely necessary to peel the apples, stew the parings and cores in a little water, and strain it to the apples subsequently; this improves their flavour fiftyfold. Or you can boil the strained water with a little sugar, till it turns pink; thicken with cornflour, and pour into a wetted mould.

Dried fruit is best cooked as follows: Wash the fruit and place it in a casserole: it should only occupy a quarter of the space. The other three-quarters should be filled up with boiling water. Leave the fruit to steep, for twelve to twenty-four hours. By that time it should have absorbed most of the liquid, and swelled out, fresh and fragrant. Drain off any of the liquid left, make a syrup of it with a little honey or sugar; let cool, and pour over the fruit in a glass dish.

All fruit-stones should be broken and the kernels extracted to use (milled or ground) for flavouring ; a very little goes a long way, because these fruit kernels contain prussic acid.

Fruit is particularly valuable now that we are eating so much constipating pulse and cereal food.

NOTE.—Many excellent puddings, etc., not included here (see " Pudding Book " of this series), can be adapted for present use.

(1) By substituting " alien " flours in the following proportions :

For baked puddings, instead of all-wheat flour, use one-third of wheat flour, one-third of maize flour, one-third of (cooked) whole rice.

For boiled puddings, one-third of wheat flour, one-third of maize flour (or flaked maize), one-third of un-cooked ground rice.

Maize flour, or maize semolina, or flaked maize should be used instead of wheat flour, or halved with it, whenever possible. It imparts a rich and delightful colour to the pudding, and is very nourishing. If you don't use maize, use barley flour. Oat flour is too pronounced in taste, except for articles to be fried, when the taste is altered by frying.

(2) By substituting cocoa-butter, or good dripping, for suet, butter, and margarine. Some people use sago instead of suet for steamed puddings, ounce for ounce ; but of course sago, though nourishing, is not *fat*, and all it does is to lighten the texture. And some people use grated raw potato (twice as much as the right amount of suet), to which exactly the same remarks apply.

(3) By substituting dried eggs (there are countless varieties of these) for real eggs. This will not answer, needless to say, for any dish requiring the yolks and white whisked separately—such as anything in the nature of a méringue or soufflé.

(4) By substituting chopped dates for currants, raisins, or sultanas—which are practically obsolete.

(5) By substituting any of the various "sweeteners" for real sugar ; and by using jam, honey, or treacle where possible.

(6) By substituting milk and water for all milk ; the water in which macaroni, rice, etc., has been cooked, comes in very handy because it is already nutritious.

(7) By using potato-pastry instead of all-flour pastry, and by employing potatoes wherever you can, in place of flour. We are only, slowly and reluctantly, beginning to guess at the great usefulness of potatoes.

(8) By using all your old scraps and crusts of bread, where "breadcrumbs" are mentioned in the recipe. Dry crumbs (for frying and for dishes *au gratin*) can be provided by baking and powdering the crusts ; crumbs for all moister purposes, by soaking the stale bread in boiling water, leaving it some hours, and *squeezing* it dry in a cloth.

485. BARLEY SHORTCRUST

To eight ounces of barley flour, add a pinch of salt and half a teaspoonful of baking-powder. Rub in four ounces of fat, and mix with as little cold water as possible.

486. POTATO SHORTCRUST, No. I

Rub three ounces of fat into eight ounces of flour ; then mix in half a pound of potatoes, boiled in their skins, peeled, and mashed, sieved, or riced, half a teaspoonful of baking-powder, a pinch of salt, enough milk and water to mix into a stiff paste. Roll out about a quarter of an inch thick.

487. POTATO SHORTCRUST, No. II

Mix two ounces of flour (household), two ounces of barley flour, and two ounces of riced potatoes. Lightly rub in three ounces of fat ; add a pinch of salt, quarter of a teaspoonful of baking-powder, and enough cold water to moisten to a stiff paste, which must only be rolled out once.

488. POTATO SHORTCRUST, No. III

Mix eight ounces of cooked riced or sieved potato with four ounces of barley flour and four ounces G.R. (household) flour and a pinch of salt ; rub in four ounces of fat ; add one teaspoonful of baking-powder. Mix with a little water into a stiff paste.

NOTE.—Many people find that ground rice, or even puffed rice, can be successfully used in pastry-making (with or without potato) instead of G.R. flour ; or half and half of rice and flour.

489. ALEXANDRA PUDDINGS

Boil six apples and mash them through a sieve ; add to them one ounce of fat, a pinch of salt, a breakfastcupful of breadcrumbs, two (dried) eggs, a little grated nutmeg, and half a cupful of milk. Sweeten to taste. Mix perfectly ; then pour into wetted cups, and bake for half an hour. Turn them out, and serve.

490. APPLE BATTER PUDDING

Pare and core some apples, and put as many into a pie-dish as will stand close together. Make some batter with two tablespoonfuls of flour, three-quarters of a pint of milk, and one egg well beaten ; sprinkle the apples with sugar and lemon juice ; add the batter, and place immediately in a hot oven for an hour and a half, when the batter should be quite set, very light, and nicely browned.

491. APPLE AND EGG PUDDING

Beat an egg well, add one gill of milk or water, seven tablespoonfuls of flour, two tablespoonfuls of sugar, one saltspoonful of salt ; mix well together. Pare and cut into pieces three middle-sized apples ; stir them into the batter. Boil in a cloth for one hour and a quarter ; if in a basin, ten minutes longer.

492. APPLE PUDDING, GRANDMOTHER'S

Take half a pound of plain flour, three ounces of minced suet or fat, three ounces of cold boiled potato, a little salt, one pound or more of apples. Peel, core, and cut up the apples, rub the potato in the flour (as you would butter), add the chopped suet and salt. Wet with a little water, roll out on to a floured board. Grease a pudding-basin, line it with the crust, put the apples in with a little sugar, wet the edges, and put on the top crust. Flour a thick pudding-cloth, tie down, put into boiling water, and boil for three hours. This can be made the day before wanted, and not boiled till the next day, when it will turn out a nice biscuit colour. Can be made two days before boiling, but no longer, as the potato turns sour. Same crust can be used for all boiled puddings.

493. APPLE AND RICE PUDDING

Boil some apples until quite tender, and some rice in a separate saucepan—in the proportion of two pounds of apples to a teacupful of rice. Butter a pie-dish, and spread the rice and apples in alternate layers (adding sugar and grated lemon rind) until the dish is full. The last layer must be rice. On this place little pieces of fat, and bake with a plate over the pie-dish for quite an hour. Can be eaten either hot or cold.

494. APPLE AND TAPIOCA PUDDING

Peel six apples; remove the core, and fill up the cavity with moist sugar and powdered nutmeg, and on the top of each apple put a small piece of cocoa-butter. Place the apples in a pie-dish, and strew round them a small teacupful of raw tapioca, sweetened with sugar. Fill the dish with water, and let the contents bake slowly in a slack oven for two hours.

495. APPLES, SCRAPED

Take one pound of good *eating* apples, peel them, and scrape them finely with a sharp knife into a glass dish. Have ready, not too hot, a nice (powder) custard, flavoured with sugar and vanilla, and pour this at once over the apples, as they discolour at once while exposed to the air. Let them be well covered with the custard. This is a most delicious and wholesome dish.

496. APPLE SHAPE

Boil about two pounds of sour apples with a little water until they are quite tender ; pass them through a sieve ; sweeten and flavour to taste.   Dissolve overnight one ounce of gelatine in one pint of cold water ; add this to the apple pulp ; place all on the fire, and boil it for twenty minutes or longer, stirring all the time.   Place in a wetted mould, and turn out when cold.

497. APPLE FOOL

Boil some apples as above.   When mashed, add sugar and lemon juice to taste, and mix with one pint of hot milk. To be eaten cold.

498. ARROWROOT PUDDING

Mix half a teacupful of arrowroot with half a pint of cold water ; put one pint of milk into a saucepan with two ounces of sugar and a stick of cinnamon ; pound six bitter almonds, and add them to the arrowroot and cold milk.   When the milk in the saucepan boils, put the arrowroot, etc., into it, stirring all the time ; boil for ten minutes, and place in a wet mould. Serve when cold.

499. AUSTRALIAN PUDDING

A quarter of a pound of suet or other fat, one pound of flour, one teaspoonful of baking-powder, a pinch of salt, and the grated rind of a lemon.   Stir these ingredients in a basin ; mix a breakfastcupful of milk with a teacupful of black treacle ; stir into the flour, etc. ; place in a greased basin, and steam for three hours and a half.   Turn out and serve.

Note.—Whenever treacle has to be used, it should be warmed first.

500. BREAD PUDDING

This is an excellent method of using up hard stale pieces, both crust and crumb.   Lay them in a large bowl or pan, pour boiling water over them, cover them with a clean cloth, and leave them overnight.   Next day strain off all moisture and add (to one pound of bread) a quarter of a pound of grated suet or good dripping, a quarter of a pound of dates or stoned raisins, two ounces of brown sugar, a pinch of salt, a little cinnamon or nutmeg at pleasure, and enough flour—very little will be required—to help bind the whole.   Either a dried egg or a very little warmed golden syrup will help to bind the mixture.   Bake in a greased baking-tin.

501. BROWN BREADCRUMB TRIFLE

Put through a fine sieve any stale brown bread, till you have at least two breakfastcupfuls of fine crumbs, which pile on a dish.   Put over about a breakfastcupful of some moist juicy jam, such as strawberry, which will soak into the crumbs.   When it has fairly soaked in, mask the whole in a (powder) custard.   This is exceedingly good if the crumbs are well saturated.

502. BROWN BETTY

Thinly slice enough large tart apples to make two break fastcupfuls ; they need not be peeled.   Put a layer of then at the bottom of a greased baking-dish, sprinkle with a little sugar, cinnamon, and shredded clarified cocoa-butter.   Put next, a layer of soaked bread, well squeezed dry ; repeat in alternate layers until the dish is nearly full.   Let the top layer be bread, strewn with bits of cocoa-butter.   Cover with a dish of equal size, and bake in moderate oven for forty-five minutes ; then remove cover and let brown quickly. Gooseberries can be treated as above.

503. CAROLINA SNOWBALLS

Boil some rice in milk until quite soft ; prepare some large apples as for apple dumplings, and having placed as much of the rice on a small cloth as will entirely cover the apple like a crust, tie each up closely, and boil for two hours.

504. CHOCOLATE MOULD

One pint of milk, two tablespoonfuls of cocoa, two table-spoonfuls of cornflour, two tablespoonfuls of sugar.

Mix the cocoa and cornflour to a smooth paste with a little cold milk ; bring the remainder to boiling point, and add the sugar ; then pour slowly on the paste, stirring all the time ; return to the saucepan and cook very slowly ; stir all the time, as it easily sticks. Pour into a wet mould.

505. CHOCOLATE PUDDING

Shred and warm three ounces of cocoa butter, and add two beaten (dried) eggs. Then mix in four ounces of cocoa, two ounces of flour, two ounces of ground rice, and one teaspoonful of baking powder. Beat well, place in mould, and steam for one and a half hours. A hot custard is nice with this.

506. DATES IN CUSTARD

Stone enough dates to cover the bottom of a glass dish, and put half a blanched almond in each ; pour over them one pint of (powder) custard and serve cold. This is particularly nutritious.

507. DEVON " STIR-UP " PUDDING

One cupful of flour, one apple cut up, one tablespoonful of currants, one tablespoonful of suet chopped, half a teaspoonful of baking-powder, and a pinch of salt.

Mix all together to a stiff paste with a little water, and steam in a basin for one and a half hours. Serve with a sauce of treacle and milk in equal parts—heated, but not boiled. This pudding is also excellent when made with rhubarb, gooseberries, or any sort of fruit. The above quantities make a small pudding sufficient for two or three persons.

508. ELIZABETH'S PUDDING

Have ready one pound of soaked stale bread, squeezed dry and broken up with a fork ; prepare one pound of stewed rhubarb, sweetened with two ounces of sugar (or any other stewed fruit). Mix with the bread one dried egg, a pinch of salt, and two ounces of suet or other fat. Put half this mixture in a greased pie-dish ; pour in the rhubarb ; place the rest of the bread mixture on top. Set in a moderate oven for one and a half hours.

509. GINGER PUDDING

Shred and warm one ounce of cocoa-butter, heat it along with half an ounce of sugar and one (dried) beaten egg. Add three ounces of boiled sieved potatoes, two ounces of flour, one flat teaspoonful of ginger. Mix well, and add one dessert-spoonful of treacle, and a quarter of a teaspoonful of carbonate of soda. Add enough tepid water to mix into a thick batter, and steam in a basin for two hours.

510. HOMINY SNOWBALLS

Take one pint of milk, and two tablespoonfuls of soaked hominy. Put it into a double boiler. Let it simmer for two and a half hours, then turn it into teacups to set ; when cold, unmould, and serve with jam.

511. LEMON CURD WITHOUT EGGS

Take eight ounces of peeled swede turnip, place in boiling water and cook until tender enough to rub through a sieve. Have ready, and add, half an ounce of fine sago which has been soaked in cold water overnight, three to four ounces of sugar, half an ounce of ground rice, a pinch of salt, the juice and grated rinds of two lemons. The ground rice should go in last. Cook over a gentle heat until the mixture thickens and the sago clears. Place in glass jars and cover closely.

512. MACARONI PUDDING

Take two ounces of macaroni and break it into half-inch pieces ; wash it. Have a pint of milk, flavoured with one ounce of white sugar and the peel of half a lemon, brought slowly to the boil in a lined saucepan, When it boils, put in the macaroni, which must simmer until it is quite tender —which will be half an hour at least. Add a little more milk if it boils away too soon. Take off the mixture and let it cool, then stir in one well-beaten (dried) egg, and let the whole be baked about ten minutes in a slow oven.

513. MAIZE PUDDING, No. I

Have ready half a pint of fast-boiling water, in a double-boiler, add a teaspoonful of salt, and gradually sprinkle in (stirring continuously) two tablespoonfuls of maize meal. Let boil gently for thirty minutes; frequent stirring will be needed. Pour it into a pie-dish, mix in one (dried) beaten egg, one breakfastcupful of milk, sugar or honey to taste, and a little nutmeg. Place in a moderate oven, and bake for thirty to forty-five minutes.

514. MAIZE PUDDING, No. II

Mix one tablespoonful of sugar with one breakfastcupful of flaked maize; add a pinch of salt; place in a pie-dish. Pour a pint of boiling milk in, and bake forty-five minutes in moderate oven.

515. MAIZE AND APPLE PUDDING

Stir one teacupful of maize meal with a pinch of salt into one pint of boiling milk and let cook gently, with frequent stirring, for thirty minutes. Remove from fire, and beat in with a fork two tablespoonfuls of treacle and one ounce of fat, or half an ounce of cocoa butter, and a pinch of soda bicarbonate. Have ready one pound of apples stewed (without peeling) in as little water as possible, and rubbed through a sieve. Put half the cooked maize in a greased fireproof dish, then put in the apple; cover with the rest of the maize, and bake for thirty minutes in a moderate oven.

516. MATTRESS

Two teacupfuls of flour, two ounces of dripping, one teaspoonful of baking powder, one (dried) beaten egg, and enough milk when added to the egg to fill a teacup.

N

Rub the dripping into flour, add the baking powder and sugar, and mix. Beat the egg, add the milk, and mix together. Bake on shallow tin from twenty to thirty minutes. Spread with jam and serve.

517. NUT PUDDING

Have ready four ounces of boiled rice, and mix into it a pinch of salt, a tablespoonful of sugar, a teaspoonful of grated lemon rind or a few drops of lemon essence, and two ounces of minced or milled nuts. Place in a greased baking-dish, and cover with half a pint (powder) custard. Place in a moderate oven for thirty minutes; when the pudding has been cooking about twenty minutes, strew it with two dessertspoonfuls of minced nuts or grated coconut.

518. NUT CUSTARD PUDDING

Boil a pint of milk and water, put in two ounces of broken macaroni, cook until quite tender. Place in a greased dish, and strew in one tablespoonful of sugar, a half lemon rind grated, a pinch of salt. Pour on top a breakfastcupful of hot (powder) custard, and strew this with some minced nuts, at least a tablespoonful. Bake in a moderate oven until the nuts brown a little.

519. OATMEAL PUDDING

Put into a greased pie-dish a little less than half a tin of Swiss milk, diluted to one pint with water; add a pinch of salt, two ounces of rolled oats, and one tablespoonful of chopped dates. Let soak in a warm place for one hour, stirring up occasionally. Then strew some shreds of fat and a little nutmeg on top, and bake two hours or so in a moderate oven.

ONE-ORANGE PUDDINGS
520. No. I

Place half a breakfastcupful of cold boiled rice at the bottom of a glass dish; peel one orange, and slice it thinly

crossways, with a silver knife, on top of the rice ; dredge
with one ounce of castor or granulated sugar ; spread another
halfcupful of boiled rice over the orange. Make a quarter
of a pint of custard powder, and when it is cooling, pour it
over the rest. Set by for two hours or until quite cold and
set.

521. No. II

Have three ounces of flaked maize made into a smooth
paste with a little cold water. Boil a pint of milk, pour it
to the maize, and put back all in the saucepan. Add a pinch
of salt, half an ounce of fat, one ounce of sugar, and the grated
rind of one orange. Let boil for five minutes or so, continually stirring. Place in a greased dish and bake for
thirty minutes.

522. No. III

Put four ounces of sago to soak overnight in three breakfastcupfuls of cold water. Turn all into a greased dish next
day, add a teaspoonful of salt, and place for an hour in
moderate oven. Then remove, and add the grated rind
and juice of one orange, and either two tablespoonfuls of
sugar or one of sugar and one of honey. Mix well and replace
in oven for thirty minutes more.

523. No. IV

Put two ounces of sago to soak overnight in two breakfastcupfuls of water. Next morning boil up all together,
add a pinch of salt, a tablespoonful of sugar, and the grated
rind and juice of one orange. Let cook a few minutes longer,
until quite thick and clear. Pour into a wetted mould,
and when cold unmould.

In Nos. 2, 3, and 4, lemon can be substituted for orange
with good effect.

With any of the above puddings, a hot or cold (powder)
custard is advisable.

524. PLAIN STEAMED PUDDING

Mix half a pound of G.R. flour with a quarter of a pound of grated raw potato, a pinch of salt, and a teaspoonful of baking powder. No fat required. Moisten with sufficient water, or milk, or both, to make a firm dough. Boil or steam in greased mould or basin, two or three hours. Serve with sweet sauce, jam, or treacle.

525. POTATO PUDDING, No. I

Boil and mash four large potatoes ; add to them a pinch of salt, two ounces of moist sugar, a quarter of a teaspoonful of vanilla essence, one ounce of fat, and two dried eggs. Pour into a greased mould, and bake for half an hour in a quick oven. Turn out of the mould, and serve with sweet sauce.

526. POTATO PUDDING, No. II

Mix eight ounces of cooked sieved potatoes with two ounces of household flour, two ounces of barley flour, two ounces of soaked drained stale bread, three ounces of shredded cocoa butter or suet, three tablespoonfuls of treacle, half a teaspoonful of carbonate of soda. Beat thoroughly till well blended, using a little milk to moisten. Steam for three hours in a greased basin.

527. POTATO PUDDING, No. III

Mix with eight ounces of cooked mashed potatoes, two ounces of fat, sugar to taste, a pinch of salt, the juice and grated rind of one lemon, and two dried eggs. Blend thoroughly, and place in a greased pie-dish (with potato-crust round edge if liked), bake for 30 minutes.

528. POTATO PUDDING, No. IV

Take half a pound of boiled and sieved (or riced) potatoes, put them into a deep bowl, and form a " well " in the middle, as if you were going to make bread. Have ready the following : four ounces of maize meal (or maize semolina) soaked in half a teacupful of milk, or in half a dried egg. Melt one ounce of cocoa butter, and stir into it two teaspoonfuls of cocoa. Put all these into the middle of the potato, along with one tablespoonful of treacle and one teaspoonful of baking powder, and beat all together until thoroughly well mixed. Then place in a greased pie-dish, and put into a moderate oven for 30 minutes.

529.   POTATO PUDDING, No V

Mash eight ounces of potatoes ; add two ounces of fat, the grated rind and the juice of one lemon, sugar to taste, two dried eggs, and a teacupful of milk. Bake in a dish (with pastry round the edge) for half an hour.

530.   POTATO AND APPLE PUDDING, No 1

Mix a pinch of salt with four ounces of G.R. flour, grate in two ounces of cocoa butter (clarified), add four ounces of cooked riced potatoes, and mix well ; moisten with as little water as possible. Roll out half an inch thick, and line a greased basin with it. To fill, take two large apples peeled and chopped small, one tablespoonful of treacle or corn syrup, rind of half a lemon grated, and one tablespoonful of crumbs (any sort). Put half the apples in the lined bowl ; sprinkle them with half the other ingredients. Put a round of the potato crust. Place greased paper over and steam for three hours.

531.   POTATO AND APPLE PUDDING, No. II

Take twelve ounces of apples, stew (but do not peel) and pulp them through a sieve. Have ready twelve ounces of potatoes, steamed, peeled and sieved ; mix well into the potato one tablespoonful of sugar, one tablespoonful of fat, one tablespoonful of milk, vanilla or almond essence to taste, and a pinch of salt. Roll out and line a greased pie-dish with part of this mixture, put in the stewed apple, sweetened to taste, and put the rest of the potato paste on top. Put the pudding in a good oven until it is a nice golden brown.

532.   POTATO AND APPLE PUDDING, No. III

Boil till tender one pound of apples (wiped but not peeled), and pass them through a sieve.   Mix with them half a pound of cooked sieved potatoes, two ounces of sugar, a pinch of salt, half an ounce of fat (any sort), one dried egg, and a little grated lemon rind (or ginger if preferred).   Place in a greased pie-dish, in a moderate oven, and bake for 30 or 40 minutes.

533.   POTATO AND APPLE PUDDING, No. IV

Boil and mash one and a half pounds of sour apples; boil three potatoes, and add them through the masher to the apples; mix well, add four ounces of sugar, a cupful of water, and the grated rind of one lemon; one or two eggs can be added, but are not necessary.   Beat well, place it in a greased basin or mould, and steam for an hour and a half.

534.   POTATO AND LEMON PUDDING, No I.

Mix two ounces of ground rice and a pinch of salt, with eight ounces of cooked riced potatoes.   Place in a basin, make a hollow in the middle, and put into it one and a half ounces of creamed or melted fat, one beaten dried egg, one tablespoonful each of treacle and of milk.   Beat all thoroughly; lastly, add one teaspoonful of baking powder.   Place in a greased dish, and bake for three-quarters of an hour in a moderate oven.

535.   POTATO AND LEMON PUDDING, No. II

Boil one teacupful of milk, put in one ounce of fat and melt it, add one beaten (dried) egg and a pinch of salt.   Stir in one pound of cooked sieved potatoes, one tablespoonful of treacle, the grated rind of one lemon.   Beat thoroughly, bake in a greased pie-dish in a moderate oven to a good brown.

536.   POTATO AND LEMON PUDDING, No. III

Have ready one pint of (powder) custard; add a pinch of salt; stir in eight ounces of cooked sieved potatoes, and

mix well, beating continually. Add half an ounce of fat,
three ounces of chopped dates, and the grated rind of half
a lemon. Bake in greased pie-dish in moderate oven.

537. RICE CREAM

Take a large heaped tablespoonful of ground rice, and rub
smooth with a little cold water. Put one pint of milk in a
saucepan, sweeten, and flavour with vanilla or lemon essence.
When the milk is hot, add the ground rice, and stir well
until it boils. Serve cold. This is an excellent accompaniment to any stewed fruit, especially rhubarb. It can either
be poured over the fruit or served alone in a glass dish.

538. RICE PUDDING (ECONOMICAL)

Wash sufficient rice to cover the bottom of a pie-dish
about half an inch deep. Add one pinch of salt, and two
teaspoonfuls of sugar. Pour boiling water in, enough to
cover the rice and leave plenty of room to swell. Place in a
moderate oven until the rice has swelled ; then put in enough
milk to fill the dish three-quarters full, give a good stir, and
add whatever flavouring is desired, and bake until set. This
takes much less milk.

539. SAGO FRUIT, No. I

Have one breakfastcupful of sago boiled in five breakfastcupfuls of water ; when it is quite clear, put in four tablespoonfuls of jam, raspberry or black currant for preference.
Pour into a mould which has been rinsed with cold water.
When cold, unmould, and serve with a (powder) custard.

540. SAGO FRUIT, No. II

Put into a casserole, three ounces of fine sago, one pint of
topped-and-tailed gooseberries, sweetening to taste (or
chopped dates), and one breakfastcupful (or a little more)
of cold water. Cover closely, bake slowly, and remove when
all is firm. This is better served cold.

541. SEMOLINA PUDDING

Boil half a pint of milk, sprinkle in one ounce of semolina, with two teaspoonfuls of sugar, and stir until the mixture is quite free from lumps ; then let it cool a little, and stir in one well-beaten dried egg (but this is not essential), and bake in a slow oven, in a greased pie-dish, for about half an hour.

Fine sago or crushed tapicoa can be treated the same way.

542. SUGAR-BEET PUDDING

Take six ounces of sugar-beet, wash well and peel, place in boiling water sufficient to cover, let simmer for two hours. Remove from water, chop small, and place in a covered casserole with a very little water, and let cook until soft enough to pulp through a sieve (or cook it to a similar condition by any of the methods on pp. 10, 11).

Add to the sieved beet the following, well mixed : two ounces of cooked sieved potatoes, four ounces of G.R. flour (or half G.R. flour and half ground rice), and a quarter of a breakfastcupful of fat ; with a'pinch of salt, and the grated rind and juice of half a lemon. Very little moisture will be needed, but if there is any of the sugar-beet liquor left from the *second* cooking, use some of that (about half a teacupful), otherwise use some from the first boiling. Last of all, moisten one teaspoonful of carbonate of soda and add. Blend thoroughly, place in a greased basin, and steam three hours.

543. SWISS PUDDING

Boil one pound of apples (wiped but not peeled) in a very little water until tender enough to put through a sieve. Have three ounces of sugar, or of treacle, mixed with three ounces of shredded clarified cocoa butter, six ounces of soaked strained crusts, a pinch of salt, and the same of cinnamon. Place half of this at the bottom of a greased pie-dish, put in the apples, then add the rest of the mixture ; strew a few

little bits of fat or cocoa butter on top. Let bake about
an hour in a moderate oven.

544. TREACLE PUDDING

Two tablespoonfuls of golden syrup, or treacle, two tablespoonfuls of chopped suet or fat, six tablespoonfuls of flour,
one teaspoonful and a half of baking-power, one egg.

Mix flour, suet, and baking-powder and pinch of salt.
Stir in treacle, beaten egg, and a little milk. Place in a
greased basin, cover with paper, and steam for about two
hours.

545. TRENCH PUDDING

Have two tablespoonfuls of rice boiled in half a pint of
milk and water, until the liquid is absorbed and the rice tender.
Mix in two ounces of shredded cocoa butter (or suet) and one
dried egg, with a few chopped dates or a little sugar, and
steam them in a greased basin.

546. VEGETABLE MARROW TART

Take a small marrow, stew it quite tender, mash it up with
fat and sugar to taste; add a little flavouring of lemon
peel, spice, and ginger, and beat a dried egg well in. Line
a dish with potato-crust and, when the pastry is baked, and
has gone cool, fill it with above mixture, and put it back
for a minute in the oven.

CHAPTER IX

BREAD, CAKES, BISCUITS

BREAD is the most important article of all. At the moment of writing we are not rationed in bread; but any day we may be.

The saving in flour, health, and happiness which can be effected by good home-made bread is unbelievable until you have ocular demonstration of it. We don't know, most of us, what good bread is. We have lost the power of perception and discernment, because we have been grumblingly content to put up so long a while, year in and year out, with a mysterious compound *called* bread (but exceedingly unlike the genuine thing), which was supplied by bakers. Some bakers' bread is worse than others. But it is very rarely that you hear of a household changing its baker. It just grumbles and—goes on.

With one's own bread, not only is great economy the immediate result—because it is so much more nourishing and satisfying, and keeps fresh so much longer, than the miserable shop stuff which is dry at twelve hours old—but you can vary it to suit your own requirements; with less or more potatoes, less or more moisture—with a little lard or fat if that can be spared—with a little sweetening of fruit (fresh or dried) if desirable.

You can vary it in shape and in size; even in colour, by the admixture of more maize, rice, oat, or barley flour (but G.R. flour will not stand *much* more admixture). And if you are rationing your house in flour, as every patriotic Briton should do, you will find that you are quite surprisingly to the good in the amount of flour left over after breadmaking.

I save five pounds out of twelve pounds of my flour rations every week.

Also you will find that minor digestive ailments disappear. The people who grouse about "War Bread" are those who only know *the bakers' version of it*.

But some will say, "All very well, but it is a troublesome job, and I haven't time." Others will hint that a dark secrecy envelops the operation of breadmaking, and that only the initiated can hope to succeed.

This is pure fallacy. It is a job which cannot, from its inherent nature, be done right off. You can sandwich its details between the labours of the busiest day. And as regards what *you* have to do, that is perfectly plain sailing. Any trifling discrepancies as regards the yeast, the G.R. flour, the temperature of the weather and the oven, you will speedily learn to recognise and get even with. . . . I wish every woman knew the pardonable pride and joy of seeing big beautiful loaves cooling off upon the table, and smelling the delicious odour of home-made bread all over the house.

For further particulars, see pp. 187–191.

Bread must never be wasted—not a scrap of it. To waste bread now is a culpable and a criminal act. As has already been stated, any crusts or broken bits must be soaked and then well squeezed as dry as possible, used for puddings, rissoles, and any of the numerous purposes for which we formerly employed fresh crumbs. Or they must be dried hard in the oven, pulverised, and used where dry crumbs are a desideratum.

Bread should not be used when you can possibly supply a substitute. At breakfast, for instance, it can be reduced to a minimum by substituting sufficient potatoes (sliced cold cooked potatoes, fried if possible, or any of the recipes in Chapter VIII.) or "cutlets" of cold boiled hominy, oatmeal, rice, maize-meal or lentils; or plenty of porridge of some sort (see Chapter VII.) ; anything, in short, which supplies bulk of a farinaceous kind. There are also a large number of hot breakfast cakes, which are used continually in Canada and the U.S.A., and are all exceedingly satisfying.

The same remarks apply to luncheon.

Bread should not be used at tea at all, if you can make shift with simple little cakes or biscuits (see Chapter VIII.). One is not hungry at tea as a rule ; most people simply eat from force of habit. *Don't eat unless you are absolutely hungry* : that is " the way to be healthy, wealthy, and wise."

Bread at dinner is a needless superfluity.

As regards the various " alien flours " of which excellent bread can be made, you will find them dealt with in the recipes *seriatim.* However, please note the following :

Wheat flour is the only flour (except rye) which " rises," *i.e.*, responds to the action of yeast. Therefore, if you mix it with any other flour (it is pretty well mixed already !) you must remember that that other flour will only rise by the wheat-flour lifting it along with itself, and you must make your calculations accordingly.

Barley flour imparts a dark, somewhat dirty-looking tone to a loaf. It is very nutritious, but inclined to promote biliousness if one is inclined that way. It is the moistest flour I know.

Maize flour has a drying effect, and gives a lovely yellow colour to the loaf. The flavour is pleasant.

Oat flour is dryer still. It whitens the loaf, and imparts a delightful oaten flavour.

Rice flour whitens the loaf, and is very drying.

Boiled rice, boiled oatmeal and *boiled maize-meal* are useful, if not ideal, adjuncts. They absorb a lot of dry flour in the kneading process ; but they greatly increase the *bulk* of a loaf, if not its quality.

Potatoes (boiled in their skins, peeled, mashed, sieved, or riced, and added to the dough—or to the yeast—while still warm), moisten the loaf, lighten it, increase the bulk, and improve the taste. The correct proportion of potatoes to flour has been the subject of Ministerial experiment; I give the result. Personally I find that one pound of potatoes to three and a half pounds of flour is an excellent admixture; but one and a half potato is also very good.

G.R. Flour.		With Potatoes.		Makes Bread.
7 lbs.	..	—	..	9 lbs.
7 lbs.	..	1 lb.	..	10 lbs. 9 ozs.
7 lbs.	..	2 lbs.	..	11 lbs. 10½ ozs.
7 lbs.	..	3½ lbs.	..	12 lbs.
7 lbs.	..	7 lbs.	..	14 lbs. 9 ozs.
7 lbs. (Wholemeal)		7 lbs.	..	13 lbs. 7½ ozs.

The old recipes for wheat-flour bread do not quite hold good now. The millers, or the bakers, or both, are allowed to mix the wheat flour with a percentage of " alien flours," barley, maize, oats, rice, and beans. Sometimes they use one, sometimes another, sometimes several; and consequently the flour varies from week to week, and the housewife never knows with what particular " aliens " she has to cope. But the net result—striking an average—is this:

(1) Less moisture is required for mixing and kneading; I should say, as a rule, nearly half a pint less than what is indicated in recipes for pure wheat flour. Barley flour is so moist and sticky in its tendency, and potatoes also contain so much moisture, that if you employ the usually stated amount of moisture, you are likely to get a dough which is most difficult to knead, and turns out pasty in the baking.

(2) Less kneading, according to some experts, is required. I don't know that I agree with this. It is quite easy to knead too little; it would be hard to knead too much. Especially now that the wheat flour is so mixed with the other flours that won't respond to the action of yeast, it is more than ever necessary that the yeast should be thoroughly incorporated. It is therefore advisable to stick to the good old-fashioned twenty minutes for kneading—(this signifies from start to finish—from the time you actually begin to

mix the flour into the risen yeast-and-potato in the
" well ").

(3) The rising of the dough is very, very slow. No wonder ;
think what a lot of " alien " flour it has got to shove up by
hook or crook. Of course, its rising varies with the weather,
the temperature, and the condition of the yeast ; but still
it is very slow. If, however, it has been properly kneaded,
the second rising, in the tins, will not be unduly prolonged.

(4) The time of baking is, as a rule, longer now than
formerly ; but this also varies very much.

I have been experimenting with various admixtures of
" alien " flours for a year ; and very nicely most of these
experiments turned out. But during that period, the G.R.
flour has become more and more coloured, or discoloured, until
now you cannot at a little distance distinguish it from
wholemeal flour (which is also considerably diluted with
beans, etc.). Of course, however, the wholemeal flour has
a different texture. . . . Well, I have come to the conclusion that it is no longer safe to try any admixtures of
one's own, lest one should upset the balance and not have
enough proportion of wheat flour—in which case the dough
cannot rise. The only safe extra ingredient, at the moment,
is potatoes. Except in the case of " mixture breads," which
see (p. 195).

Potatoes are a distinct improvement in every way. Not
only do they, as already mentioned, increase the bulk, but they
improve the taste and colour, and they lighten the texture.

They should be boiled or steamed in their skins ; then you
must remove the skins, and mash, sieve, or pass the potatoes
through a ricer. The last is the quickest. Anyhow, get them
perfectly free from lumps.

Opinions vary as to *when* you should add the potatoes ;
though all agree that they should be warm (not scalding hot)
when you add them. Some put them into the flour before
making a " well " for the yeast ; some mix them with the
dough while kneading. I follow a third course. " The middle

way is the safest," says the old proverb, and certainly I think this is as safe as any. I mix them into the creamed yeast-and-sugar after the tepid water has been added to it; and pour the whole lot into the "well." No flour need be stirred in to make a "sponge"; the potatoes suffice. Sprinkle some flour over the top, and cover up with a cloth.

NOTE.—The stalest loaf may be revived and made eatable, by treatment as follows. Plunge it for a minute into fresh cold water; and *immediately* place it in a *very hot* oven. It should begin to steam, and when it has finished steaming, it should (theoretically) be ready to take out. But the time varies with different breads.

YEAST

NOTE.—It is advisable, if not absolutely necessary, to understand *something* about yeast; otherwise one is working in the dark.

Yeast is a plant, "a collection of living, one-celled organisms"—though most people are unaware of this. It grows, by perpetual budding out of itself; this is what raises the flour. Like any plant, it needs certain favourable conditions for growth, and these conditions are mild warmth, a certain amount of moisture, and suitable food. The favourite food of the yeast-plant is sugar; which it finds, or rather manufactures for itself, in wheat flour. It digests this sugar, so to speak, and turns it into carbonic-acid-gas and alcohol, which, in their efforts to escape from the glutinous walls of the cells enclosing them, expand, inflate, or swell the dough, as the yeast grows and grows. It is a most interesting and mysterious process.

If you let the yeast (at any stage) stand in a draught, which all plants hate, it will deteriorate. If you check the growth of the yeast at the wrong moment by too fierce a heat, or too intense a cold, it will die; just as any plant will. It *does* die, at a certain moment, when it has done its duty by raising the dough. The heat of the oven eventually kills the yeast; the size of the air-cells which it has evolved remains fixed; the alcohol and carbonic gas are driven off; in other words, the bread is properly raised, aerated, and baked. Several other things happen; but this is the simplest way of stating it.

If, however, the dough is left too long before baking, its condition will change. The alcoholic fermentation produced by the yeast will be followed by a break-up of the alcohol into acetic acid and water (just as wine changes to vinegar), and the bread, when baked, will be sour. This souring is more likely to happen in warm weather.

But as the longer time of fermentation or rising that you can allow, will secure the best bread, if it be necessary to leave the dough a good while, "cut it down" once or twice after it has doubled in bulk. This lets out some of the gas and improves the flavour. "Cutting down" is the clean cut, with a sharp knife, across, north to south, and east to west, mentioned in the general formula for bread-making.

Yeast may be (1) that known as brewer's or liquid yeast, which is the best, but which *must* be used fresh, and is rather hard nowadays to come by. Or (2) compressed, formerly known as German, yeast, which is now more than twice its old price; this will keep two, sometimes three days, but is much the best when fresh. It should be of a light even colour like good dripping, with no dark veinings in it. (3) Home-made yeast, which is invaluable when you can't procure either of the others; only, note well, you must *start* your home-made yeast with No. 1 or No. 2. I give several recipes for this. It is of most use to those who have to make bread often and to a considerable amount. It won't keep longer than three days open, but may be good for six weeks, bottled; and you can always start a fresh supply from a little of the old stuff. Having once obtained the yeast plant, you can go on propagating it for ever.

A piece of dough held over unbaked, will serve as leaven for a new lot, and some people swear by it; but I don't recommend it, because obviously the chances are that it will make the bread sour.

In these hard times we must not run the least risk of wasting any of our materials. We must try and make sure that we are giving our bread the best possible conditions; so that every scrap of it shall be eatable, wholesome, and enjoyable.

The right proportion of yeast to be used is stated so differently by different experts, that the subject might well bewilder an amateur. You may, however, be sure you are safe in allowing one ounce of compressed yeast to three and a half pounds of flour, or one and a half ounces to seven pounds of flour. Two ounces is said to suffice for fourteen pounds of flour. But I had rather be on the safe side by using a little more.

One ounce of compressed yeast equals about two-thirds of a breakfast cup of liquid (brewers') yeast; or about half a pint of home-made yeast.

547. HOME-MADE YEAST, No. I

Put a heaped tablespoonful of dried hops, and a pinch of salt into a bowl, pour on one pint of boiling water (water in which potatoes have been boiled is best); let this grow cold, then strain and boil it up again, all but a tablespoonful or so, which you can use (cold) to mix to a smooth paste one heaped teaspoonful each of flour and of sugar. When the liquid boils, pour it over the sugar, etc., stirring continually. Bottle, cork closely, and set in a warm place. It should ferment on the third day. A breakfastcupful will suffice for three and a half pounds of flour.

548. HOME-MADE YEAST, No. II

Wash and chop up three good-sized potatoes, without peeling them. Put them, along with one and a half handfuls of dried hops, into four and a half pints of cold water, and bring to the boil. When the potatoes are done enough,

O

mash them well, and let all cool down to lukewarm or blood heat. Then stir in smoothly one and a half handfuls of sugar and two large handfuls of flour, also one ounce of compressed yeast (but this last is only needed the first time you start making it), which should be creamed with a little sugar and lukewarm water. Pour all into a jar, and set in a cool place. Before using, shake it up and strain it through a gravy strainer or a piece of muslin. Half a pint will raise seven pounds of flour.

Some of this yeast must always be kept to begin the next lot with (instead of buying more compressed yeast).

(" Handfuls " is rather vague ; but as bread-making matters are usually run by men, I should say that " handful " was about a large tablespoonful.)

549. HOME-MADE YEAST, No. III

Take eight or nine good-sized potatoes ; peel, and boil them along with a large handful of hops tied up in muslin ; have enough water to cover them completely. Strain off the water when the potatoes are done, remove the hops, mash the potatoes, put them back, with the water, into the saucepan, mixing thoroughly. Then put in two table-spoonfuls of flour, half a cupful of granulated sugar, and one tablespoonful of salt. Stir well, and dredge in more flour, until you have a thin batter. Let cook for four or five minutes, then add two ounces of compressed yeast (creamed). Mix all well, pour off into an earthenware jar, let stand ten or twelve hours in a warm place, stirring every four hours. Then cover closely and put into a cool place.

550. HOME-MADE YEAST, No. IV

Have one and a half pints of water boiling in a pan. Add a full teacupful of hops, tied up in butter-muslin, and one and a half pounds of potatoes. Boil these till the potatoes are tender, then press them through a colander, and add one breakfastcupful of wheat flour, one and a half teacupfuls of

Demerara sugar, one teaspoonful of ground ginger, one ditto salt. Take two and a quarter ounces of ordinary yeast, melt it in a little warm water, and mix it with the other ingredients. Leave the mixture in a cool place for twenty-four hours, then mix in as much cornflour as will enable you to roll it out into a paste. Roll out the paste, cut it into small rounds with the top of a flour-dredger or a wine-glass, and dry them on a dish, taking care that both sides become thoroughly dry and hard. They must then be wrapped in butter-paper and put away in closed tins in a dry place. For bread-making, one and a half ounces of this compressed yeast can be used to seven pounds of flour; dissolve it in half a pint of warm water, adding a good teaspoonful of brown sugar, and let it stand in a warm place for five minutes or so; when the yeast rises to the top of the water, it is ready for use.

HOW TO MAKE WAR BREAD OF G.R. FLOUR IN 1918

NOTE.—I have explained this (really very simple matter) most carefully and at considerable length, so that it may appear quite plain sailing. After you have done it once or twice, you will be able to do it almost mechanically, fitting in the various bits between your other jobs. It will present no more difficulty than doing up your hair in the morning. Every woman knows that some days her hair *won't* be done up satisfactorily. Even so, some days bread-dough turns obstinate and is slow in rising. In both cases, Patience is a virtue.

THE MIXING

Take three and a half pounds of G.R. flour [if you have no means of weighing, remember that four (heaped) break-fastcupfuls are about equal to one pound of flour; one pint of flour weighs fourteen ounces] and set aside half a pound of it on a plate. Put the three pounds in an earthenware pan, or large bowl, and mix well into it one teaspoonful of salt. Stand the bowl in some place where the flour can get warmed through; either in front of the fire, or out in the sun (on a chair), or in the gas oven. Stir it up now and then, that it may get warmed right through. Meanwhile weigh one pound of potatoes (a little over will not hurt, but if you can't weigh them, say five medium-sized ones). Scrub them, and boil or steam them; when they are done, put them through a sieve, or through a ricer, or mash them quite free from lumps. Let them cool off a little, so as not to be scalding hot; but on no account let them be cold.

Put one ounce of fresh compressed yeast into a bowl, cream it with one dessertspoonful of sugar; and mix into it about two breakfastcupfuls (rather less than more) of lukewarm water. Then stir in the sieved potato, a little at a time. Don't get the yeast ready as above until the flour is warmed.

Make a hollow in the centre of the flour, with your knuckles or with a wooden spoon. (This hollow is known as a " bay," or " well," or " fountain.") Make it fairly deep ànd wide, but not right down to the bottom of the pan. Pour, into this hollow, the yeast and potato mixture. Sprinkle some flour over the yeast, from the sides of the hollow. Cover the pan with a thick cloth or towel, and put it in a warm place, out of a draught; such as a kitchen chair beside the fire; or on the fender before the fire; or out in the sun on a chair, in summer. If you have none of these places handy, anyhow put it in the warmest, most sheltered place you have got. In about a quarter of an hour you should find that the yeast mixture has broken through the sprinkled flour, and is working and moving about with big bubbles—often making funny little noises. (But if the yeast is not very fresh, or the weather is cold, it may take longer.)

You then lift the pan to a table out of a draught. Have ready a pint of lukewarm water (you may not want it all), and the half pound of flour which you set aside at the beginning.

THE KNEADING

You now mix into the yeast in the middle all the flour from the sides, doing this gradually and deliberately, and adding more lukewarm water as you need it. It is not possible to explain in words the exact state of softness to which you must bring your dough, especially as some flour requires more moisture than others. It is better to have the dough too stiff than too wet; but try to have it what appears just right.

You now proceed to knead it, with your clenched fists and the back of your knuckles. Bring in the sides of the dough continually towards the centre, and throw the whole weight of your body into each part of the dough which you tackle. Do not use your hands too close to each other. The object of the kneading is to distribute the yeast equally throughout the flour, and to give the bread a uniform texture, with neither holes nor pasty places, so that it shall be equally light and porous all over. Some people do their kneading on a paste-board, but it is easier in the pan.

As you knead, you will find that sometimes a little more water is required, sometimes more flour. Whichever you add, do it *gradually*—don't splash it in anywhere. You should thus, by degrees, add at least another breakfastcupful (half-pint) of tepid water, and all the rest of the half pound of flour. Be careful not to get the dough too moist; it is better too stiff than too moist. But you may need a whole pint of tepid water.

You must go on kneading until the bread is a smooth, elastic ball, which comes right clean away from the bottom and sides of the pan. For the above quantity of flour, about fifteen to twenty minutes' kneading should be necessary.

When the dough seems just right, turn it upside down in the pan, cut it across twice with a sharp knife—north to south and east to west; cover it up again with the cloth and return it to the warm place as before, *well out of a draught,* to rise till it is at least double in size. This may take an hour, or an hour and a half, or even more, according to the state of the weather, the freshness of the yeast, the quality of the flour, and the warmth of the place.

Have ready, out of a draught, a pasteboard, or clean table, dredged with a little flour, and two half-quartern bread-tins, or a large flat baking-tin. Whichever tins you use, they should be well warmed and greased. (Some people say, if you warm the tins properly, you need not grease them. But I don't think that applies to G.R. flour, which has a lot of sticky barley flour in it.)

Lift out your dough upon the board, divide it into two equal parts, and knead it *only just enough* to get it into the proper shape for your tins, or, round for " cake " loaves. (But if cake loaves are made where potatoes are used, the dough is apt to be too soft, and spreads out too thin.) *Only half-fill the tins.* Prick the top of the loaves sharply with a steel fork, in three or four places; and put them into a warm sheltered place to rise again. The kitchen rack is a good place. You will find that the dough has gone much smaller while you were handling it. Let the loaves double in size and rise to the top of the tins before you bake them. This will probably take half an hour.

THE BAKING

If you use a coal fire oven, it must be very hot at the beginning. Put half a teaspoonful of flour into the oven; if it goes brown in three to five minutes, the heat is right for the loaves. You must keep up a good heat all the time, but especially the first half hour.

A gas-oven requires to have the gas turned *full on for fifteen minutes* before you put the bread in, when you must turn it down to half. When the bread has been in for half an hour, reduce the heat much further, turning it quite low.

The baking should take about an hour; it may be more, or a little less. The time depends chiefly on the oven, and on the weather, but also on the amount of moisture in the dough. You can tell if a loaf is done by taking it out, and tapping the bottom of it with the back of your fingers. If it sounds hollow, it is done.

If there is anything not quite right with your bread first time, you must find out whether it was the yeast, the risings, too much water, too little kneading, or the oven. But it *should* be just right.

When the loaves are done, turn them upside down, or on their sides, upon a sieve or grating of some sort, *out of a draught,* until they are quite cool. Then wrap them in a thick dry cloth, and put them on a shelf or in a bread-pan. Loaves kept as above are quite moist after several days. What is left of the bread I make one week, is beautifully fresh the following week, when I bake again. (Think of the bought bread after twelve hours !)

*   *   *   *   *

The above recipe should result in about six pounds of bread ; because, in addition to the three and a half pounds of flour, you have one pound of potatoes, also one and a half pints (equal to one and a half pounds) water; also the creamed yeast and sugar. Of course a lot of the moisture evaporates in the oven. The bread, therefore, goes very much further than two half-quartern baker's loaves ; and it is so much nicer, wholesome, more nourishing, and better-keeping, that you wonder why the baker's loaves should be called " bread " by the side of yours.

Now, the above may appear a lengthy, complicated, and arduous undertaking. Yet I assure you that it's nothing of the sort, but ridiculously simple. You can just sandwich it in between the various details of your daily work. For instance, two or three days ago I made my bread in the intervals of (1) an hour's (very important) odd jobs about the house, (2) two hours' (very difficult) shopping and carrying things home, (3) transplanting large rose bushes to make

room for vegetables, and (4) writing parts of this book. . . .
I often remember an account of Mrs. Beecher Stowe writing
"Uncle Tom's Cabin," in bits and snatches, and simul-
taneously attending to her baby of a few months old—doing
all the housework—*and making the bread*.

Reduced to its usual cook-book formula, the above "How
to Make War Bread" would read thus :

> Three and a half pounds of G.R. flour, one pound of
> boiled sieved potatoes, one teaspoonful of salt, one dessert-
> spoonful of sugar, one ounce of yeast, lukewarm water.
> Make as for ordinary yeast bread.

And you would probably be none the wiser. . . . It is
because I am so anxious that every woman should have
home-made war bread, and that all likelihood of its going
wrong in the making should be reduced to vanishing point,
that the foregoing minute instructions have been given.

There are, of course, many other ways of making bread ;
but this is the best for the present emergency, as regards
dealing with G.R. flour.

BREAD MADE WITH BAKING-POWDER AND OTHER ARTIFICIAL LEAVENS

NOTE.—This is not so good from any point of view as
yeast-bread ; especially, because it gets dry so much sooner.
But in some cases it is Hobson's Choice.

Artificial leavens include baking-powder (bought or home-
made) and bicarbonate of soda combined with cream of
tartar (sometimes with sour milk, with treacle, or with lemon
juice).

The proportions usually given for these vary as widely
and astoundingly as do those given for yeast. But you will
find it safe to use either

> One large heaped tablespoonful of baking-powder
> to one pound of flour. The flour, salt, and baking
> powder must be well mixed together, *dry* ;

Or, one teaspoonful of carbonate of soda, and three and a half teaspoonfuls of cream of tartar, to one quart of flour (this is under two pounds, see p. 230).

As baking powder is made of bicarbonate of soda and cream of tartar, in a little rice flour, you will find it cheaper to use that instead of buying the ingredients, because cream of tartar is now so very expensive. Cream of tartar, or tartaric acid, is a deposit which forms inside wine-casks ; and there are not many wine-casks available nowadays.

One teaspoonful of soda may also be combined with one pint of thick sour milk, for one quart of flour. Never mind about treacle—it is too scarce ; or lemon juice—too dear.

Please note that (1) *Baking-powder bread is not kneaded any more than you can help*—only just enough to get it into a decent dough ; so that in this respect it is exactly opposite to yeast-bread, which likes all the kneading (at the right stage) that you can give it.

(2) That it must be *baked the minute you have mixed it*—opposite to yeast-bread again.

(3) That it is best made into *small* loaves.

(4) That the oven must be hot and the *heat kept up the same till the end.* So, you see, on all these points it radically differs from yeast bread ; and in America it is not called bread, but " biscuit."

. 552. BAKING-POWDER BREAD, No. I

Mix two pounds of flour with two large teaspoonfuls, *heaped,* of baking-powder ; add one teaspoonful of salt ; mix thoroughly. Some people add a teaspoonful of sugar. Pour in by degrees about two breakfastcupfuls of cold water, or more, enough to moisten the flour into a firm dough. Mix quickly, and knead as little as possible. Make it into small loaves, place in greased tins or on a flat tin, and put them *at once* into a quick oven for an hour.

553. BAKING-POWDER BREAD, No. II

Take one pound of flour, one ounce of sugar, one teaspoonful of salt, two level teaspoonfuls of baking-powder. Mix very thoroughly. Moisten with about half a pint of milk and water, knead very quickly, divide into two loaves, place in greased tins. Bake in quick oven for one hour.

554. BAKING-POWDER BREAD, No. III

Take half a pound of flour, mix thoroughly with a pinch of salt, and a good half-teaspoonful of baking-powder. Pour to this one breakfastcupful of milk, stirring well all the time. Knead quickly and lightly, handling as little as possible; divide into four to six equal pieces, place on a flat tin (floured) in a very hot oven; bake a quarter of an hour.

555. RICE BREAD (BAKING-POWDER)

Have three ounces of rice boiled until you can pulp it through a sieve. While it is still warm, rub in one ounce of fat to fourteen ounces of flour, to which has been added half a teaspoonful of salt, and one teaspoonful of sugar. Add two teaspoonfuls of baking powder, and mix in the rice. More liquid (milk or water) or more flour, may be added in order to make the dough of the right consistency. When it is stiff enough, shape into little rolls, and bake in a quick oven.

556. SODA BREAD

To one pound of flour, add a *small* teaspoonful each of salt and of bicarbonate of soda, and a *heaped* teaspoonful of cream of tartar. Mix thoroughly; then add half a pint of milk, and mix quickly into a softish dough. *Do not knead.* Place in greased tin and bake immediately in a quick oven, for about forty-five minutes.

557. SODA BREAD (WHOLEMEAL)

One pound of wholemeal, one teaspoonful each of sugar and of salt, half a teaspoonful of bicarbonate of soda, one teaspoonful of cream of tartar, one ounce of margarine (or other fat) rubbed in. Moisten with milk or water; mix to a nice dough, roll out quickly two inches thick, bake in a shallow warmed greased tin for half an hour to forty minutes.

558. LITTLE SODA LOAVES

One quart of flour, one small teaspoonful of soda, one large teaspoonful of cream of tartar, a pinch of salt. Mix the salt and soda with the flour, then dissolve the cream of tartar in a little milk, and make your dough. Shape into very small loaves, and bake in hot oven.

559. WHOLEMEAL BREAD (YEAST), No. I

Requires to be made a trifle moister than bread of G.R. flour; also it takes rather longer to bake. To three pounds of wholemeal, allow half a pound of flour for the mixing, and one pound of sieved potatoes; one dessertspoonful of sugar, one ounce of yeast, and two to three level teaspoonfuls of salt. Proceed as for War Bread.

MIXTURE BREADS (FLOUR-SAVING)

Note.—For these, the extra ingredient—*warm cooked* rice, pearl barley, oatmeal, etc.—is incorporated into the flour before the yeast is put in; and a different procedure from that of G.R. bread is adopted, *i.e.*, you *mix and knead when you put the yeast in*, and then let rise two or three hours.

As two ounces of oatmeal (uncooked) make one pound when cooked; and three ounces of pearl barley yield one pound, and eight ounces of rice similarly result in two pounds, it will be seen what a large quantity of bread can be produced by this means. I haven't tried these mixture breads myself; but a great many experts pronounce them admirable. It is possible that they are better in quantity than in quality.

More salt is required in the flour—two and a half teaspoonfuls instead of one—and less sugar. A hot oven, *with the heat well maintained*, is advisable for these mixture breads.

560. BARLEY BREAD

Cook three ounces of pearl barley in two pints of water, until it can absorb no more water ; drain, and add it while warm to two and a quarter pounds of G.R. flour, warmed and well salted. Cream three quarters of an ounce of yeast with one teaspoonful of sugar ; add half a pint of (tepid) water in which the barley was boiled. Mix with the flour and barley, and make a dough ; leave to rise for two or three hours. Knead, add more flour if need be ; form into loaves, and let these rise for half an hour. Bake in a hot oven. Forty minutes should suffice.

561. MAIZE BREAD

Make a stiff maize porridge with one and a half break-fastcupfuls of maize meal, one tablespoonful of salt, and one pint of water. (See Maize Porridge, pp. 143–4.) Have ready—this is better made overnight—a "sponge," made with three quarters of an ounce of yeast creamed in one tablespoonful of sugar, and diluted with one pint of tepid water. Stir in one breakfastcupful each of G.R. flour and of maize meal, and beat it well until it is quite smooth and elastic. Put it, covered closely, in a warm place to rise. When it is light and spongy—which will not be for nine or ten hours, mix it with the lukewarm porridge ; add one and a half cupfuls more meal and three cups more flour, and, if need be, more tepid water. Knead, and proceed as for War Bread. Will take at least an hour in a hot oven.

562. OATMEAL BREAD

Put two ounces of oatmeal into one pint of boiling water, in a double saucepan, and cook, stirring well, until you have a stiff porridge. Let cool a little, and mix it into two and a quarter pounds of G.R. flour, salted and warmed. Have three quarters to one ounce of yeast, creamed with one tea-spoonful of sugar, and diluted with half a pint of tepid water. Mix into the flour and oatmeal, making a nice dough. Set

to rise two to three hours. Then knead, adding more flour
if need be ; shape into loaves, leave them to rise again ; bake
in a hot oven for about forty minutes.

563. RICE BREAD, No. I

Boil one and a half pounds of rice gently in four quarts
of water, until it is tender enough to beat into a smooth
paste, or rub through a sieve. Have four pounds of salted
flour ready warmed ; have one ounce of fresh yeast creamed
with one dessertspoonful of sugar, and set to rise in a " well "
in the flour. When the yeast bubbles, add the rice while
still warm, kneading very thoroughly ; and proceed as per
formula for War Bread.

564. RICE BREAD, No. II

Boil eight ounces of rice until soft enough to beat smooth.
It will by then be about two pounds in weight. Mix it while
warm into two and a half pounds of warm salted flour.
Cream one ounce of yeast with one dessertspoonful of sugar,
place it in the " well " and sprinkle it with flour, or mix it right
in to the flour and rice. Let stand one hour. Then knead,
and let stand for two hours. Proceed as for War Bread,
and bake in hot oven for one and a half hours.

VARIOUS BREADS

NOTE.—These recipes are included for the sake of completeness ; but unless made with pure wheat flour instead
of G.R. flour, they are not certain to be satisfactory.

565. BARLEY BREAD

(1) Mix two and a half pounds of G.R. flour, with two
and a half pounds of barley flour, one ounce of salt, one
teaspoonful of sugar, one ounce of yeast, about two pints
of tepid water (but remember that barley flour is rather
moist and sticky in itself). Proceed as for War Bread,

Or (2) One and three-quarters of a pound of G.R. flour, one and three quarters of a pound of barley flour ; one teaspoonful each of sugar and of salt ; one and a quarter ounces of yeast.

Or (3) Two pounds of barley flour to one pound of G.R. flour ; one ounce of yeast.

Or (4) Two pounds of barley flour to two and a quarter pounds of G.R. flour ; two ounces of yeast.

(It will be seen that these recipes vary very greatly as regards proportions. I may add that they have each been recommended by experts. Barley bread is largely used in Wales. I understand that it doesn't suit " liverish " persons ; just as oatmeal is, for some, too heating to the blood.)

566. MAIZE BREAD

Proceed as for Barley Bread, No. 1.

567. OATMEAL BREAD

Mix three pounds of G.R. flour with one and a half pounds of (dry) oatmeal, and one ounce of salt. Set it to warm, and make a " well " in the middle. Pour into this one and a half ounces of yeast, creamed with a dessertspoonful of sugar, and diluted with one breakfastcupful of lukewarm water. Sprinkle with flour ; and when the yeast works through the flour, knead (using more tepid water as required) for half an hour. Set in a warm place to rise, and proceed as for other yeast bread. Should take one hour in a good oven.

568. RYE BREAD

Rye is the only flour besides wheat which rises under the action of yeast. Cream one ounce of yeast with one dessertspoonful of sugar ; meanwhile have three pounds of rye meal, to which has been added one teaspoonful of salt, warming by the fire. Add half a pint of tepid water to the yeast, make a " well " in the rye-meal, and pour it in. Proceed as for other bread. It should not take so long to bake as

G.R. flour. If preferred, use two pounds of rye and one pound of wheat flour.

569. POTATO BREAD

Take the quantity of potatoes required; boil them in their skins. When done, peel them, and bruise them with a rolling-pin to the consistence of a paste. To this add as much flour as there is potato pulp, salt—at least one teaspoonful—and yeast (creamed with sugar) in the proportions of one ounce to three and a half or four pounds of flour and potatoes. Knead them well, putting as much water as may be necessary. When properly kneaded, form into loaves, and place in the oven, taking care that it be not quite so hot as for common bread, or it will become hard on the outside before the inside is properly baked. This bread must be allowed longer time to bake than any other.

570. WHOLEMEAL BREAD, No. II

Take two pounds of wholemeal flour, twelve ounces of white flour, two large teaspoonfuls of sugar, and the same amount of salt, three-quarters of an ounce of yeast, one quart of warm water. Mix the yeast with the sugar; add in the water and salt, and gradually stir in the wholemeal flour, till all is thoroughly mixed and absorbed. Sprinkle a little white flour over the dough, and put it aside in a warm place to rise. When it has risen enough, add in the rest of the white flour, sufficient to make it into a firm dough when kneaded; make it into two loaves; put it again to rise; then bake in a moderate oven for one hour and a quarter.

FRUIT BREADS

Note.—These are useful and wholesome for a variety. Apples, gooseberries, and dates are the fruits most fre-quently used, because (as a rule) they are the cheapest. Chopped figs are very good, so are raisins—when one can get them—or currants.

The dough in which fruit has been intermixed takes a long while to rise—from six to eight hours.

571. APPLE BREAD

Take one pound of apples to two pounds of flour. Boil the apples to a pulp (using as little water as possible) and sieve them. Meanwhile have half an ounce of yeast creamed with sugar, and set to rise in the warmed flour. Knead the dough with the warm apple-pulp, instead of water. Set the dough to rise for a long while, six hours at least; shape into long loaves, and bake.

572. DATE BREAD

For this, yeast dough made with milk instead of water is the best. Work into it, when thoroughly risen, a little fat, say two ounces to the pound. Then add stoned chopped dates, as many as you like; eight ounces to the pound of dough will suffice. Work in the dates thoroughly, and place the dough to rise again in greased tins. It will take longer to rise and to bake than plain bread.

573. GOOSEBERRY BREAD

Cook half a pound of gooseberries in a very little water until they are soft enough to rub through a sieve. Have one and a half pounds of flour, mixed with half a teaspoonful of salt, warmed; make a "well" and put in half an ounce of yeast, creamed with a teaspoonful of sugar, and a little tepid water. Let the yeast rise in the usual way—add the gooseberries, while they are still warmish, in kneading. Leave six or eight hours to rise, and put into tins to rise again.

Sugar and spice may be added at pleasure (cinnamon, cloves, or ground ginger); and two to four ounces of lard or other fat may be added in the kneading.

CAKES AND BISCUITS

These at first sight seem a woeful extravagance in war time. But they're not really. A plain cake may go just

as far, and use up very much less flour, than a plain loaf.
Also, it supplies wholesome variety—and variety is wholesome in itself. Cocoa butter lends itself to biscuit-making,
but is apt to be rather hard of effect in cakes. Eggs, of
course, are out of the question; but egg substitutes are
handy here as elsewhere.

The following recipes are very plain and simple; yet they
will produce nourishing and appetising results.

Your attention is especially directed to the hot cakes
and scones of true scone nature, *i.e.*, fried, not baked. These
may be either salt or sweet. A very little fat suffices for them.
A number of other suitable recipes are to be found in the
"Cake Book" of this series, which can be adapted for
present use.

574. JOHNNY CAKE, No. I

Stir one pint of scalded milk or water, or half of each,
into one cup of yellow or white cornmeal, to which a teaspoonful of salt has been added. Bake in a shallow greased pan
or on a griddle.

575. JOHNNY CAKE, No. II

Into one pint of meal and one teaspoonful of salt stir
boiling water to make a thick drop batter; thin to a thick
pour batter with cold milk; drop by tablespoonfuls on to a
hot greased frying-pan and bake as griddle cakes; or cook
as No. 1.

576. MAIZE CAKE

Have one pint of maize meal and half a pint of G.R. flour
thoroughly mixed with two teaspoonfuls of baking powder,
one teaspoonful of salt, two tablespoonfuls of sugar. Add
one (dried) beaten egg, one tablespoonful of fat (creamed)
and three-quarters of a pint of milk or milk and water. Put
the mixture into a greased tin, and bake in hot oven.

577. COFFEE CAKE

Into two breakfastcupfuls of bread dough, mix one beaten
(dried) egg, one tablespoonful of fat, one teacupful of sugar.

P

Mix thoroughly, moistening if necessary with tepid water. Let rise, cover in a warm place, until double in size ; roll out very lightly and quickly, an inch thick, place in a greased flat baking tin, and let rise again. Then spread the top with half a dried egg, beaten up with one teaspoonful of sugar, and some chopped nuts. Bake in a fairly hot oven for at least half an hour.

578. OATMEAL CAKE

Mix four ounces of fine oatmeal with eight ounces of G.R. flour ; add a pinch of salt, any spice desired, and one teaspoonful of baking powder.   When all is well blended, moisten with four tablespoonfuls of treacle and a little milk (tinned will do).   Beat, pour into a greased cake-tin, and bake in moderate oven for an hour.

579. PARKIN

Mix one pound of fine oatmeal with one teaspoonful of salt, one teaspoonful of soda bicarbonate, four teaspoonfuls of ground ginger.   Heat in a pan four tablespoonfuls of milk, four ounces of fat, one tablespoonful of treacle, two tablespoonfuls of sugar.   Pour this liquid to the dry ingredients, mix into a soft paste, bake in a shallow greased baking-tin, in a moderate oven.   Half an hour should suffice.

580. POTATO CAKE

Take eight ounces each of G.R. flour and of cooked sieved potatoes ; and a pinch of salt, two ounces of sugar creamed with two ounces of fat, four ounces of chopped dates, and a teaspoonful of baking powder.   Mix thoroughly, moisten with a very little milk, place in a greased tin, bake in a fairly hot oven to a nice light brown.

581. SEMOLINA CAKE

Two ounces of flour, two ounces of semolina, two ounces of lard or dripping, one ounce of Demerara sugar, a dozen raisins, a teaspoonful of baking-powder, a pinch of salt, one dried egg.

Mix flour, semolina, sugar, baking powder, salt together, rub in dripping, add raisins, and mix with the egg, well-beaten. Bake in greased and papered tin in hot oven.

582. BARLEY BANNOCKS

Put one pint of milk into a lined pan, add two ounces of fat and a pinch of salt. Let boil, then stir in barley meal until the whole is a thick dough. Turn out on a floured board, let cool a little, roll thin, cut into rounds, cook on a heated greased griddle over a sharp fire. Both sides must be browned. Serve at once.

583. BUCKWHEAT CAKES

Take one pound of buckwheat flour, add one full teaspoon of baking powder, a quarter of a teaspoonful of salt, two dried eggs, and cold water enough to mix all into a deep batter; beat this well—then drop the batter by table-spoonfuls into boiling fat in a frying pan, and cook over a clear hot fire. Drain and serve at once.

584. CORN DODGERS

Mix one teaspoonful of salt with two breakfastcupfuls of maize meal. Put these ingredients into a bowl, make a hollow in the middle of them, put one tablespoonful of lard or other fat into the hollow ; then pour in boiling water (about three quarters of a pint) to wet the meal thoroughly and melt the lard. Beat one (dry) egg with one tablespoonful of milk, and stir it into the meal when that has cooled off a bit. Mix thoroughly, beat well, and either drop in spoonfuls on a greased tin, or roll out a quarter of an inch thick and cut into rounds. Bake in a very hot oven for fifteen minutes, or in a hot oven for thirty minutes, according to whether the dough is dropped or rolled out.

585. CORN PONES

Mix a pinch of salt into two pints of maizemeal, moisten with enough cold water to make a soft but firm dough.

Melt one and a half teaspoonfuls of lard, stir it into the dough ; shape it into little oval cakes and bake in greased tin in hot oven for fifteen minutes, or until well browned.

586. ELLEN CAKES

Mix eight ounces of G.R. flour with a pinch of salt, three ounces of sugar, and half a teaspoonful of baking-powder. Then rub in three ounces of fat—lard will do ; flavour with a few drops of lemon essence or the grated rind of half a lemon, and moisten with a dried egg and a very little milk. Bake in little patty pans, or on a greased tin.   Above quantity should make sixteen little cakes.

587. GINGER CAKE

Mix six ounces of flour with six ounces of medium oatmeal, a pinch of salt, and a teaspoonful each of ground ginger and of baking powder. Rub in four ounces of fat, or two ounces of grated cocoa butter. Put four tablespoonfuls of treacle into a teacupful of milk, and warm it, but do not boil ; then stir in two beaten dried eggs, and blend thoroughly. Moisten the other ingredients with this liquid mixture, mixing well ; bake in a greased cake-tin. It should take one and a half hours in a moderate oven. Chopped preserved ginger can be added at discretion.

588. HOMINY CAKES, No. I

Take some cold boiled hominy, and to each breakfastcupful allow one pint of self-raising flour, one teaspoonful of salt, one dried egg, two ounces of fat. Moisten with a little milk, mix well into a not too stiff paste. Shape into buns, and place on greased tin in hot oven. Cold boiled rice may be treated the same way.

589. HOMINY CAKES, No. II

Take two breakfastcupfuls of cold boiled hominy (see p. 143), seven breakfastcupfuls of self-raising flour, two well-beaten

dried eggs, one teaspoonful of salt, one quart of milk. Mix
thoroughly and bake immediately.

590. HOMINY CAKES, No. III

Boil one breakfastcupful of hominy (soaked) for two hours
in one quart of milk. Remove, and stir in half a teaspoonful
of salt, two beaten dried eggs, two tablespoonfuls of fat.
Mix thoroughly, drop in little heaps upon a greased baking
tin, and bake a pale brown.

591. HOMINY CAKES, No. IV

Take some cold boiled hominy, and to each breakfastcupful
allow two ounces of fat, one beaten dried egg, one teaspoonful of salt, and one pint of self-raising flour. Moisten
with enough milk to make a soft paste. Shape into buns,
and bake in hot oven on greased tin.

Cold boiled rice may be used in the same way.

Sugar to taste may be added to any of above.

592. MAIZE ROCK CAKES, No. I

Mix four ounces of maize flour, four ounces of G.R. flour,
a pinch of salt, three ounces of sugar, half a teaspoonful of
mixed spice. Rub three ounces of fat ; moisten with two
beaten dried eggs ; beat all thoroughly. If more moisture
is required, use a little milk. Drop in rough heaps, using
two forks instead of a spoon, on a greased baking tin. Cook
for twenty minutes in hot oven.

593. MAIZE ROCK CAKES, No. II

Take two breakfastcupfuls of maize meal and one of G.R.
flour. Mix thoroughly with one and a half teaspoonfuls of
baking powder and a good pinch of salt. Then rub in one
tablespoonful of fat, and add chopped dates to taste and a
little sugar if you can spare it. Mix into a very stiff batter,
drop in lumps upon a flat tin (greased), and bake in a good
oven to a nice golden brown.

594.　OAT CAKES, No. I

Take a walnut-size piece of dripping or other fat, and melt it in a saucepan containing one breakfastcupful of boiling water. Flour well blended, one large tablespoonful of brown sugar, one dessertspoonful of salt, three teaspoonfuls of ground ginger, half a teaspoonful of bi-carbonate of soda. Pour the fat and water to these; and immediately sprinkle in two breakfastcupfuls of oatmeal. When the dough is firm enough to knead with the fingers, and the ingredients are well mixed, roll out very thin, dusting with a little flour if need be. Cut into shapes as desired; bake a light brown in a moderate oven.

595.　OAT CAKES, No. II

Have one ounce of lard melted in one pint of boiling water; add one pound of medium oatmeal, and make into a stiff dough. Knead slightly, divide into equal portions (eight or ten), make each into a ball, roll out thinly, and cook in a greased frying-pan, or bake in a cool oven, until the edges curl up. Put in a warm place until dry. Store in a tin. The cakes should not brown.

596.　OAT CAKES (SOFT), No. III

Mix one pound of medium oatmeal with half a pound of self-raising flour, and one ounce of salt. Cream one ounce of yeast, add one breakfastcupful of warm water to it, let stand till it begins to work. Make a "well" in the meal and pour it in, and mix with lukewarm water to a thin batter. Cover, and let stand three hours or more. Pour a teacupful at a time into a thick greased frying pan, and cook over a clear fire or on a gas stove. Let one side cook about six minutes, then turn it over with a knife, and cook the other side about four minutes.

597.　RICE AND MAIZE MEAL CAKES

Take half a breakfastcupful each of maize meal and of flour; one cup of cold boiled rice, two teaspoonfuls of baking powder, one teaspoonful of salt, two dried eggs, one cup of new milk.

Mix the dry ingredients well, add the mixed eggs with milk. Roll out, shape into cakes, cook on griddle ; serve hot.

598. POTATO CAKES, No. I

Take about one pound of cold boiled potatoes. Mash well with salt, add two ounces of fat, and moisten with a little milk into a thick batter. Then work in about double the quantity of flour, mixed with one dessertspoonful of baking powder. Sweeten to taste. Work until all is quite soft ; roll out, cut into small cakes, and bake in a good oven.

599. POTATO CAKES, No. II

Take an equal weight of cold boiled potatoes, pressed through a sieve, and of flour. Mix well ; rub in dripping, two ounces to the pound, and salt to taste. Moisten with a little milk ; roll out about half an inch thick ; cut into rounds with the top of the flour dredger. Put the cakes into a good hot oven till they are a golden brown ; serve piping hot. Serve with treacle.

600. WALNUT CAKES

Take three tablespoonfuls of flour, rub in two ounces of fat, add half a teaspoonful of baking powder, and eight ounces of shelled walnuts, blanched, skinned, and broken very small. A pinch of salt must then be mixed in, and two eggs. Blend thoroughly ; drop teaspoonfuls of the mixture on a greased paper or tin, and brown in a good oven.

BISCUITS

601. CHOCOLATE BISCUITS, No. I

Mix one ounce of flour with four ounces of ground rice rub in one and a half ounces of cocoa butter. Add half a teaspoonful of cocoa, four ounces of boiled sieved potatoes ;

mix well. Add a few drops of vanilla essence, and beat in half a dried egg and one tablespoonful of treacle. Lastly, mix in half a teaspoonful of baking powder. Roll out half an inch thick, cut into small rounds. Bake about fifteen minutes (or more) in a hot oven.

602. CHOCOLATE BISCUITS, No. II

Cream two ounces (melted) cocoa butter along with two to four ounces of sugar (according to taste). Stir in two ounces of cocoa, one beaten (dried) egg, and enough cornflour to make the mixture into a stiff paste. Lastly, add half a teaspoonful of baking powder. Roll out half an inch thick, cut into small rounds, bake ten to fifteen minutes in good oven.

603. MAIZE BISCUITS

Mix one breakfastcupful of maize meal with half that quantity in G.R. flour. Add one ounce of castor sugar, creamed with four ounces of cocoa butter, one beaten (dried) egg, one teaspoonful of baking powder. Moisten with half a breakfastcupful of water. Roll out a quarter of an inch thick, cut into rounds, bake about fifteen minutes in moderate oven.

604. OATMEAL BISCUITS, No. I

Mix eight ounces of oatmeal with the same quantity of G.R. flour, into which two ounces of fat has been rubbed. Add one flat teaspoonful of salt, and the same of baking powder. Mix into a stiff paste with water or milk. Roll out a quarter of an inch thick, cut into biscuit shapes, bake on a tin in a moderate oven for about twenty minutes.

605. OATMEAL BISCUITS, No. II

Mix half a pound of medium oatmeal with half a pound of risen dough. Add four ounces of fat, half a teaspoonful of salt, one teaspoonful of baking powder. Knead well into a smooth dough, roll out half an inch thick, cut into small rounds, bake in a rather slow oven.

606. OATMEAL GINGER BISCUITS

Melt three ounces of fat with one tablespoonful of treacle. Have ready mixed eight ounces of flour and four ounces of oatmeal, with two ounces of sugar, one small teaspoonful of ground ginger, and a quarter of a teaspoonful (or rather less) of cream of tartar. Add the treacle, etc., blend thoroughly; roll out half an inch thick, cut into biscuits, bake on a greased tin in a quick oven for twenty minutes.

607. OATMEAL WAFER BISCUITS

Mix one breakfastcupful of oatmeal, one of rolled oats, and two ounces of flour, with a quarter of a cup of sugar, one teaspoonful of salt, two-thirds of a teaspoonful of bicarbonate of soda, and enough hot water (about half a cupful) to moisten into a stiff paste. Roll out very thin ; cut into biscuits, bake on a tin in a moderate oven.

608. OATMEAL CRACKNELS

Mix thoroughly half a pound each of oatmeal and of flour, with one teaspoonful of baking powder and half a teaspoonful of salt. Rub in four ounces of fat, till the whole is like breadcrumbs. Moisten with milk till you have a firm but not stiff paste ; mix with a knife. Turn out on floured board, knead lightly into a round, roll out thin, cut into shapes, place on a greased tin, prick with a fork, and bake till hard, in a moderate oven. Do not let the cracknels brown, except slightly underneath. Remove from oven and place in a wire sieve till cold.

609. POTATO AND CHOCOLATE BISCUITS

Mix three ounces of ground rice with two ounces of G.R. flour, rub in one and a half ounces of fat (cocoa butter can well be used), add a pinch of salt, four ounces of cooked riced potatoes, and a teaspoonful of cocoa. Blend well, and add one teaspoonful of treacle and half a dried egg. Beat till the ingredients are thoroughly incorporated, then put in vanilla essence to taste, and a half-teaspoonful of baking powder. Mix, roll out half an inch thick, cut into desired shapes; bake about twenty minutes on greased tin in quick oven.

610. POTATO AND OATMEAL BISCUITS

Mix two ounces of G.R. flour with three ounces of medium oatmeal, and a pinch of salt. Rub in one ounce of fat; add two ounces of cooked sieved potatoes. Mix thoroughly, adding half a teaspoonful of baking powder. Moisten with sufficient water (about a teacupful) to make a paste firm enough to roll out a quarter of an inch thick. Cut into desired shapes, bake on greased tin for about twenty minutes in moderate oven.

611. WHOLEMEAL BISCUITS

Mix three ounces of wholemeal flour with three ounces of G.R. flour, a pinch of salt, a quarter of a teaspoonful of bi-carbonate of soda, and one tablespoonful of sugar. Rub in two ounces of lard or other fat; bind with a beaten (dried) egg and a little milk-and-water. Mix into a firm dough; roll out a quarter of an inch thick or a little more; cut into desired shapes; bake on a greased tin in a hot oven.

612. BARLEY FLOUR SCONES, No. I

Rub one tablespoonful of fat into four breakfastcupfuls of barley flour: add half a teaspoonful of salt, one and a half teaspoonfuls of sugar, two teaspoonfuls of sugar: moisten with enough milk-and-water to make a stiff dough. Roll out, cut into desired shapes, and bake.

613. BARLEY FLOUR SCONES, No. II

Mix six ounces of barley flour with two ounces of fine oat-meal, one dessertspoonful of sugar, a teaspoonful of salt, two ounces of dripping or other fat, and one teaspoonful of baking powder. Moisten with warm milk-and-water sufficiently to make a firm but not stiff dough. Roll out half an inch thick, cut into any shapes desired, and cook the scones for twenty minutes in a rather hot oven.

614. BARLEY MEAL SCONES

Mix four ounces of barley meal and two ounces of G.R. flour. Rub in one ounce of dripping or other fat ; then add half a teaspoonful of bicarbonate of soda and one teaspoonful of salt. Moisten with sour milk into a workable dough. Knead quickly for a minute or two, roll out half an inch thick, cut into any shapes desired ; set in a hot oven for a quarter of an hour.

615. RICE SCONES

Put eight ounces of rice, one teaspoonful of sugar, and a good pinch of salt, into a saucepan, with a pint of cold water. When it boils, draw aside and let it steam two hours or so till the water is absorbed and the rice perfectly soft. Turn it on to a floured pasteboard until cold : then add enough flour to help shape it into thin scones, and bake on greased tin in good oven.

616. MAIZE MEAL SCONES

Mix into one pint of maize meal, one teaspoonful of salt, one tablespoonful of sugar, and two teaspoonfuls of baking powder. Rub in one tablespoonful of fat, then stir with cold milk into a batter which will drop stiffly from a spoon. Bake at once in a greased tin in a hot oven or on a griddle.

617. POTATO SCONES

Boil eight medium-sized potatoes in their jackets : peel and sieve, and mix whilst hot with two ounces of sugar creamed with half an ounce of yeast and dissolved in a break-fastcupful of warm milk. Beat until well mixed, then beat in enough flour to make a soft dough : let it stand until light and double in size. Roll out quickly half an inch thick, cut into squares, and bake in greased tin in hot oven.

618. WHOLEMEAL SCONES

Mix one pound of wholemeal flour with twelve ounces of barley flour, a pinch of salt, two teaspoonfuls of baking powder. Rub in two ounces of fat, and moisten with a beaten dried egg and a little milk. Make into a soft dough, knead for a minute very lightly, roll out half an inch thick, cut into shapes, bake in a hot oven, or cook on a griddle.

CHAPTER X

VARIOUS: NUTS, JAMS, BEVERAGES, HAYBOX COOKERY, WEIGHTS AND MEASURES, ETC.

NUTS

NUTS are of great food value, and are not, as a rule, used half so much as they ought to be, except by strict vegetarians. They are disproportionately dear at present: still, they are worth buying occasionally—if only for variety. They include walnuts, hazel-nuts, filberts, almonds, chestnuts (practically unprocurable), Brazils, and pea-nuts (which are not really nuts at all).

They can be employed, blanched, peeled, chopped (or better still, milled or grated) in cakes, biscuits, and puddings: in some kinds of bread: in salads: and even separately as vegetables. Not to mention " cutlets " and other vegetable make-believes.

Almond-meal, walnut-meal, etc., are to be purchased at the bigger stores: but they are distinctly expensive.

Some people cannot digest nuts at all: they result in skin eruptions, boils and swellings. This is, I presume, because nuts contain oil in too highly concentrated a form. However, to most digestions they are safe and wholesome—if properly prepared by blanching and grating.

619. CHESTNUT CURRY

Shell one pound of Spanish chestnuts, put them into a saucepan of cold water, bring to the boil, and remove the inner skin. Replace in the water and boil for a quarter of an hour, then drain off the water. Have ready the following sauce : Fry one sliced onion in a little fat ; add one table-spoonful of flour, one ounce each of curry powder and of curry paste, and mix smooth ; proceed to add and cook one sliced tomato, two teaspoonfuls of ground almonds, salt, pepper, and nutmeg to taste, and one breakfastcupful of stock (any sort). Boil up fast, and strain the liquor upon the chestnuts, or rub all through a sieve over them. Simmer the whole mixture for twenty minutes or so. Serve at once, with rice.

Half above quantities will suffice for three people.

620. CHESTNUT STEW

Boil twelve ounces of shelled chestnuts, remove inner skins. Have a minced onion and a sliced tomato fried in a little fat. Take them out, and put in one ounce of cornflour ; when it is brown, add half a pint of stock or water, and let boil. Add the onions and tomatoes, also half a small turnip, half a small carrot, and two or three mush-rooms, all chopped small, a small teaspoonful of Worcester sauce, and the chestnuts. Cover and simmer slowly for one and a half hours. Then add salt and pepper, and (at pleasure) a wineglass of claret and a tablespoonful of red currant jelly.

Serve with boiled rice.

621. NUT OMELETTE

Shell and peel the skin off one pound of fresh walnuts. Mill them, or pound into a paste. Have one teacupful of soaked drained bread, beaten into crumb, mixed with four beaten dried eggs, and seasoned with salt and pepper. Have a little fat very hot in a frying-pan, put in the bread mixture (which should be just liquid enough to pour), and cook it carefully or it will burn. When it is almost cooked, strew the walnut over it, put a plate over the pan to cover it for an instant, then roll up the omelet and serve.

This is, of course, better with real eggs; in which case, beat yolks and whites separately, and add the latter just before frying the mixture.

622. NUT ROAST

Boil a pint of stock (any sort), sprinkle in three table-spoonfuls of semolina, and let cook for five minutes, or until it thickens. Add two teaspoonfuls of grated cheese, and stir well for five minutes more; then remove the pan from the fire, and put in three ounces of milled nuts, two teaspoonfuls of grated onion, one tablespoonful of tapioca (previously soaked for an hour) and half a breakfastcupful of soaked drained crumbs; with seasoning to taste, and half an ounce of fat. Mix very thoroughly, shape into a thick roll, smear with little bits of fat, and bake thirty minutes, or until nicely browned, in a hot oven.

623. NUT SAUSAGE

Mix one breakfastcupful of milled or minced nuts with one breakfastcupful of riced potato. Add salt and pepper, moisten with one beaten (dried) egg, blend thoroughly, shape into sausages, dust with fine oatmeal, and bake a nice brown in a hot oven.

624. NUT SCALLOP

Mill two ounces of shelled nuts. Cut one pound of cooked potatoes into little cubes. Have half an ounce of fat melted in a saucepan; stir in half an ounce of flour, continue stirring for a minute or two; then put in a breakfastcupful of milk and water, and go on stirring till it boils. Add salt, pepper and (made) mustard to taste. Put in the nuts and potato, and one teaspoonful of grated cheese; thoroughly blend, and pour into a greased dish. Strew the top with another teaspoonful of grated cheese, a little grated crust, and some tiny bits of fat. Place in a moderate oven; when nicely browned and well heated through, serve at once.

625. PEA-NUTS

These nourishing articles are not really nuts at all, but are produced by a leguminous plant (hence "pea"). They should be boiled for twenty minutes, then drained and spread out on a dish for some hours until dry ; then put in a baking-tin in the oven until rather brown ; and if rubbed in a dry cloth when you take them from the oven, the skins will come off. Keep in a dry tin.

626. PEA-NUTS AND RICE

Melt three tablespoonfuls of fat in a saucepan, stir in three tablespoonfuls of flour and cook until the mixture is quite smooth. Add three breakfastcupfuls of milk and water, stirring continually. When this thickens, season with pepper and salt. Have ready some hot boiled rice (one breakfast-cupful, cooked as per any of the recipes on p. 152, etc.), two breakfastcups of chopped or minced pea-nuts, two tea-spoonfuls of salt, and pepper to taste. Mix thoroughly with the sauce, pour into a greased pie-dish, bake twenty minutes in a moderate oven.

Half the above quantities would suffice for a small family.

627. PEA-NUTS AND RICE RISSOLES

Prepare the following : four ounces of pea-nuts, roasted, skinned, and minced ; eight ounces of hot rice, boiled and drained ; four ounces of hot cooked sieved potatoes ; half an ounce of melted fat ; pepper and salt to taste. Mix thoroughly and let cool. Shape into rissoles, roll in fine oatmeal or grated crusts, and bake or fry to a nice brown.

628. PEA-NUTS, STEAMED

Shell, blanch, and skin one pint of pea-nuts ; mill them, and mix a little fat in. Have ready two breakfastcupfuls of tomato purée, one breakfastcupful of cornflour, salt and pepper to taste. Mix thoroughly for at least five minutes. Place in mould or basin, and steam for four to five hours.

629. PEA-NUTS, STEWED

Shell one pint of pea-nuts and blanch them, either by boiling water or by oven-heat ; rub off the red skins. Put them into a casserole with enough water to cover them well (about two quarts), bring to the boil ; place in a slow oven and bake for eight hours or so, or until tender. Season with salt and pepper, and serve.

630. WALNUT PIE

Line the bottom of a greased pie-dish with hot mashed or sieved potatoes ; over these, put four ounces of grated walnuts ; add salt and pepper. Heat and thicken a quarter of a pint of stock (any sort) and a quarter of a pint of mushroom ketchup, and pour over walnuts ; cover with a layer of mashed potatoes, dab with bits of fat, bake to a golden brown.

631. WALNUT ROAST

Take one breakfastcupful of blanched, ground, or grated walnuts ; add two breakfastcupfuls of soaked drained crumbs, one tablespoonful of finely chopped onion, one teaspoonful of minced parsley, and a pinch of minced lemon-thyme. Season to taste with salt and pepper. Mix thoroughly, and bind with one (dried) egg. Place in greased basin, and cook for one hour (at least) in a good oven. Serve with apple sauce and green vegetables.

WAR-TIME JAMS AND MARMALADES

NOTE.—See the remarks on sugar. If you have saved sugar from your ration, and can eke it out with glucose (one part to three parts sugar), or if you can use dates as a sweetener (for instance, with rhubarb or with apples), or if you cook the fruit in sugar-beet syrup instead of plain water, plus a little sugar, you will be able to provide yourself with jam. Readers of the " Jam Book " in this series will remember the essential principle there laid down, that it is the

Q

fruit which requires cooking, not the *sugar ;* so, that to follow the usual method and cook both together, is great waste of the sugar. Whereas, if you *first cook the fruit* and then give it a boil up with the sugar, twelve ounces of the latter per pound of fruit will be found amply sufficient. The old-fashioned " pound for pound " is " na-poo."

The less sugar is used, the shorter time the jam will keep, because sugar is a preservative.

In using dates as a sweetener, wash them, steep a while in a little cold water ; stone, chop, and weigh along with the other fruit, using the water they were in. To each pound of mixed fruit, allow four ounces of sugar.

Where sugar for jam is out of the question, you can use glucose (corn syrup) as follows :

To ten pounds of fruit, allow seven pounds of corn syrup ; boil it with the fruit (after cooking the fruit first) and add a small teaspoonful of tartaric acid, citric acid, or white vinegar. This helps to set the jam. Let it stop boiling two or three minutes, stir thoroughly and pour off into pots.

Another method employs one pound of glucose to one pound of fruit (the sweeter fruits being best for the purpose). The fruit is cooked gently until the juice runs, then boiled up fast until soft ; the glucose is then well stirred in, and the mixture boiled and skimmed, until it sets.

This will not keep so well as preserve made with half-and-half glucose and sugar.

In making jam with combined sugar and glucose, put the sugar in first and let it dissolve *slowly,* simmering, Then add the glucose, and let it dissolve fast, *boiling.*

Treacle can be used, four and a half pounds to six pounds of fruit. But it is only advisable for mixture jams and the coarser fruits. I do not recommend it for choice, but for Hobson's choice.

In using saxin, for every pound of fruit allow forty tablets of saxin, and about one ounce of gelatine (a little less will do). When the fruit is cooked, add the saxin, and boil for thirty minutes; then put in the gelatine, and stir well until it is dissolved.

It is said that 1 teaspoonful of salt to every pound of fruit makes it less acid.

Raspberry or black currant jam can be diluted by mixing it with a double quantity of cooked beetroot (put through the mincer), and soaked boiled sago (allow one ounce to each one pound of original jam, and three breakfastcupfuls of the water in which the sago has been boiled), and the juice and grated rind of one lemon per pound of the original jam. Boil up all together until the jam will set. This is all right for cooking purposes, but hardly for table use.

See also the sugar-beet syrup recipes in Chapter I.; these may be used instead of water in making jam, and considerably less sugar will be needed, but it will not be so good for keeping.

632. APPLE AND GINGER JAM

Well wipe, peel, core and slice, four pounds of cooking apples. Place in preserving pan with one teacupful of water, the grated rind and juice of two lemons, and a quarter of a teaspoonful of ground ginger. Cook till nearly a pulp; then add one pound of glucose and two pounds of Demerara sugar; boil up again until the jam will set; put into pots, and cover whilst hot.

633. APPLE AND GINGER JELLY

Take the peel and the cores of the apples, used for above, place in a covered jar, with enough water to cover them, and simmer for six hours. Strain, and to each pint allow the grated rind and juice of one lemon, a pinch of ground ginger, and twelve ounces of sugar. Boil the juice separately for forty-five minutes; add the sugar, and boil up until it sets. Place in jars, and do not cover until cold.

634. BLACKBERRY JELLY (French Sugarless)

Place the picked blackberries (four to six pounds) in a preserving pan, covered with water; boil until tender enough to strain through a muslin. Return strained juice to pan; and add three carrots, two beetroots or one sugar-beet, and one lemon; all coarsely sliced. Boil up until the jelly will set, remove the vegetables, pour off into jars, do not cover until cold.

635. CARROT MARMALADE, No. I

Take two and a half pounds of peeled sliced carrots (weigh after preparing), six lemons thinly sliced, with the pips removed, a heaped saltspoonful of salt and four quarts of water. Boil all together till they can be pulped through a sieve; say about two and a half hours; then add two pounds of sugar, and boil up until the marmalade will set.

636. CARROT MARMALADE, No. II

Take six oranges and four lemons, put them to soak for twenty-four hours in a quart of water, soaking the pips separately in a breakfastcupful of water. Peel and chop one and a half pounds of carrots, pass them through a mincer, put them with the oranges and water and boil for two hours, along with the pips in a muslin bag. Remove bag, add one teaspoonful of salt and two and a half to three pounds of sugar. Boil fast until set.

637. MIXED FRUIT JAM

Peel and slice six bananas, peel and cut up the pulp of four oranges (removing pips), thinly slice four lemons (removing pips), halve and core (but do not peel) six cooking apples. Place all in a preserving pan with eight pints cold water, bring to the boil, let cook steadily for two hours, or until all is soft enough to pulp through a sieve. Weigh and add twelve ounces of sugar for every pound of pulp. Boil up again until the mixture will set or jelly; proceed as for other jam.

If preferred, the jam need not be sieved; in that case the apples must be peeled and sliced.

638. ORANGE JAM

Take ten sweet oranges, peel, remove pips and white " rag," and cut into chunks, using a silver knife. Weigh, and set aside eight ounces of sugar for every pound of fruit ; if the jam is not intended for long keeping, six ounces of sugar will suffice. Add a pint of cold water, place in a preserving pan ; bring to the boil and boil until quite tender.

Stir in one ounce of gelatine dissolved in a little warm water ; then add the sugar, and boil up until the jam sets, which will not be long because of the gelatine. Do not cover the pots until the jam is cold.

639. ORANGE MARMALADE JELLY

Take six oranges and two good lemons ; clean carefully, and grate the peel into one quart of cold water. Remove any superfluous white inner lining, and slice the fruit across, in thin rounds. Place the fruit in a jar of two quarts of cold water, and the pips in a breakfastcupful of water. Leave for a day and a night. Then put the fruit and water to boil in a preserving-pan, with the strained water from the pips. Let boil for thirty minutes ; rub through a fine sieve ; replace the liquid in the preserving-pan. Then strain off the water from the grated peels, and add them to the liquid in the pan. Boil this for ten minutes, then measure, and for every pint allow twelve ounces of sugar, or eight ounces of sugar and four ounces of glucose. Stir well until the sugar is dissolved, and boil fast for half an hour or until the jelly sets when tested.

Do not cover the pots until cold.

640. PARSNIP MARMALADE

Peel and slice enough parsnips to make two pounds when weighed subsequently, place in boiling water, and boil steadily for an hour. Strain off the water, and set aside half a pint. Sieve or rice the parsnips, and return the half pint of water to the jam, along with the grated rind and juice

of two lemons, and eight ounces of sugar, or six ounces of
sugar, and two ounces of glucose. Stir thoroughly until
the sugar is dissolved; then add the parsnips, and boil,
stirring often, for thirty minutes.

BEVERAGES

641. BARLEY WATER

Pour one quart of boiling water upon two full tablespoons
of pearl barley; let it steep a little at the side of the stove;
then turn all into a saucepan and simmer with the thinly
pared rind of a lemon, till it is as thick as desired, which may
take from half an hour to two hours according to what you
want. Strain off the liquor (the barley can be then used for
a milk pudding) and sweeten to taste; adding any flavour
preferred. One large apple can be sliced, boiled separately,
and added with its liquor to the barley water before straining.

642. BLACKBERRY SYRUP

Stew the blackberries with a quarter of a pint of water to
every three pounds, until the juice is drawn. Strain, and to
every pint of juice add six ounces of sugar. Boil sugar and
juice together for fifteen minutes, and bottle for use when
cold.

643. BLACKBERRY VINEGAR

Take three quarts of ripe blackberries, crush them, pour
over them two quarts of good white vinegar. Let them stand
twenty-four hours, then strain through a muslin, and add
the liquor to three quarts of fresh blackberries. Stand and
strain these as before, and if the liquid does not seem strong
enough, repeat a third time with fresh berries. Pour it into
a jar, to stand in a pan of boiling water which must boil fast
for one hour; then bottle it for use.

644. GINGER BEER, No. I

Take two and a half pounds of loaf sugar, two ounces of
best whole ginger, two sliced lemons, and one ounce of cream

of tartar. Put one gallon of water on the fire, and when it boils, add the ginger and the lemons, let it boil a quarter of an hour, then turn it into a pan, and add six quarts of water and the sugar. When cool, set it to ferment with half a breakfastcup of good yeast, or piece of compressed yeast the size of a chestnut. After it has done fermenting, which will be in thirteen or fifteen hours, strain through a muslin rag, and beat the cream of tartar and the white of an egg together, and add just before bottling.

645. GINGER BEER, No. II

Have powdered ginger, one ounce; cream of tartar, half an ounce; a large lemon sliced; two pounds of lump sugar; and one gallon of water, added together, and simmered over the fire for half an hour. Then ferment it in the usual way with a tablespoonful of yeast, and bottle it for use, tightly corked.

646. GINGER BEER, No. III

Take two ounces of cream of tartar, one ounce and a half of white ginger well beaten (not ground), one lemon shred fine, one pound and a half of sugar. Put them all together in an earthen vessel, and pour on them ten quarts of boiling water. Let stand till nearly cold, then add two table-spoonfuls of good yeast; mix it well; let it stand for thirty hours, then strain it through a flannel bag, pressing it well through. Bottle it, and confine the corks with twine. It will be fit for use in two days.

647. LEMON SYRUP

Rub one pound of loaf sugar upon the rinds of six lemons, until all the yellow part is absorbed, and place the sugar in a preserving pan with half a pint of cold water. Boil until the syrup is clear; then add the strained juice of twelve lemons. Let it simmer for five minutes very carefully; it must not boil again. Pour off into clean dry bottles; let the syrup grow cold, and cork closely.

648. RASPBERRY SYRUP

Take two quarts of good ripe raspberries, pour one quart of good vinegar over them ; cover them closely and let them stand for two days. Then mash up the berries in the vinegar, and strain off the liquid on to two quarts of fresh fruit. Let this stand another two days, then mash and strain as before. To every pint of liquid, add two teacupfuls of white sugar. Let it simmer very gently for fifteen minutes in a lined saucepan over the fire, keeping it well skimmed. Then strain it, bottle it, cork, and cover closely ; seal the cork. This should be taken with cold water.

APPENDIX

649. BLACKBERRY AND APPLE CUSTARD

Peel some good-sized apples, core them, put them in a baking-tin with a little water and sugar, bake until done. Have ready some cooked blackberries, flavoured with a little grated lemon-rind ; fill up the hollows of the apples with these, and return to the oven for a little while. Then place on a glass dish ; pour over them any syrup that was formed ; and cover with a (powder) custard.

650. BREAD PANCAKES

Take enough stale soaked bread, well-squeezed, to make two breakfastcupfuls. Add two beaten (dried) eggs, one teaspoonful of flour, one teaspoonful of salt, and sufficient milk to make a thin batter. Beat until very smooth ; then mix in one teaspoonful of baking powder, and cook on a griddle or in a frying pan.

651. BREAD STEAKS

Cut slices of stale bread in pieces about a quarter of an inch thick, two inches wide, and four to six inches long. Dip them into ketchup and water (but do not let them soak or they will break), have ready a (dried) beaten egg, seasoned with pepper, salt, and finely minced parsley : dip the steaks into this, and fry in boiling fat. Serve with fried onions.

652. CURRIED SAVOURY TOAST

Take two dried eggs, one ounce of fat, one salt spoon of curry powder, three tablespoonfuls of milk. Heat the fat in a stewpan, add the curry powder to this when it boils and a little milk. Beat the eggs a little, add to the ingredients in the pan, stir altogether, add the three tablespoonfuls of milk and salt to taste. Directly the mixture is thick, pile it on to squares of fried or toasted bread and serve garnished with small dice of beetroot.

653. FISH OR CHICKEN WITH MAYONNAISE

This is a good way[a] of employing an almost infinitesimal quantity of any kind of choice fish or poultry. First place in little china or paper cases a layer of broken lettuce, very lightly dressed with oil, vinegar, pepper, and salt. Next a slice of tomato. On this place a little heap of chopped chicken or turkey, flaked salmon, turbot, halibut, lobster, or crab. Over all pour some rather thick mayonnaise sauce or salad dressing, and garnish, as may be convenient, with an olive, a few strips of gherkin, and chilli, or whatever may be at hand.

654. GRAVY WITHOUT MEAT

Allow four large onions sliced to two quarts of water, a bundle of sweet herbs, a burnt crust of bread, two ounces of fat, some pepper and salt. When boiling, strain it, and add to it a tablespoonful of ketchup.

655. OATMEAL JELLY

Have two breakfastcupfuls of boiling water in a double-boiler. Have one and a half ounces of fine oatmeal mixed smooth with a little cold water, stir it in, let boil, add a pinch of salt, and thin lemon rind to taste. Cover the inner pan, and let boil about forty-five minutes, with frequent stirring. Strain through a muslin jelly-bag into a rinsed mould; put in any extra flavouring desired, and let grow cold, then unmould.

656. RICE SHORTCRUST

Mix four ounces of flour with two ounces of fat, rubbing well in; add a pinch of salt, stir in four ounces of well-drained boiled rice; mix to a stiff dough, using a little cold water to moisten, roll out and use.

657. SAUSAGE AND CARROT SAVOURY

Grate eight ounces of raw carrots, and mix with one pound of boiled sieved potatoes, eight ounces of sausage meat, a small onion finely minced, a teaspoonful of minced parsley. Mix well, then add salt, pepper, and nutmeg to taste, a teaspoonful of meat extract, and a beaten dried egg. Blend thoroughly, and moisten if necessary with a little stock. Place in a greased basin, covered with greaseproof paper, and steam for two hours.

HAYBOX COOKERY

NOTE.—There is a distinct variety of opinion on this subject—some people maintaining that they cannot be bothered with haybox cookery, because it does not abolish the use of a fire, and can only be used for dishes which have to be cooked very long and slowly, but which *must* be started and finished by means of stronger heat than a haybox can afford. Also, that unless you remove these dishes at the psychological moment, they will go bad.

Others, again, declare that they were " perishing in the snow " before they discovered the invaluable haybox; that it has made life much easier to them, saved no end of fuel, and resulted in most appetising meals.

However, this is what a haybox will and will not do. It *will* cook, most effectually, stews, soups, and such porridges as require a lengthy process; under certain conditions, it will cook suet puddings; it will cook such vegetables as are stewed *en casserole* with next to no liquid. And it will keep other things warm for several hours.

It *won't* roast or bake, boil or steam or simmer, broil or grill, fry or sauter. All these operations require strong heat, in varying degrees of intensity. So that you must cook the food by one of above methods before putting it in the haybox; and you must make it thoroughly hot, after taking it out of the box, before you can serve it.

This is how you make it—get an old cube-sugar box or other box about the same strength and size, *with a lid*. This lid must be fixed on by hinges of some sort at back, and a hasp or fastener in front. If no wooden box be obtainable, a little old tin one will do.

Line the inside with two or three thicknesses of newspaper. Then you put a layer of hay all over bottom and sides—the hay must be at least four inches thick; and it must be covered with flannel; and you must arrange two little nests in it (or three, if there is room), into which your casseroles or stew-jars will fit, exactly and just-so. And you then provide cushions of thick tight hay to fit over each jar in its nest, or one cushion to cover the entire top over the nests. The idea is that there shall not be the smallest chance of any heat escaping, and not the least chink or crack through which it might escape.

There are other ways of making a haybox, but the above is about the best; and while you are about it, you may as well play for safety.

Remember (1) that you must transfer your food, whatever it is, in the casserole, straight from the fire to the haybox whilst the liquid is actually boiling.

And (2) that you must not open the haybox until it is time to take the casserole out.

To this end, you must go by a definite time-table as follows:

Dish.	Cooked on the Fire or Gas.	In Hay-Box.
Lentil Soup	¾ hour	4 hrs.
Potato Soup	¼ hour	1½ hrs.
Fish, stewed	3 minutes boiling ..	½ hr.
Irish Stew	{ ½ hour Meat— Potatoes 5 minutes }	1½ hrs.
Beef Stew with Vegetables	¾ hour	3 hrs.
Potatoes	5 minutes	1½ hrs.

Dish.	Cooked on the Fire or Gas.	In Hay-Box.
Haricot Beans, soaked ..	1 hour	2 hrs.
Boiled Rice	2-3 minutes boiling	2½ hrs.
Stewed Apples	2-3 minutes boiling	1-2 hrs.
Stewed Prunes	2-3 minutes boiling	3½ hrs.
Coarse Oatmeal Porridge	5 minutes boiling ..	All night
Quaker Oats	5 minutes boiling ..	2½ hrs.
Suet Pudding	30 minutes ..	2½ hrs.
Meat Pudding (Suet) ..	45 minutes ..	3 hrs.
Boiled Bacon or Mutton	45 minutes ..	4-5 hrs.
Vegetables—Young ..	10 minutes ..	2 hrs.
Old	18-20 minutes ..	2½-3 hrs.

The meat for stews must be absolutely fresh for haybox cookery.

Suet-puddings must be placed in a basin with a screw-down top, set in a pan of *boiling* water, and, after thirty to forty-five minutes boiling, put, pan and all, into box.

Porridge can be cooked overnight, by boiling fast for five minutes, placing in the haybox, and heating up in the morning.

Vegetables, as already stated, require very little water or stock.

You understand, the food must not be shunted or *shifted* from a pan into a jar or casserole to go into the box. Whatever it is boiling in, must go *straight in, just as it is*.

WEIGHTS AND MEASURES

2 saltspoons full	equal	1 coffee spoon
2 coffee spoons full	,,	1 teaspoon
5 teaspoons (dry) full	,,	1 tablespoon

WEIGHTS AND MEASURES—*continued*.

4 teaspoons (liquid) full	equal	1 tablespoon
4 tablespoons (liquid) full	,,	1 wineglass, or half a breakfast cup.
8 large tablespoons full	,,	1 gill
2 gills	,,	1 breakfastcup, or half a pint.
2 breakfastcups full	,,	1 pint
2 pints (4 cups) full	,,	1 quart
1 tablespoonful (liquid)	,,	½ ounce
1 heaped tablespoonful of sugar or butter	,,	1 ounce
1 breakfastcupful of sugar (granulated)	,,	8 ounces
1 breakfastcupful of butter (solid)	,,	8 ounces

Roughly speaking :

1 pint (milk or water) equals 1 pound of dry material.

The same applies to small articles such as beans, peas, nuts, and small berries.

For making roux, *i.e.*, thickening sauce, use one tablespoonful of flour and one tablespoonful of fat to half a breakfastcupful of liquid.

Remember that one breakfastcup of rice will absorb three times its amount if water be used, and more in the ᵉe of milk or stock.

FLOUR WEIGHTS

1 pint of flour	weighs	14 ounces
1 quart (½ quartern)	,,	1¾ pounds
1 quartern (½ gallon, or ¼ stone)	,,	3½ pounds
1 gallon (2 quarterns or ½ stone)	,,	7 pounds

FLOUR WEIGHTS—*continued.*

1 stone (2 gallons, or 1 peck)	weighs	14 pounds
2 stones (2 stones)	,,	28 pounds ($\frac{1}{2}$ bushel)
1 bushel (4 pecks)	,,	56 pounds
1 sack (5 bushels)	,,	280 pounds